VOCATIONAL
EDUCATION

Officers of the Society
1964–65

(*Term of office expires March 1 of the year indicated.*)

STEPHEN M. COREY
(1967)
Teachers College, Columbia University, New York, New York

EDGAR DALE
(1965)
Ohio State University, Columbus, Ohio

JOHN I. GOODLAD
(1966)
University of California, Los Angeles, California

ROBERT J. HAVIGHURST
(1967)
University of Chicago, Chicago, Illinois

HERMAN G. RICHEY
(1965) (*Ex-officio*)
University of Chicago, Chicago, Illinois

RALPH W. TYLER
(1965)
Center for Advanced Study in Behavioral Sciences, Stanford, California

PAUL A. WITTY
(1966)
Northwestern University, Evanston, Illinois

Secretary-Treasurer
HERMAN G. RICHEY
5835 Kimbark Avenue, Chicago, Illinois 60637

VOCATIONAL
EDUCATION

The Sixty-fourth Yearbook of the
National Society for the Study of Education *Committee*
on vocational education,

PART I

By

THE YEARBOOK COMMITTEE

and

ASSOCIATED CONTRIBUTORS

Edited by

MELVIN L. BARLOW

Editor for the Society

HERMAN G. RICHEY

19 NSSE 65

Distributed by THE UNIVERSITY OF CHICAGO PRESS · CHICAGO, ILLINOIS

The responsibilities of the Board of Directors of the National Society for the Study of Education in the case of yearbooks prepared by the Society's committees are (1) to select the subjects to be investigated, (2) to appoint committees calculated in their personnel to insure consideration of all significant points of view, (3) to provide appropriate subsidies for necessary expenses, (4) to publish and distribute the committees' reports, and (5) to arrange for their discussion at the annual meeting.

The responsibility of the Society's editor is to prepare the submitted manuscripts for publication in accordance with the principles and regulations approved by the Board of Directors.

Neither the Board of Directors, nor the Society's editor, nor the Society is responsible for the conclusions reached or the opinions expressed by the Society's yearbook committees.

Published 1965 by

THE NATIONAL SOCIETY FOR THE STUDY OF EDUCATION

5835 Kimbark Avenue, Chicago, Illinois 60637

The Society's Committee on Vocational Education

MELVIN L. BARLOW
Professor of Education
Director, Division of Vocational Education
University of California
Los Angeles, California

HERBERT M. HAMLIN
Professor Emeritus of Agricultural Education
University of Illinois
Urbana, Illinois

LAURENCE D. HASKEW
Professor of Educational Administration
University of Texas
Austin, Texas

FRANKLIN J. KELLER
Principal Emeritus, Metropolitan Vocational High School
New York, New York

WILLIAM P. MCLURE
Professor of Educational Administration
Director, Bureau of Educational Research
University of Illinois
Urbana, Illinois

Consultants to the Committee on Vocational Education

ERNEST G. KRAMER
Chief, Bureau of Industrial Education
California State Department of Education
Sacramento, California

MAYOR D. MOBLEY
Executive Secretary, American Vocational Association
Washington, D.C.

WILLIAM SELDEN
Consultant, Business Education
Commonwealth of Pennsylvania
Department of Public Instruction
Harrisburg, Pennsylvania

ELIZABETH J. SIMPSON
Associate Professor of Home Economics Education
University of Illinois
Urbana, Illinois

v

INEZ WALLACE TUMLIN
State Supervisor, Home Economics Education
Georgia State Department of Education
Atlanta, Georgia

JOHN PATRICK WALSH
Deputy Director, Office of Manpower, Automation, and Training
United States Department of Labor
Washington, D.C.

Associated Contributors

GEORGE E. ARNSTEIN
Associate Director, Project on the Educational Implications of Automation
National Education Association
Washington, D.C.

GEORGE L. BRANDON
Head, Department of Vocational Education
Pennsylvania State University
University Park, Pennsylvania

RUPERT N. EVANS
Dean, College of Education and
Professor of Vocational and Technical Education
University of Illinois
Urbana, Illinois

CLAUDE W. FAWCETT
Associate Professor of Education
University of California
Los Angeles, California

ELI GINZBERG
Director, Conservation of Human Resources, Professor of Economics
Columbia University
New York, New York

WILLIAM B. LOGAN
Professor of Distributive Education
Ohio State University
Columbus, Ohio

MARY S. RESH
Special Assistant to the Director, Office of Manpower, Automation
and Training
Department of Labor
Washington, D.C.

J. CHESTER SWANSON
Professor of Educational Administration
University of California
Berkeley, California

A. W. TENNEY
Director, Agricultural Education Branch, Division of Vocational and
Technical Education, Office of Education
Department of Health, Education, and Welfare
Washington, D.C.

Editor's Preface

The National Society for the Study of Education manifested an early interest in vocational education. Even before the passage of the Smith-Hughes Act in 1917, it had devoted several of its yearbooks to the problems of vocational education: *The Place of Vocational Subjects in the High-School Curriculum* (1905), *Vocational Studies for College Entrance* (1907), *Industrial Education: Typical Experiments Described and Interpreted* (1912), and *Agricultural Education in Secondary Schools* (1912).

After vocational education became firmly fixed as a part of the school curriculum, it was treated in *Vocational Guidance and Vocational Education* (1924), in volumes on units of the educational enterprise, the curriculum, and other subjects, but an entire volume was not devoted to a comprehensive treatment of the subject until 1943, when the Society published *Vocational Education*, prepared by a committee under the chairmanship of Franklin J. Keller.

The Board of Directors discussed, in its meetings of 1959 and 1960, the desirability and feasibility of bringing out a new volume on the subject. In the autumn of 1960, the Board received a letter from Mr. Keller urging that such a volume be prepared, and shortly thereafter Professor Melvin L. Barlow submitted a proposal for a yearbook. The Board invited Professor Barlow to attend its meeting in February, 1962, to present the proposal more fully and to join in its deliberations. The Board approved the proposal and appointed Professor Barlow chairman of the Society's committee on the yearbook.

Recent legislation and other events have made clear the validity of Professor Barlow's conviction that the need was great and the time was right for a comprehensive treatment of vocational education. The present yearbook is the product of his and the committee's labors, the advice and assistance of a group of special consultants, and the contributions of the associated contributors.

To paraphrase Professor Barlow, the yearbook neither praises vocational education nor defends it. The volume was written by persons with different backgrounds of education and experience, from different parts of the nation, and having different philosophical bents and views. All who contributed to the yearbook, however, were deeply concerned that it contribute to clearer thinking about vocational education in the context of contemporary American life.

HERMAN G. RICHEY
Editor for the Society

Table of Contents

ix

CHAPTER I

The Challenge to Vocational Education

MELVIN L. BARLOW

The Rationale for Vocational Education

INTRODUCTION

In the progress of the human race, the vocational education of man has been a consistent and identifiable element. Vocational education has been part of the foundation of man's creative and progressive development. Its position in society has been as varied as its forms. One needs only to recall that, while apprenticeship held an exalted position during the time of Hammurabi, it was more or less shunned by Sparta fifteen centuries later. During the golden age of Pericles, Athenian financial resources produced not only a marvelous public works program but also a significant economic advancement, due in part to the fact that craftsmen were paid for their services. Nevertheless, development of vocational education did not become an element of Greek policy.

Early Jewish law made the father responsible for providing trade instruction for his son. Throughout the Middle Ages, skills of craftsmanship continued to be passed from father to son with little collective effort to provide instruction in them. After 1061, however, in which year the Candlemakers' Guild was founded in Paris, organizations of craftsmen appeared which had among their purposes some forms of vocational education. Society developed the need for vocational education, and its modern roots appeared in the educational reforms of Rousseau, Pestalozzi, and Fellenberg. These reforms, as they related to vocational education, were slow to filter into formal education, and forms of apprenticeship continued to be the chief means of vocational education.

In our own colonial period, apprenticeship was a fundamental educational institution. It was directly related to the social and economic stability of the colonies. A system of involuntary apprenticeship laws prevented orphans and children of the poor from becoming public charges by providing them with a means to become economically independent. But apprenticeship was not for these social unfortunates alone; it flourished also as a voluntary system of education, which produced craftsmen for the colonies.

During our national period, the development of vocational education paralleled our economic growth. Absorption of vocational education into the public education curriculum was a natural product of the American goal of education for all the children of all the people. The claim of vocational education to be considered a significant portion of the public school curriculum was strengthened by extraordinary developments in business, industry, and technology.

Freedom of occupational choice is an American ideal and, consequently, a national concern. The Smith-Hughes Act (1917) sought specifically to facilitate occupational choice by providing funds to the states for the promotion and development of programs of vocational education. It was in the interest of the "general welfare" of the nation that states were urged to provide occupational instruction for youth in school and for youth and adults who were out of school. The commonly accepted justifications for new or improved programs of vocational education are based on (a) the right of each individual to a total education, (b) the responsibility of society (through the public education system) to provide such instruction, and (c) the effect of vocational education on the economic strength of the nation.

TOTAL EDUCATION FOR EACH INDIVIDUAL

Although theory and practice as they relate to a program of total education for each individual have been slow to merge, agreement about theory is relatively easy to reach. The "cardinal principles of education," the "imperative needs of youth," and similar contemporary statements of purpose are broad enough to provide generously for each individual. To so provide is society's intent, and to such purposes its schools are dedicated.

The problem at mid-twentieth century was not theory but, rather, implementation. The mass of subjects, experiences, and environments to which the student was subjected reached critical proportions. The fact was, and still is, that there was a lot to learn, and many subjects, experiences, and environments were valuable in contributing to the total education of each student. But the available time in which to provide the appropriate instruction had not changed. Competition for instructional time resulted in assignment of more value to some areas of instruction than to others. Some subjects were accorded a high status and became largely standard equipment in recommended programs leading to high-school graduation. Vocational education, as a part of the total education for each individual, became entangled in a dichotomy of subject-matter values. Some "academicians" and vocationalists expressed extreme points of view; others expressed a need for a balanced position. An example of the latter position is found in a statement by Geiger:

> That concern with the present is illiberal is of a piece with the idea that "vocational education" presents the grand antithesis: Here is the illiberal bogey always available for drubbing. Now, it is very easy to sneer at the alleged vocationalizing of much modern education. Lofty contempt for practical subjects is the watermark of too many self-defined scholars. The examples chosen are calculated to get a laugh—pie-making, camp leadership, window-cleaning, pre-pharmacy, salesmanship. Certainly there will be no apology here for the evident abuses of overvocationalism in many sections of present-day education. But to assume that training for making a living has no place in liberal education is to assume that education has no context.[1]

As another example, Greene viewed liberal education and vocational training as "two essential and complementary aspects of the total preparation of the individual for his total life" and not "as hostile rivals nor as mutually exclusive enterprises." Greene offered the following solution:

> What is obviously needed is a truly liberal academic community in which the study of art and typewriting, of philosophy and accounting, of theology and medicine, of pure and applied science are, though admittedly very different, judged to be equally honorable and valuable in their several ways.[2]

1. George R. Geiger, "An Experimentalist Approach to Education," in *Modern Philosophies and Education*, p. 153. Fifty-fourth Yearbook of the National Society for the Study of Education, Part I. Chicago: Distributed by University of Chicago Press, 1955.

2. Theodore M. Greene, "A Liberal Christian Idealist Philosophy of Education," in *ibid.*, p. 119.

The vocational educator's concept of the total education required for each individual is not particularly different in theory from that of the "liberalist." It is deplorable to find a high-school graduate, or even a dropout, who cannot read, write, speak, or calculate with facility. It is similarly deplorable if he does not have a thorough understanding of the American way of life or of his cultural heritage. It is further deplorable if he cannot find employment because he has not been prepared to enter the world of work. Educating the good citizen, in the minds of vocational educators, includes preparing him to become a producer of the goods and services which society requires.

VOCATIONAL EDUCATION IN THE PUBLIC EDUCATION SYSTEM

The national movement in the interest of vocational education, initiated during the period 1906–17, focused attention upon the public school system as the logical institution for the development of vocational education. In 1914, the Commission on National Aid to Vocational Education reported:

Equality of opportunity in our present system of education is not afforded to the mass of our children. While our schools are opened freely to every child, their aims and purposes are such that a majority of the children are unable to take advantage of them beyond a certain grade and hence do not secure at public expense a preparation for their work in life. Although here and there we see the beginnings of change, it is still true that the schools are largely planned for the few who prepare for college rather than for the large number who go into industry.[3]

Industry, labor, education, and the public at large supported the general position that a public school program of vocational education was imperative. Within a short time all of the states were participants in the federally aided program of vocational education. By the middle of the twentieth century enrolments in the program of vocational education had increased significantly, but the contribution of the public schools to the actual needs of the labor force was small.

The place of vocational education in the public school program had been accepted in principle, but availability of vocational education to the youth of the nation varied from state to state and with

3. *Report of the Commission on National Aid to Vocational Education*, Part I, pp. 23–24. Washington: Government Printing Office, 1914.

the size of the community in which the school was located. Obviously major problems had to be solved in many schools in order that vocational education could be made available to all who needed such instruction. Only a few school districts or states had attempted to make comprehensive vocational education available. Furthermore, in the public schools where vocational education was available, many students were denied access to these programs by subject-matter prejudices of school personnel and, perhaps to an even greater extent, by unrealistic parental attitudes.

ECONOMIC STRENGTH OF THE NATION

A central tenet of vocational education is often expressed by the phrase "to fit for useful employment." This implies an economic future for the individual which will be better than what he might have had without vocational education. Economic improvement leads toward a better standard of living for the individual, and this in turn becomes a gain for society as a whole. Vocational education has, therefore, been thought of as a "wise business investment" both for the nation and for the individual.

The general rationale emphasizes also the development and conservation of natural resources, the prevention of waste of human labor, and the defense of the nation as other natural products of vocational education. Such rationale was dramatically validated by the performance of vocational education in World War II. And so, our national dedication "to provide for the common defense and to promote the general welfare" found a measure of realization in the national program of vocational education.

EVOLVING VIEWS

It is logical to think that vocational education in its broadest sense pertains to all occupations and to all people, but (because of the influence of federal participation in vocational education) it is customary to think of this type of education in a more restricted sense. However, even with the elimination of education for those occupations which require a prolonged learning period (the professions, for example), the contemporary program of vocational education encompasses the vocational needs of 85 per cent of the persons who enter and work in the nation's labor force.

Defining vocational education presents some problems to the layman. The total program provides for in-school youth, largely at the high-school level, and for out-of-school youth and adults. However, over a period of nearly a half-century some common understandings have emerged, are frequently repeated with few variations, and have become generally acceptable. Conant's pronouncement about the place of vocational education in the high school was formulated from such often-repeated and generally accepted statements. He wrote:

The controlling purpose of vocational education programs at the high school level is to develop skills for useful employment. These programs relate schoolwork to a specific occupational goal but involve more than training for specific job skills.

Vocational education is not offered in lieu of general academic education, but grows out of it, supplementing and enhancing it. Vocational education is an integral part of the total education program and requires aptitude that students at the lowest academic level do not have. Slow readers, for example, are not able to benefit from regular vocational programs.[4]

Such views about vocational education are or are rapidly becoming the dominant ideas of a commonly accepted rationale for vocational education. However, this rationale is challenged by some contemporary educators.

Mid-Century Controversy

By mid-century, America had rediscovered its schools, and the public plunged deep into educational controversy. The enrolment bulge of war babies brought to light the critical shortage of classrooms. An equally critical shortage of qualified teachers existed. Startling facts about education were presented to the public; the implications were even more startling.

American high schools had changed in a half-century from institutions enrolling less than 20 per cent of the youth of high-school age to institutions enrolling nearly 90 per cent of that age group. The large increase of enrolment was unevenly distributed among the subject-matter areas. The public was critical of the end product of the high school and the subject-matter specialists denounced each other.

4. James B. Conant, *The American High School Today*, p. 123. New York: McGraw-Hill Book Co., 1959.

The plight of poor "Johnny" was described endlessly—he couldn't read; he couldn't go to college; he couldn't get a job; he was anti-intellectual; he was the victim of creeping vocationalism; ad infinitum.

Age-old arguments concerning liberal education, fundamental disciplines, basic sciences, applied arts, and the humanities blazed anew, providing much heat but little light. The educational path toward the future was far from clear, and the public at large was confused by an array of claims, counterclaims, contradictory values, and misinformation. The struggle was definitely for control of the high-school curriculum, and value of subject matter was measured in terms of its relationship to college-entrance requirements. College enrolment had quadrupled during the first half of the twentieth century, and college attendance had become a symbol of highest value in the American mind.

The flood of either-or debate which reached the American people did little to solve the problem and did much to add to the confusion. Should the school program consist of a rich cultural experience or should it emphasize camping? Should the student study physics or personal grooming? Do you want your son to go to college or to take vocational education? Such forced-choice, yes-or-no questions were little related to the major problem. It is not surprising that the American educational crisis produced a variety of opinions. *Newsweek* summed up the situation in its December 5, 1955, issue by its cover title, "Johnny in a Jam."

Vocational education was challenged in four different ways:

First. As America looked at its schools, the cold finger of suspicion was pointed toward vocational education with the implication that it represented an unwanted element in the curriculum which could, and should, be dispensed with. In the minds of some critics, skill development had had its day.

Second. Studies and reports dealing with the purposes of American education appeared to place emphasis upon intellectual, moral, spiritual, and social values. Achievement of these goals was identified clearly as the task of the so-called academic education; that it was also the task of vocational education was not clear. In effect, this represented a challenge by omission, something like being dressed to go to a party but not receiving an invitation.

Third. The third challenge was generally constructive. It did not question the right of vocational education to exist but placed great stress upon related goals and little upon its particular role. For example, it demanded that students in vocational education develop stronger backgrounds in science, mathematics, English, and in the general social environment. Such suggestions were completely acceptable to vocational educators except when presented with the implication that this was new information and was an addition to vocational education. Vocational education had always sought the attainment of these values. However, the challenge to strengthen the program of vocational education in the ways suggested was readily accepted.

Despite the long history of aristocratic contempt for manual labor, vocational educators have held steadfast to their belief in the value of the practical arts, not to the exclusion of other values but with the point of view that man's contribution to society depends in a large measure upon his practical bent.

Fourth. The fourth challenge to vocational education at mid-century arose from the evidence that a large majority of American youth needed instruction of a practical nature in order to enter the world of work and from the evidence that the American labor force must upgrade and update itself in order to change with the technological age.

Johnny, as a dropout from high school, was most certainly in a predicament: He was too young to retire, and he was too short on skills to bargain for employment. Johnny as a high-school graduate was only slightly better off. The inescapable fact about "Johnny in a Jam" was that he must work or be dependent upon someone who did work. The challenge to vocational education is to help Johnny prepare for the occupation of his choice, but he must "fit" into the occupational structure as it is.

Johnny as a college student also represented a challenge to vocational education. Going to college is, in part, inspired by occupational need. The post-high-school program for American youth is manifested in a variety of ways. Area schools, junior colleges, technical institutes, community colleges, and other similar institutions provide occupational instruction in one- and two-year programs through which one can prepare for a career which will determine largely how he participates in social and civic life and how he makes his contribution to the world of work.

Significant Challenges

The reconstruction and development following World War II brought two kinds of challenges to vocational education. First, there were challenges in accord with the general purposes of vocational education, which urged improvements and expansion. Second, there were challenges that questioned the foundations of vocational education as a public school enterprise and which led to an emphasis upon vocational education outside the traditional administrative pattern of public school control.

Vocational educators reacted to the first challenge without delay. Renewal of public interest in vocational education made certain improvements and expansion possible. The second challenge was not consistent with the general needs of the mid-century society and was reminiscent of arguments from an older age; some writers have labeled the view as the "archaic dichotomy."

Since all education today is, and must be, both liberal and vocational, the task is not that of finding the appropriate proportions of each but rather of reappraising and re-defining all courses so that they contribute to both. We have, in fact, begun to do this; we have only failed to realize and commit ourselves wholeheartedly to the process.[5]

Although all of the specific challenges may be important and significant in the future development of vocational education, only four have been selected for further review.

THE STUDENT AND THE CENTRAL PURPOSE OF EDUCATION

Every society has struggled with concepts of education. Should attention be given to the individual or to society at large? Some societies pay more attention to one than the other; our society pays attention to both. Social gains are sought which provide benefits to the individual and to the group as a whole. Attention focused upon the student as the central concern of education does not neglect the total social environment and its needs.

In 1958, the challenge to American education, in all its parts, was

5. Paul L. Dressel, "Liberal and Vocational Education," *College and University Bulletin* (Association for Higher Education), XI (May 1, 1959), 4.

closely related to the shock to the American dignity by the extraordinary achievements of Russian science. The United States took stock of its educational needs and reaffirmed its fundamental faith in free public education for all. Identification of giftedness in students and their guidance into programs that would challenge their abilities became immediate tasks of American education. Giftedness was frequently discussed in terms of programs which were academic in nature. To forestall narrowness in the search for talent, the Educational Policies Commission pointed out:

> It must be recognized that a student's gifts may lie in areas other than the academic. Artistic and creative talent must also be sought out and developed. Guidance should also involve the co-operation of parents, for parental attitudes strongly influence the school plans of all students.[6]

The challenges of the 1950's led frequently to reidentification of the purposes of American education. General objectives of education charge the school with a vast range of responsibility with respect to the total development of students. Within this framework, vocational education has a significant responsibility to the American people. The Educational Policies Commission stated:

> More than ever before, and for an ever increasing proportion of the population, *vocational competence* requires developed rational capacities. The march of technology and science in the modern society progressively eliminates the positions open to low-level talents. The man able to use only his hands is at a growing disadvantage as compared with the man who can also use his head. Today even the simplest use of hands is coming to require the simultaneous employment of the mind.[7]

The Commission identified the central purpose of education as the development of the ability to think. It was also pointed out that achievement of the central purpose required concentrated attention by the agencies concerned and that "the development of every student's rational powers must be recognized as centrally important."

Development of the ability to think rationally is independent of subject matter and is the responsibility of all subject-matter specialists if appropriate integration and articulation are to be attained.

6. *The Contemporary Challenge to American Education*, p. 11. Washington: National Education Association, Educational Policies Commission, 1958.

7. *The Central Purpose of American Education*, p. 6. Washington: National Education Association, Educational Policies Commission, 1961.

Increase in the retention of students in school was one of the major factors that led to great concern for the student and the central purpose of education. A study by the United States Office of Education indicated that in the thirty-year period, 1932–62, the number of high-school graduates increased 110 per cent, and the number entering college increased 185 per cent.[8] Such dramatic change in the retention of students in school is evidence that attention to the student's future occupational life is increasingly a significant responsibility of the school.

THE SEARCH FOR QUALITY AND EXCELLENCE

The challenge of the 50's to American education concentrated attention upon the need for attainment of quality in education with due regard for the concepts of *universality* and *diversity*. "The diverse needs of society also demand diversified education. A society which strives to maintain high standards of living and culture needs developed talents of every type."[9] Expansion of programs of instruction was urged for all subject-matter areas, including those of a practical nature. "There should be commercial, vocational, technical, and homemaking courses designed to develop skills which have social or economic value."[10]

In many respects education groped blindly for quality, unable to identify specific requirements but able to describe conditions and environments in which it was believed that quality could germinate and grow. On the other hand, society was becoming more sophisticated in its conception of the appropriate design of the educational machinery needed to supply the desired goals of quality.

Individualized programs to provide for differences among students and to accommodate different social needs were necessary. Competent teaching staffs were essential. Dynamic leadership was needed. Small schools were unable to offer appropriate programs. Development of any degree of progress in quality was dependent upon the extent to which the American people financed their schools.

8. *Progress of Public Education in the United States of America, 1962–63,* p. 7. United States Department of Health, Education, and Welfare, Office of Education. Washington: Government Printing Office, 1963.

9. *An Essay on Quality in Public Education,* p. 7. Washington: National Education Association, Educational Policies Commission, 1959.

10. *Ibid.,* p. 9.

The stinging criticisms of education forced the subject-matter specialists to run for cover and to re-examine purposes, content, and methods. The wave of enthusiasm for quality and excellence in education was projected over the entire range of subject matter from kindergarten to the graduate school. Improvement was thought to be as imperative in the academic areas as in the vocational areas. Public and private funds were directed toward experimentation. New views concerning the efficient use of teachers' time and talents were sought. Course content was reviewed and updated. Considerable attention was devoted to methods of instruction, the use of TV, programed learning, and team teaching.

DISADVANTAGED YOUTH

The student who cannot fit into a general pattern of studies becomes a troublesome problem for the school administrator. This student's plight has received much more attention in recent years than formerly, but movement toward the solution of his problems has been slow. No one term will describe adequately these youth as a group, but the fact remains that a significant number of them have been crowded into an educational no-man's land, and little has been done to help them escape. When age releases them from school, the problem is changed from a school problem to a social problem because a large majority of them cannot find work. It would appear that a program of prevention by the school is preferable to remedial measures by civic groups. "If the dropout is to teach us any abiding lesson it is the lesson of individual differences and infinite variation and the impossibility of expecting this variety to conform to a single standard or to perform with equal acceptability according to an externally imposed criterion."[11]

The Panel of Consultants on Vocational Education brought into view the complex problems of "Youth with Special Needs."[12] It urged the federal government to promote and develop programs for

---

11. Benjamin C. Willis, *Perspectives on Industrial Education*, p. 10. Twenty-fifth Annual Conference on Industrial Education, San Francisco, California, March 13–15, 1963.

12. *Education for a Changing World of Work*, pp. 227–30, 257–58. (Report of the Panel of Consultants on Vocational Education.) United States Department of Health, Education, and Welfare, Office of Education, OE-80021. Washington: Government Printing Office, 1963.

these youth. Education in general has failed to help the disadvantaged youth, and vocational education has largely eliminated the group by imposing selection devices. Now the vocational educators of the nation, well aware that these students want to, or should, go to work, are attempting to meet the challenge. But vocational education alone cannot solve the problem. Several areas of education must combine their efforts and work co-operatively if effective action is to result.

If the student cannot acquire command of the three R's, something must change in his educational environment. If he cannot make his way with the masses in crowded classrooms and cannot keep pace with instruction, something must change so he can learn. If the student can find his way to the classroom by himself, he can most certainly learn something about the subject matter; but possibly the environment must change in order to enhance learning. The student failures of general education are not employable. The conjecture that vocational education can help to create a desire to learn the three R's is supported by just enough evidence to make that possibility an enticing problem for co-operative study by representatives of the subject-matter areas.

Certain problems of cultural disadvantage are centered in the inability of an individual to become a producer of the goods or services which society requires. Many of these fall logically within the province of vocational education.

A strong program of vocational education can serve several important purposes. Opportunities to learn job skills are relatively easy for the pupil to value. They can increase his interest in school. They can help him to consider himself a useful and respected person. They can develop the initiative and sense of responsibility that are basic to preparation for college as well as for new jobs. And they can be designed to introduce or incorporate lessons in science, economics, or other subjects.

Programs of part-time work and part-time study are advisable for many children who are likely to benefit little from an almost exclusively classroom-oriented education. Such programs hold out the hope that many pupils whose handicaps the schools have not otherwise been able to overcome will become contributing, self-supporting adults. The planning of work-study programs demands considerable flexibility and close contact between school and community.[13]

13. *Education and the Disadvantaged American*, p. 18. Washington: National Education Association, Educational Policies Commission, 1962.

The real challenge to vocational education arising from increased attention to the disadvantaged American is the need for the nation in the future to provide occupational instruction to a greater variety of workers and potential workers than ever before and to provide also for a wider variation of individual need because of the complexities of cultural disadvantage. It is obvious, however, that vocational education is only one of the facets of the solution; the home, the school, and the community have equally challenging responsibilities.

... the fact remains that the economy has less and less need for the poorly educated. As the technology becomes more complex, it becomes harder to help the poorly educated to develop marketable skills. When the society fails to develop an American's potentials, it is limiting his chances for productive employment to a disappearing segment of the economy. A public works program can merely compensate for the failures of a society; it cannot correct them. The long-range solution is an increase in the length and effectiveness of schooling.[14]

MANPOWER AND EMPLOYMENT

It is recognized that the defense of the nation is based on two main ingredients—material and manpower. An abundance of one, if the other is scarce, provides little contribution to the national security. How the nation treats these essential elements is a measure of its ability to defend itself.

Manpower is usually considered from a broad point of view and is positively related to such factors as health and civic loyalty. Important among the factors is *vocational efficiency*. The importance of vocational education, properly conceived, in relation to the total manpower resources was a point of emphasis in the 1950's.

The choice of useful work which will most completely enlist the talents and interests of each individual is an important outcome of a well-rounded education. The discovery and development of these abilities and interests by appropriate guidance, training, refresher courses for increased vocational efficiency, and re-training for workers who need to change occupations are other aspects of good schools which are directly related to vocational efficiency. That the United States, with only 7 per cent of the world's population, produces 50 per cent of the world's mechanical energy, is partly due to our system of general and vocational education.[15]

14. *Ibid.*, pp. 35–36.

15. *Public Schools a Top Priority*, p. 9. Washington: National Education Association, Educational Policies Commission, June 1951.

The clear implication of this statement is that *vocational efficiency* of the nation's manpower is a general national responsibility and a specific responsibility of more than one area of education.

In theory, vocational education is available to a large majority of the labor force. However, the enrolment record indicates that vocational education has not provided all the job training it is theoretically capable of providing. Furthermore, such training has not always matched critical employment needs. This situation is not a defect in vocational education alone but is the result of a vast array of complexities, including parental attitudes, lack of adequate financing, and general failure of the schools and the public to recognize that preparation for occupational life is a legitimate function of public education.

The relationship of vocational education to manpower and employment is often misunderstood. Vocational education cannot create job opportunities; this has never been a function of vocational education. All that it can possibly do is to provide appropriate training for jobs that exist; and this it has been doing for many people for a half-century. However, if one reads the critics of vocational education, he finds it is taking an undeserved drubbing. Robert Hutchins writes about "Vocational Training: A Soothing Syrup but No Cure for the Jobless."[16] Of course not! But if jobs are available, vocational education can be and has been remarkably successful in providing the training required for the occupation. Sylvia Porter, in a national syndicated column, writes that "Vocational schools fail to focus on jobless solutions."[17] The emphasis was placed upon what had not been done, with no indication of the extent to which vocational education had dealt with the national problem. An equally misinforming article by Chase, "Learning To Be Unemployable," states that "Good auto mechanics, . . . plumbers, . . . and business-machine repairmen are hard to find. They will be even scarcer in the years ahead unless we stop training young people in obsolete skills and start preparing them for real jobs which remain unfilled while millions are unemployed."[18]

16. *Los Angeles Times*, July 22, 1963, Part II, p. 6.

17. *Chicago Daily News*, April 10, 1963, p. 47.

18. Edward T. Chase, "Learning To Be Unemployable," *Harper's Magazine*, April, 1963, p. 33.

On the other hand, the president of the United Association of Journeymen and Apprentices of the Plumbing and Pipe Fitting Industry sees the problem of vocational education in an entirely different light. He is well aware of the weaknesses of vocational education, but he is also well informed about its strengths. He supports the view that "money spent on vocational education is an indispensable investment in the future manpower of America, which is the real basis for adequate economic growth."[19] Conant, an astute educational observer and commentator, after a thorough study of vocational education, said, "When I hear adverse criticism of vocational education, I cannot help concluding that the critic just has not taken the trouble to find out what he is talking about!"[20]

Obviously, vocational education is not without sin in the matter of manpower and employment, but these factors are central to the existence of vocational education and have had the undivided attention of a large number of persons. Unfortunately maximum achievement is exceedingly difficult when the trump cards of attitude, prejudice, and finance are held in other hands.

Manpower and employment are major concerns of vocational education and are significantly affected by its progress. There is evidence for the conclusion that a greater variety of vocational education available to more people in more schools of the nation could contribute to the solution of manpower and employment problems.

Impact of These Challenges upon Vocational Education

Out of a decade of national self-examination and concern for education a variety of challenges have evolved. The American concept of education for all, with due regard for the individual, is based upon the belief that the maximum social good can be achieved through education. The diverse nature and needs of the total population require that this concept of education find an expression in an equally diverse manner. Recognition of value is awarded to every area and level of education, and it is important that each of these areas and

19. Peter T. Schoemann, "The Changing Needs of Vocational Education," p. 13. A statement presented to the Panel of Consultants on Vocational Education, August 10, 1962, Washington, D.C.

20. James B. Conant, "Vocational Education and the National Need," *American Vocational Journal*, XXXV (January, 1960), 15.

levels assume responsibility for making its maximum contribution to the social good. The central theme of this yearbook is vocational education in the context of many modern forces and values. The challenges to vocational education require that this area of education be reviewed, with emphasis upon a number of forces and facts which appear to have an impact upon the direction of vocational education.

The socioeconomic context of vocational education in an era of technological change provides for an expansion of its scope. Program content must be closely related to the occupational environment of those employed. Worker obsolescence, displacement, mobility, and automation are new dimensions for concern by vocational educators.

The general school program has always had an influence upon the development of many competencies required for successful employment. It is important that the general school program be developed with due regard for its impact upon the occupational world. One of the major contributions which the general school program can make to this end is in the area of vocational and educational guidance. This contribution must be made with increasing effectiveness in the years ahead.

The challenges of the present and their implications for the future call for increased attention to vocational education beyond the high school. Particularly critical are programs of one or two years' duration for students who are preparing to enter the labor force and programs for out-of-school youth and adults.

Recent activity on the part of the federal government has presented a challenge to vocational education. A national study of vocational education was requested by the late President Kennedy in his message to Congress in February, 1961. A panel of consultants was appointed with the assignment to review and evaluate vocational education and to make recommendations for its redirection in terms of the general impact of technological change.

The national study, together with state and local studies, will focus attention upon and lead to the improvement of many aspects of vocational education—policy-formation, organization, administration, and support. Planning to provide for the total national needs in vocational education must take into account the role of nonpublic agencies and the contribution which can come from research in vocational education.

The challenges to vocational education have created a nation-wide interest in it and in its total role in society. Vocational education is a means, in the judgment of many persons, of meeting an important need of American society.

A platform for vocational education in the future will be constructed upon the strength of renewed commitments to the American ideal of education for all. Vocational education must figure prominently in the attainment of this goal. The end product is not solely the responsibility of vocational educators. Successful vocational-education programs, to contribute maximally to the social and economic stability of the nation, must evolve from many relevant sources.

CHAPTER II

Social and Economic Trends

ELI GINZBERG

Introduction

Before entering upon a large-scale social appraisal, it is necessary to select a vantage point from which to launch the assessment, even if during the course of the inquiry incursions are made from multiple points. And here is the first difficulty. Even before the process of analysis can begin and long before the consequences of the evaluation can be verified, it is difficult to obtain agreement about the proper approach. Some leaders of education believe that most of the efforts subsumed under the heading "vocational education" have been not only puerile but downright dangerous; the young people exposed to it have not only failed to acquire an order of technical skill which would assure them success in the labor market but have also been deprived of the opportunity to acquire the elements of a general education which are the birthright of every citizen in a democracy.

To the severity of this judgment can be juxtaposed the equally strong views of leaders of vocational education who maintain that vocational education, especially at the secondary-school level, has never attempted to produce a skilled worker. Its objectives have been much more modest: to afford certain youngsters an alternative to the conventional college-preparatory curriculum by offering them a balanced program of general education, an introduction to applied mathematics and basic scientific theory, and at least the rudiments of specific manual skills or preliminary training as a technician.

Numerous other professional educators are not ideologically opposed to vocational education but are loath to support it because of their serious doubts about its accomplishments in fact. They question whether more than a very small percentage of all those in vocational-education programs actually secure even a small part of the many benefits that proponents claim.

In the face of such differences of opinion about theory and practice, it is difficult for the outsider to find a vantage point and to adopt a stance acceptable to or that can gain the confidence of all these groups. I will set out below my basic assumptions about education in contemporary United States so that my later analysis of important trends in the social and economic environment and the implications of these trends for the future of education, in general, and vocational education, in particular, can be objectively appraised.

Basic Assumptions

Every worth-while educational program contains both a cultural and a vocational element. For a long time mastery of the classics was the key to occupational advancement. One of the principal routes to a preferred career for able but impecunious youths in many countries of the Western world has long begun with a start in the clergy. And achievement in a ministerial career requires competence in the classics. Parenthetically, in the United States the Catholic Church has encountered difficulty in manpower recruitment because of the failure of many novitiates to master Latin. Another example is provided by the detailed reports of contemporary Soviet education, which indicate that the young people who do very well in their studies in secondary school are admitted to the better universities and that, if they continue to do superior work there, their later careers are practically assured. Never before has mastery of mathematics, the sciences, or even the humanities been the one key to occupational preferment.

The overriding challenge that every educational system has always faced is to awaken a love of learning in students and to provide them with the basic tools, above all an ability to read, which will enable them to continue their education when they are no longer enrolled in school. To the extent that the system accomplishes this objective, it succeeds; if this objective is not achieved, it has fundamentally failed, no matter how many other accomplishments it can point to.

The commitment of a society to provide secondary schooling, not only for a small minority who are preparing for scientific or professional occupations but also for the entire population, implies the necessity for differentiated curricula. There is no point in complaining that there has been an intellectual emasculation of the curriculum of secondary schools in the United States during the past several decades. To compare the course of studies pursued by the small percentage of students who graduated from high school at the time of World War I with the 80 to 90 per cent who graduate in many communities today is not relevant. This becomes clear as soon as we introduce into the equation the range in intellectual potential, educational motivation, and occupational objectives that exists between the most talented sixth in the population and the average. The postulate, however, of the essentiality of differentiated curricula is by itself a predisposing but not an overwhelming basis for justifying the elaboration of vocational-education programs; it is intended even less to justify specific programs.

Young people and adults can learn in different ways—from classroom instruction and from less formally structured environments—particularly in connection with their jobs. If the objective of the instruction is to master a particular technique, it is likely that they can make greater progress in a real life situation than in the simulated environment of a classroom, especially in a school that has no organic relation to the work setting. It is simply not possible to simulate within most schools the subtle and, frequently, not even the gross qualities that permeate a work environment. Adult work is carried on in order to establish a profit; in nonprofit and governmental organizations work is conducted in order to provide a basic community service. Much of what the worker needs to know can be learned only in the concrete situation affected by time, supervision, competition and co-operation between workers, emergencies, and many other pervasive reality factors. Most of these conditions cannot be simulated in a school environment. This fact, together with the costliness of maintaining up-to-date physical equipment and the difficulties of attracting and retaining competent instructors, places severe limitations on the elaboration of strong vocational programs within the educational structure. This does not argue that it cannot be done; it simply points to the difficulties.

The additional assumption is that the United States has been more successful in extending the educational cycle than in evolving its content or establishing the conditions under which both general education and vocational instruction can most effectively be provided. We have a serious unsolved problem. But there would be little point in trying to solve it in terms of today's conditions and circumstances. Significant educational reforms require time, and, while they are being introduced, the basic contours of the society and economy undergo rapid change. Hence, it is always wise to gear reforms of the general educational structure and, more particularly, of the vocational-educational structure to the transformations which are under way in the large social framework. The delineation of some of these more important changes is our next task.

Key Trends

It is fashionable in these early years of the space age to stress the rate at which our world is experiencing fundamental and rapid changes, particularly because the breakthroughs in space occurred before the spectacular manifestations of the nuclear age had much opportunity to alter the quality of civilian life and work. We still have not found a way to mass-produce the inexpensive nuclear reactor which is eventually to provide very low-cost fuel to the impoverished nations of the world. Nor have we found the key to inexpensive desalinization, the parallel development which holds such great promise for the world's poor. While we wait for these promises to be turned into reality we see regrettably that the numbers of the world's poor are increasing ever more rapidly. Science and technology are potent forces to use in our efforts to increase the effectiveness with which we use the world's resources, but they may not be potent enough to win the race against the multiplication of man himself.

Another facet of contemporary change is the contradiction to the assumption of rapid change. Let us consider the simple question of the extent to which the life of a middle-class family has been transformed by technological advances since the end of the New Era (1929). The answer is, "Relatively little." There have been only two developments of major import—air travel and television. The pattern of daily life for the minority who do not like television and who have no occasion to travel has not been significantly altered in the last third of a century. Technology aside, significant changes have, of course, taken place as a result of the Depression, the New Deal,

World War II, the advances in the economy, and the demographic and cultural changes which have accompanied these political and economic shifts. But the recent historical record indicates that even a society as dynamic as ours is not transformed very rapidly or radically. In forecasting for the decade ahead, we must place even more stress on the elements of continuity than on those of change. To this end we will focus, first, on those aspects of change that relate to demography and the labor force; next, to those associated with the alterations in the demand for labor as a consequence of developments in science, technology, and income; and, finally, on transformations in the value structure of the society, particularly as these are reflected in the actions of individuals, groups, and government. Only after these several dimensions of change have been identified and delineated will we be in a position to inquire into the opportunities and the challenges which these developments offer to vocational education.

On the demographic front, one of the most important developments is the significant increase which will occur in 1964–65 in the number of eighteen-year-olds. In that one year they will increase by approximately one-third—from three to four million; and when the basis of comparison is the population of that age group in the early 1950's, the order of change will be more than 100 per cent. The impact of this trend will be noticeable. High schools and colleges will face a noticeably increased work load, and the number of young people who will be available for work will increase substantially. In a delicately articulated economy in which it is never easy to establish and still more difficult to maintain a balance between those who seek jobs and the jobs available, sudden and large-scale increase in the supply of young job applicants would always present a serious challenge. And since this increase will take place against a background of relatively high and chronic unemployment, particularly among those in their teens and early twenties, the difficulties that loom ahead appear almost ominous. It is easy to understand, on the basis of this single phenomenon, why President Kennedy repeatedly stated that the major economic challenge facing the United States in the 1960's was employment or, as he sometimes referred to the issue, economic growth at a rate sufficient to furnish an adequate number of jobs for prospective job seekers.

In releasing the disturbingly high unemployment rate for September, 1962, the spokesman for the Department of Labor called attention to the fact that the unexpectedly large number of women seeking employment was in considerable measure responsible for the rate of 5.8 per cent. The behavior of women with respect to the labor market has been undergoing a revolutionary change since the onset of World War II. Prior to that time it was only the exceptional married woman who worked. Today the majority of the more than 24 million women workers who are employed at any one time during the year—the number employed at some time during the course of a year exceeds 30 million—is composed of married women, many of whom have children under eighteen. While many women do not seek full-time employment and are interested in employment only during certain periods of the day, week, or year, the fact remains that more and more married women are interested in working out of the home during much of their lives, except for the rather short period during which they have young children to care for. Because of the young age at which most women in the United States marry— one-quarter are married by eighteen, and half are married before their twenty-first birthday—they are likely to complete their families by their late twenties and to have their youngest in school before they are thirty-five. Early marriage has greatly increased the availability of women for work.

Immediately after the end of World War II it was possible to ignore or discount the rapid increase in womanpower, but during the last eighteen years the importance of women in the labor force has been firmly fixed. Despite the opposition of certain powerful religious groups, Congress recently took note of the large numbers of women at work and authorized a grant-in-aid program for the purpose of expanding and improving day-care centers for the children of working mothers. Trends definitely indicate that many young women will cease or interrupt their education or training in their late teens or early twenties to marry and have their families; and many of them will want to pick up their studies again or get a job in their thirties. No planning with respect to education or employment should neglect one-half of the nation's human potential and one-third of its current manpower resources. An appropriate education for women—as for men, but even more so for women—must be related to the totality of the challenges which they will meet in life. Since more and more married women will eventually be employed part-time or full-time, the desirability of their securing an educational base from which they can more readily acquire skills is evident.

The United States has long been characterized by a very mobile population, and recent data indicate that this feature of our experience is continuing and will be present and potent in the decades ahead. Seymour Wolfbein of the United States Department of Labor has stated that one out of every six jobs in the country is now found within the three states of California, Texas, and Florida. In 1962, California moved ahead of New York as the most populous state in the union.

The basic pattern of mobility is from the Southeast and South Central states and from the North Central region to the West and Southwest. Florida is the exception on the eastern seaboard; it has been drawing substantial numbers from many sections of the country.

Additional facets of mobility have an important bearing on education and employment. There is a great and continuing amount of family relocation within counties, between counties, and between states. The census reports indicate that in a recent twelve-month period for which data are available (March, 1960, to March, 1961), over 35 million persons above the age of one year, or one out of every five persons in the population, moved. The record for this period was consistent with each of the preceding surveys undertaken since 1948. Although most people moved within the same county, more than 11 million moved from one county to another or from one state to another. While many moves within a county did not involve job changes for adults or school shifts for children, a high proportion of moves did involve shifts in employment and school and were concomitants of the family's relocation. The mobility rates are high for the early-twenties age group. It is about 45 per cent for this group of young people who are at the start of their careers. Other facts about mobility are that the unemployed and those in the lower-income ranges are more mobile than those with jobs, particularly those who earn more than $5,000 a year; nonwhites are somewhat more mobile than whites, although the difference is accounted for solely by higher rates of intracounty mobility; and since there is very little movement to the farm, the rates for the rural population are relatively low for they reflect primarily a one-way movement—off the farm.

There is every reason to postulate the continuance of a high mobility rate, particularly among young adults and their children. This means that our historic, although diminishing, reliance on local government as the principal instrument for providing education has serious drawbacks. In certain areas the school authorities are confronted with the necessity of preparing many of their young people for life and for jobs which they will pursue in distant places and which may be vastly different from those anticipated. Wise educational planning, therefore, must allow for continued high mobility.

This discussion of mobility brings us to a consideration of two remaining aspects of broad demographic trends—the future of the farm population and the outlook for minority groups, particularly Negroes. With regard to the farm population, the United States presents a striking paradox. On the one hand, our steady advance in science, technology, and instruction in agricultural skills for young people and adults has enabled this country to develop an agriculture that has led the world in productivity. It has enabled this country to feed much better an ever larger population with an ever diminishing proportion of the total work force. Today, approximately 5.5 million in a labor force of 75 million are in agriculture.

But even this absolute and relative shrinkage of the agricultural labor force still leaves too many people attached to agriculture. Many families struggle to eke out a living from a soil which has been mined of its richness, without adequate resources to either replenish it or to shift its use. In the richer farm sections, the steady forward march of technology precludes the employment of all, or even most, of the farmer's offspring. A recent report by the Committee on Economic Development has argued persuasively that the only way in which American agriculture can escape from continued dependence on the present costly and burdensome system of controls and subsidies is through a substantial relocation of many who now seek a livelihood on the land.

Although the desirability and feasibility of particular remedies for a problem that has been attacked by three decades of political experimentation could be argued, most specialists would agree that a successful program would have to include a reduction in the number of persons engaged in agriculture. Hence, in the years ahead, with respect to both economic policy and educational planning, it is essential that one assumption be built into any proposal—the relocation of many people, especially young people, from the farm to the cities.

The last important demographic dimension relates to minority groups. We noted earlier that nonwhites are more mobile than whites. Another fact about these groups is that a high proportion of the large numbers who now live on farms at a subsistence level belong to minority groups—primarily Negroes, but also Mexican-Americans and Indians. However, the last two decades have seen an accelerated movement of southern Negroes into the larger urban communities within the South and even more into the large cities of the North and West. There is every indication that these movements will continue until Negroes are almost exclusively urban dwellers.

There is also mounting evidence that population pressure is increasing on Indian reservations to a point where many Indians will have to seek employment elsewhere. There is little prospect, even with increased help from the federal and state governments, of establishing on the reservations a sufficiently high level of economic activity to provide a livelihood for all who are born and reared on them.

The last decade has seen a substantial movement of Mexican-Americans out of the Southwest into California. With the continued mechanization of agriculture, the relocation of rural and nonfarm families into the larger centers of California and other Pacific and Mountain states is likely to continue.

The patterns of mobility of minority groups characteristic of the recent past are likely to continue in the decade ahead with the single exception of those of the Puerto Rican population. The peak in the inflow from Puerto Rico to the mainland occurred in the first half of the 1950's, and it diminished radically thereafter to a point where it recently reached a negative figure—more were returning to the island than were arriving. But the continuing great pressure of population in Puerto Rico itself may lead to a renewed substantial inflow into the continental United States, particularly if a strong demand for labor should develop and persist in New York City and environs. In fact, if employment opportunities were to be noticeably better in

New York than in Puerto Rico for a number of consecutive years, a large migration might be expected again.

Another aspect of Puerto Rican population movement is that the very heavy concentration of that population in New York City has begun to lessen. It is dispersing over wide areas in the Northeast, and this dispersion is likely to continue. This means that more and more communities are likely to find, among their school-age population, youngsters who have little and sometimes no facility with English.

Members of minority groups are thrice handicapped. First, certain of their attributes impede their ready acceptance by the dominant population, and this makes their search for employment more difficult. Next, many of them are migrants, who always face special difficulties in adjustment as they attempt to shed earlier patterns of adjustment and acquire new ones. Finally, members of minority groups tend to come from environments which failed to provide the range of opportunities available in the communities in which they settle, and this places them at a further disadvantage both in school and in the labor market. Our society has been conspicuously obtuse about the weight of these cumulative hardships and about the necessity of making major efforts to help members of minority groups overcome them.

The preceding review has sought to identify some of the important changes in the size and location of groups in the population that are under way. Demography will provide one of the important parameters for vocational education in the years ahead. Another parameter, which we will now consider, relates to changes in science, technology, and the economy. For convenience we will subsume these changes under the rubric of the changing demands for skills.

We do not need detailed manpower forecasts to substantiate the premise that the future will witness the continuation of a strong demand for a high quality of technological manpower. Only a sudden and drastic cut-back in defense- and space-spending could change this trend, and then only slightly.

During the last decades there has been not only a substantial increase in the absolute numbers engaged in scientific, professional, and technical work but also a more than proportionate gain in these categories as a part of the total labor force. Reliable projections for 1970 and 1975 suggest that this trend will continue and that the absolute and relative number of persons engaged in such fields of work will continue to show large increases.

In addition to the ever broader permeation of the economy by science and the new and improved technologies based on science, there is a related development that contributes to the consistently strong demand for recent science graduates. The very rate at which scientific knowledge is accumulating and then applied is resulting in a stepped-up obsolescence of the knowledge and know-how of persons already in the labor market. By dint of effort and work experience, some are able to keep abreast of the latest developments, but the great majority is likely to fall further and further behind and eventually be unable to cope with current problems. Industry, therefore, scrambles for the promising, recent graduate. First, he has attributes which most older persons in the labor force do not have; second, he may be one of those rare persons who will be able to discover a new method or design a new product which will catch the public's fancy. Industry's interest in the young graduate, although based on his superior training, contains an element of gambling. Many employers are willing to hire large numbers of recent graduates in the hope of finding the exceptional man who may succeed in making a major breakthrough.

A consideration of the problems presented by the speeded-up obsolescence of knowledge and skills should include the warning that, since the proportion of current science graduates to the total existing supply is about 1 to 20, or even less, a major challenge in improving manpower development and utilization is to insure that adequate resources are devoted to keeping the existing supply of trained manpower vital.

The obverse of the foregoing discussion is the impact of the rapid advances of technology on the unskilled end of the occupational structure. Here the evidence from the recent past also casts a powerful shadow ahead. At the turn of this century and up to the time when labor shortages were engendered by World War I, there was a substantial demand in the American economy for men with strong backs. But advances in technology soon reduced the demand for unskilled laborers until today it is relatively small. In recent years the advances in technology, which currently are subsumed under the term "automation," have moved toward liquidating, especially in the manufacturing section of the economy, a high proportion of semi-skilled jobs—those held by operatives.

More recently automation has resulted in a similar trend in various service sectors of the economy, especially in insurance, banking, and related fields. The new technology has eliminated a great number of clerical positions, particularly those which involve a great amount of record-keeping.

In recent data about the labor force, there are indications, but nothing more as yet, that the earlier impact of automation on the employment of men in the automobile industry, in steel, and in meat-packing is beginning to be repeated in areas where women have, for a long time, found ample employment opportunities. Because of the much greater mobility of women in and out of the labor force, the impact is not so much on those currently employed as on those who are ready to enter or re-enter the labor market and who will find fewer jobs available.

The impact of technology is also felt by poorly educated persons with limited skills, who now find it particularly difficult to locate work. The characteristics of the unemployed leave no doubt that it is the poorly prepared and those with limited skills who find it most difficult to secure and keep a niche for themselves in our highly dynamic economy. To find a place for persons of limited capacity and competence in an economy which is increasingly interested only in persons with skill or the potential for the acquisition of skill remains a major challenge.

If we shift from the employment to the productivity aspects of an affluent economy, we find that the steady reduction in the hours of work, which have characterized our economy in the past, will continue and possibly accelerate in the years ahead. Some recent contracts provide for three months' vacation for workers who have been on the payroll for fifteen years. During the past years, in both the unionized and nonunionized sectors of the economy, management has been paying for more and more hours that are not worked—holidays and vacations with pay. Many white-collar workers already work a 35-hour week. There is every reason to anticipate that within the foreseeable future, the average hours of work per week may drop to 32 or even to 30; workers will enjoy more holidays with pay; and four weeks' vacation for workers with a few years of service may be the norm.

It has surprised some students, including the writer, that the trade-union movement has acted so slowly to exert pressure to reduce the hours of work, although it recently committed itself to do so. The American economy has historically absorbed about two-fifths of its increasing productivity in more leisure rather than in more goods. In the face of increasing stringencies of employment, organized labor has no option but to make use of this mechanism for adjusting demand and supply. The oft-repeated fear that a reduced work week, if accompanied by the same weekly pay, will lead to a serious wage inflation is not irrelevant, but it may be considerably exaggerated. With continued technological improvements, it should be possible to absorb part of the reduction in work hours without any rise in labor costs. Moreover, the slack which exists in most work situations should make possible the absorption of another part of the potential cost increases by more effective manpower utilization. We may not be able to fulfil the prophecy of John Maynard Keynes that, by the end of this century, a basic work week of 15 hours will suffice for producing all the essential goods required by an advanced technological society, but we may not be very far from that goal. A 20-hour week is well within the realm of possibility.

A series of broad social trends and institutional arrangements that are developing will also help to determine the parameters within which vocational education must work out its answers in the years ahead. The first is the continuing nation-wide emphasis on the lengthening of formal education with an ever higher percentage of the high-school graduates seeking admission to college. Although the most optimistic figures about future college enrolments may prove too high—for they do not consider adequately the steeply rising costs of tuition, the difficulties presented by a college curriculum to many with only modest intellectual endowment, or the possibility of a narrowing wage differential between high-school and college graduates —a substantial increase in both the absolute and relative numbers who will attend college and graduate school will surely occur.

Part of this expansion will undoubtedly be reflected in the rapid proliferation of junior and community colleges. California has already set the pattern, and before long other rich states with a tradition of strong support for education will undoubtedly move toward the development of community colleges that will blanket all areas within their borders. This prospect presents an excellent opportunity for the restructuring of vocational and technical education.

Professor Harold Clark of Teachers College, Columbia University, was among the first to call attention several years ago to the fact that the costs of education and training provided by industry had reached a magnitude which approximated the total expenditures within the formal school system. He acknowledged the difficulty of deriving a clear estimate of the value of this industrial-education effort and pointed to important distinctions concerning the breadth and depth of the education and training in school and in plant, but he concluded that all of the advantages were not necessarily with school instruction. Issues of quality aside, the incontrovertible conclusion emerging from Clark's survey was that American industry is conducting a very elaborate and large-scale educational and training effort. Planning for vocational education in coming years must take into account the probability that the future will witness an ever greater involvement of industry in the total training effort.

A third related dimension is the continuing educational role played by the Armed Services through the large-scale training of recruits, career personnel, and reservists. By far the largest sector of military training has been the training of men who have been drafted or have enlisted for one tour of duty and who return to civilian life as soon as their two-, three-, or four-year commitments are completed. While the Armed Services have made a strenuous and, to some degree, a successful effort to raise their re-enlistment rates, the fact remains that most of the men leave as soon as they have served the required minimum. As a consequence, the military must engage in a great amount of first- and second-level skill training.

It is not easy to make qualitative and quantitative comparisons between this military training in skills and that provided through civilian vocational institutions, but in many areas the contribution of the military is outstanding, and its total contribution has been and will undoubtedly continue to be very substantial.

The last decade has seen a growing awareness on the part of management as well as other community leaders, of the fact that the economic well-being of their firm or of a locality hinges to a marked degree on the skill level of the population. Communities with good schools increasingly have the advantage in attracting and expanding industries that depend on the utilization of trained manpower. While some industries, such as textiles, that use a relatively high proportion of unskilled and easily trained workers continue to locate in low-wage and low-tax areas; many others, such as the new electronics companies, are more concerned about the availability of a large supply of trained and trainable labor. The rapid expansion of electronics in California, Massachusetts, and New York is directly related to the availability of good educational facilities and a trained labor supply. In the years ahead, communities will find that cutting corners on educational and other services to keep taxes low is less and less an effective means of attracting new industry; it will be the progressive community that will have the advantage.

Despite recent untoward disturbances in the deep South, it may be that the counterrevolution in the South is reaching its peak and that we may soon be launched on a process of compliance with the law. The determination of the Negro leadership, North and South, to insist on all legal and civic rights for Negroes—and their mounting ability to reinforce this insistence with their newly aggrandized political power—foreshadows the eventual collapse of the remaining vestiges of segregation, at least in all the larger communities of the nation.

An aspect of this long-delayed but now high-priority item on the nation's agenda is the increasing awareness on the part of thoughtful leaders, both white and Negro, of the special efforts that must be put forth on behalf of minority groups if they are to be able to compete successfully in a nonsegregated society. This means special assistance on every front: in school, in training programs, in employment. The only way to help correct the imbalance resulting from three hundred years of exploitation is to pursue a policy which recognizes the inherent inequality of "equality" for severely handicapped groups and which provides special programs to establish the preconditions for effective integration. Because most vocational-education efforts have a history of racial discrimination, adjustment in line with our new national policy is essential.

Implications for Vocational Education

The outline of our basic assumptions about education and the detailing of the specific social, economic, and related trends, which will determine the shape of the occupational structure, places us in a position to indicate some of the more important implications of these appraisals for the future of vocational education. The key considerations are what should be taught to different groups and under what conditions the instruction should be provided.

Since the advances in science and technology foreshadow a continuing increase in skill requirements, the employability of young people in the future will depend on their preparation in fundamentals. Control over fundamentals is essential for continued learning throughout adult life. And continued learning is necessary if adults are to play their proper roles in the economy and the larger society. Even a Ph.D. who stops learning after his graduation will soon become ill-informed. Most young people who have the intellectual capacity to complete an academic high-school curriculum, and perhaps to attend a junior college, should postpone vocational education until they complete high school. Until then, most young people should concentrate on acquiring control over the rudiments and simple academic subjects.

If, as we hope, a large part of the more intellectually capable sector of the population pursues a primarily academic curriculum in high school and spends an average of two years in a community college, it seems reasonable to provide them with a range of opportunities that are vocationally oriented during the years in which they are in college. Some will prefer to continue to study academic subjects, but many others will undoubtedly prefer to prepare more specifically for occupations which require specialized education and training. The California junior and community colleges have developed a wide range of solid offerings which suggest what can and should be done.

The task required by the foregoing recommendation may be related to conventional training for secretarial work and for the distributive trades that have for so long attracted such a considerable number of girl students during their high-school years. Girls who are capable of pursuing an academic curriculum should be encouraged to postpone their specific vocational training until after graduation from high school—although all students, boys and girls alike, should be encouraged to learn to type. Girls who are less inclined to academic work probably need good work-study programs as much as do boys, perhaps more so, since girls mature more quickly.

What about the very sizable proportion, between one-quarter and one-third or even more, who do not have the intellectual prerequisites for this much academic education? Currently the nation's educational and political leaders are pleading with the youngsters who drop out before completing high school to remain in school. But these pleas miss the point. The school, as presently constituted, does not meet the needs of these young people. Long before they drop out, most of them cease to profit from classroom instruction. Only radical adjustments can meet the challenge presented by adolescents who are neither intellectually capable of advanced academic work nor motivated to continue classroom study. So far educators have found it very difficult to work out appropriate curricula for young people who are intellectually slow and often backward.

Moreover, the school alone probably cannot solve all of their problems. By the time these young people become 15 or 16 years of age, surely before they are 18, they are straining at the bit to join adult society—to get a job, earn money, and enjoy the freedom of adulthood. Our society is blocking the accomplishment of these legitimate aspirations. So far it has swept the problem under the rug and held the teachers responsible for the poor preparation for work and life now offered to these adolescents. The challenge goes beyond the school and involves management, labor, and government. While a few communities have demonstrated initiative in developing experimental prevocational training for many of these young people, and others have developed effective work-study programs, the vast majority of communities have not even recognized the existence of the problem. The major challenge to vocational education below the college level is to help develop imaginative solutions for the difficult problem presented by this sizable group of young people who are being stultified by the present system.

Special note should be taken of the educational needs of young people growing up in rural areas. This has long been the arena for one of the more ambitious long-range programs in vocational education which has successfully given instruction in the agricultural arts and sciences in home economics. While there is still need for both of these programs in some rural high schools, the majority of the youngsters currently in such schools and of those who will attend in the future have needs that are not being adequately met by these conventional programs. It should be noted in passing that, since agriculture is increasingly becoming agro-business, the type of preparation which the farmer of tomorrow will need includes solid instruction in the fundamentals so that he can acquire additional education and training in such fields as economics, accounting, and genetics.

The acquistion of a solid core of academic subjects is even more necessary for those who will have to earn their livelihood in the burgeoning industrial and commercial centers of population which will continue to receive in the future, as in the past, the substantial surplus of population born and brought up on the farms. Consequently, there is indication of a need to supplement the present agricultural-vocational program with others that are city oriented and to adjust the agricultural instruction to the changing realities of modern farm technology and economics. It is never easy to make adjustments, but this is an area in which adjustments are essential, and new programs that will help the future industrial migrant are sorely needed.

The foregoing adjustments concern the young person in high school or junior college. But vocational education must make provision for adults as well. One of the largest groups in need of help is made up of mature women in their thirties or early forties who are entering or re-entering the labor force. Since the responsibilities of these women at home tend to be reduced gradually as their children grow up and become more self-sufficient, many of them would welcome an opportunity to return to school on a part- or even full-time basis before seeking employment. The community college can meet the needs of many by offering the type of general- and vocational-education courses which will help them sharpen their old skills or acquire new ones.

Similarly, community colleges are suited to provide the educational and vocational training facilities required by many adult men who are seeking to improve their positions or who, by choice or necessity, must acquire a new skill. Congruent with the suggestion advanced earlier, to limit vocational preparation in high schools to the less intellectually inclined adolescents, is a recommendation to shift the bulk of adult vocational training for employed men to the community college. In this connection it is suggested that admission into various programs for both adult men and women be made more flexible than that for regular students and that requirements and credits be liberally interpreted so that work experience is accepted in lieu of formal courses. As education pervades the whole of adulthood, it becomes important to break through the rigidities of academic life.

Apprenticeship has long played an important, if necessarily minor, role in the development of skill. One of the weaker aspects of even strong apprenticeship programs has been the quality of supplemental instruction. If the community college is to become the center of much of the adult vocational effort, it will have to provide strong supplemental instruction in connection with approved apprenticeship programs. But it must do more. Increasingly, journeymen will find it necessary to return to school periodically to acquire additional specialized knowledge and techniques. We must, therefore, attempt to strengthen the relationships among vocational education, management, and labor in order to broaden and deepen the range of this supplemental instruction. In this connection it becomes essential that past practices involving racial and other types of discrimination be eliminated.

There are approximately 10 million persons in our civilian labor force of slightly more than 70 million who did not graduate from elementary school. Some of this group are totally illiterate; others are semiliterate; most of the others cannot adequately read, write, or do simple sums. We know from various efforts to retrain the unemployed that a major barrier is their low level of general knowledge. It is essential, therefore, that any comprehensive planning for vocational education on a community level provide for instruction in literacy for all adults. Literacy training frequently founders because of the difficulty of eliciting the co-operation of those who need it. Many illiterates are ashamed to announce their handicap by enrolling in a course which by its title identifies them as illiterate. Here the community college or even the high school could make a significant contribution to overcoming this major psychological barrier by appropriately disguising such courses. Instruction in basic skills might be part and parcel of a program with a broad reach, such as citizenship.

One of the trends that was identified in the preceding section was the steady reduction in the amount of time that people will devote to work in the future. The corollary of this is the almost certain increase in the number and proportion of people who will want to put their leisure time to constructive use. The demand on the part of the adult population for general and specialized education in addition to specific courses geared to enhance employability will undoubtedly grow by leaps and bounds. Since formal adult education in this country is underdeveloped, major effort should first be devoted to surveying latent needs, to exploring alternative ways of meeting these needs, and to providing the requisite facilities and instructors. The community college appears to be the logical center for such an expansion. In this, general adult education and vocational education should not be sharply divided, for many will undoubtedly be able to turn what begins as an avocational interest into the foundation for an occupational skill.

Community Co-ordination

Implicit in the foregoing discussion is the need for much closer correlation among the many different sectors of society that have a direct concern with one or another facet of vocational education. There should be closer liaison among the several levels of government—federal, state, and local—as well as in industry, among the individual company, the trade association, and the large national employer groups; in labor, among the local union, the trades council, the international, and the AFL-CIO; in education, among high schools, junior and community colleges, state education departments, and the United States Office of Education.

Equally important is improved articulation in planning and execution of programs among government, education, management, labor, and representatives of the public. We know the many complexities involved in strengthening these relationships at each of several levels: local, state, regional, national. But the need for major revisions in vocational education is clear, and the required changes cannot be undertaken or even identified by any one group alone. To raise the skill level of the American people requires the co-operative effort of the principal groups involved. The scholar can help identify and evaluate the need for action, but only interested citizen groups can carry the action through to a successful conclusion.

CHAPTER III

The Technological Context of Vocational Education

GEORGE E. ARNSTEIN

Introduction

There is increasing realization today that we are living in the middle of a major revolution, every bit as far-reaching as the Industrial Revolution some two hundred years ago. Because of its radical nature and rapid pace, this technological or scientific revolution has had, and no doubt will continue to have, major influence on vocational education.

There is also increasing realization that the old patterns of vocational education, based in a large part on the Smith-Hughes Act of 1917 and subsequent federal legislation, are not adequate to prepare youngsters and adults for today's technological needs. The Panel of Consultants on Vocational Education, appointed at the request of the President, spent more than a year surveying the whole field of technical education. The Manpower Development and Training Act (PL 87-415) was passed in 1962 to hasten efforts to upgrade the work skills of the nation. The roots of the present imbalance between manpower supply and demand are, of course, very complex; they were explored in some detail in a series of 1963 hearings held by the Subcommittee on Manpower and Employment of the Senate Committee on Labor and Public Welfare.

The list of hearings, studies, and surveys could be extended. Publication of the present volume is in itself a manifestation of the widespread concern with technical education, technical manpower, and manpower-planning in general. We find ourselves in the midst of a sweeping technological revolution, which we are trying to understand and control before it overwhelms us. In a way, our continuing quest for progress and amelioration has brought us to this point.

The Impact of Research and Development

Among the most significant events in the history of modern man is the invention of invention, the systematic quest for new ways of doing things, for new products and ideas. The rise of American investment in research and development (R&D) is an illustration of this quest. The following quotation indicates the dimensions of the enterprise and, equally important, the trend which has made possible the new industrial revolution in which we are now living.

> In its first 150 years as a nation, the United States—government and industry combined—spent some $18 billion for R&D. That total was matched in the five-year period, 1950 to 1955, and almost matched again in the single fiscal year of 1962.[1]

The figures continue to rise, with estimates that annual R&D expenditures will double in the next ten years.

There is evidence that many areas of American life have been the beneficiaries of concerted efforts toward amelioration. Our present agricultural surpluses may cast some doubt on the idea of amelioration, but the fact remains that the surpluses arise from a deliberate decision, made about a century ago, to stimulate agriculture. The Morrill Act of 1862, which laid the groundwork for our land-grant colleges and universities, called for the establishment of new agricultural and mechanical colleges in each of the states. To stimulate agricultural research, a later act also provided funds for the specific purpose of establishing agricultural experiment stations to be linked to the agricultural colleges. In more recent years, the Agricultural Extension Service has brought the fruits of agricultural research to the farmers themselves.

These efforts are part of an impressive record of American attempts to promote research, development, and education in order to achieve beneficial results in selected areas of the economy.

Especially in the light of this experience, our current, sharp increases in R&D should cause careful scrutiny of the rapid march of technology and of the total movement which has been described as a scientific, technological, or second industrial revolution.

The original Industrial Revolution, based largely on the steam

1. Lawrence Galton, "Will Space Research Pay Off on Earth," *New York Times Magazine*, May 26, 1963, p. 29.

engine, made evident the fact that mechanical power could replace human and animal muscular effort. Today's revolution, featuring the electronic computer as its most visible mainspring, is demonstrating that machines can replace human mental effort. A less visible but possibly more important difference was the relatively slow spread of the impact of the Industrial Revolution—urbanization, rail transportation, the factory system, and the novel idea of standardization introduced by Eli Whitney, who produced rifles with interchangeable parts,[2] in contrast to the revolutionary swiftness of today's technological change, as evidenced by the development and impact of the computer.

The Computer and Its Applications

Until about 1950, most computing machines were hand operated, mildly complex adding and calculating machines which sat on the

TABLE 1*

COMPUTER INSTALLATIONS, 1960–63

DATE	TOTAL NUMBER		INCREASE IN NUMBER OF COMPUTERS INSTALLED IN SIX-MONTH PERIOD	NET CHANGE IN ON-ORDER POSITION IN SIX-MONTH PERIOD	NEW ORDERS RECEIVED IN SIX-MONTH PERIOD
	Installed	On Order			
January, 1960....	3,612	1,364	1,578	127	1,705
July, 1960.......	4,257	4,377	645	3,013	3,658
January, 1961....	4,528	6,246	271	1,869	2,140
July, 1961.......	5,371	7,437	843	1,191	2,034
January, 1962....	7,305	7,904	1,934	467	2,401
July, 1962.......	9,495	7,286	2,190	− 618	1,572
January, 1963....	11,078	7,097	1,583	− 189	1,394
July, 1963.......	11,926	5,889	848	−1,208	360

* Testimony of John Diebold, President, the Diebold Group, Inc., before the U.S. House of Representatives Committee on Education and Labor, Select Subcommittee on Labor, August 5, 1963.

desk. They were in the same class as other mechanical office and billing machines that have been used for many years. Today, computers are electronic, digital, transistorized machines which are evolving from magnetic tape to random-access memory discs, including miniaturization, thin-film memories, and applications of cryogenics. Table 1 indicates how recently and how rapidly computer installations have grown.

2. T. S. Ashton, *The Industrial Revolution, 1760–1830*. London: Oxford University Press, 1948.

To some extent, the computer still carries with it the notion of a resplendent calculating machine, sometimes denounced as a stupid beast, sometimes praised as a superhuman information-processor. In the present state of computer development both of these views are correct, although the future potential of these machines appears evident.

Stupid beast.—There is no getting away from the fact that computers are created, used, and manipulated by human beings. Among system analysts there is the pithy expression GIGO—Garbage In, Garbage Out—to indicate that the output will be just as good or as bad as the input, consisting of program, data, and memory. In this sense, Sir Josiah Stamp's statement of some thirty years ago concerning the government and its statistics could be applied to the modern computer and its products:

> The government are very keen on amassing statistics. They collect them, add them, raise them to the Nth power, take the cube root and prepare wonderful diagrams. But you must never forget that every one of these figures comes in the first instance from the village watchman, who puts down what he damn pleases.[3]

Mental giant.—Computers, however, can do things no human being can ever hope to do. They can perform calculations never before possible. Their memories are nearly infallible and their operation is all but perfect.[4] Given a program to play checkers, computers soon can beat their human opponents, if only because their attention does not lapse, their memory does not fail, and their program has instructed them to profit from every mistake—never to make the same mistake twice. Granted, computers have not quite "learned" to play a decent game of chess, but this inability rests on the limits of memory and program. As soon as the human masters devise the proper machines and program, the machine will "learn" to outplay its master as well as other opponents.

3. Comment of an English judge on the subject of Indian statistics, as quoted by Sir Josiah Stamp in *Some Economic Factors in Modern Life*, pp. 258-59. London: P. S. King & Son, 1929.

4. In the days of vacuum tubes, malfunctions were far more prevalent than with today's transistors. Computers may be programed incorrectly and suffer from other defects. However, as a general proposition, computers approximate flawless performance, after debugging, especially because they can diagnose and correct some of their own defects.

The transcending importance of the computer lies in the variety of applications and our expectations of still greater performance in the future. Relatively simple programs now operate elevators, a routine task once performed by human beings. Punch cards instruct a computer, which produces mailing labels at greater speed and with greater efficiency than was possible when embossed addressing plates were used. In the telephone industry, the dial system has not only reduced the need for operators but there is increasing use of automatic recording devices to collect the information needed to process toll calls and other special charges. Even space travel and missiles would be impossible without on-line computers.

Technological change is not necessarily tied to the computer, although manifestations of such change may have far-reaching manpower consequences. Particularly noteworthy is the process of numerical control, representing a great refinement of the historic Jacquard loom or the perforated tape of player pianos. Whether the input is in the form of paper tape, punched cards, or magnetic-electronic impulses, the result is the remote instruction and control of machines which stamp out mechanical parts, drill holes, or squirt fruit fillings into doughy shells. Significantly, these numerically controlled routines may be used over and over again—with precision and dependability greater than can be achieved by experienced journeymen. They can also be replaced by a new and different routine with a minimum of delay and adjustment, whether the change is from large to small holes to be bored by a drillpress, or whether the change involves a switch from filling apple rather than cherry pies. Progress in numerical control has reduced "down time" and has introduced elements of flexibility which exceed those of human workers whose efforts are limited by physical endurance, occasional lapses in attention, and other human frailties.

In these and other ways the computer and its allies often improve on human performance of routine tasks and make possible complex calculations which heretofore, for lack of human ability or for economic reasons, had been beyond the reach of man. Every schoolman who has struggled with the task of class scheduling (of assigning a group of students to the requested and required courses, rooms, and teachers) knows the task to be formidable and that better assignments could have been made, were it not for the limits of human endurance, memory, and ingenuity. Not surprisingly, class assignments are now being made by computers, with results which equal or better earlier human achievements, and require much less effort and patience on the part of the teachers or administrators who were formerly burdened with this chore.

While the computer can manage exceptions, every exception becomes disproportionately expensive. The result is that the computer uses a program which has a tendency to turn out a homogeneous product, to be corrected manually later on an individual basis. The need for handling exceptions in such a manner may be illustrated by the case of a one-legged boy who is to be excused from physical education; this exception is best handled by human intervention.

This illustration also lends some substance to the frequently heard charge that computers eliminate the personal touch in human relations and contribute to the dehumanization of our culture. In part, this charge is true; to an even greater extent, it need not be true, for the machine can service more students more nearly according to their needs than was possible under the less-than-perfect personal, human arrangement which preceded it.

By making complex information more manageable, the computer is helping man conquer new frontiers and, therefore, deserves to be called a giant brain.

Information Retrieval

THE EXPLOSION OF KNOWLEDGE

From the accomplishments of the computer and our investment in research and development, there has resulted a tremendous increase in knowledge, commonly described as an explosion. President Kennedy illustrated the dimensions of the explosion in his 1963 "Message to Congress" on education: "In the last 20 years, mankind has acquired more scientific information than in all of previous history. Ninety per cent of all the scientists that ever lived are alive and working today."[5]

5. "President Kennedy's Message on Education," submitted to Congress January 29, 1963, *Congressional Quarterly*, XXI, No. 5, p. 129.

Still another measure of the increase in knowledge can be found in the publication of scientific papers; the number of papers has doubled every 15 years since 1700, as has the number of scientific journals. Still more tellingly, there has appeared the abstracting journal; the number of these, too, has doubled every 15 years (since 1900), as shown in the accompanying logarithmic charts.

This phenomenal growth of knowledge has brought with it a problem of its own, which is designated as "Information Retrieval." Loosely speaking, every library is organized as an information-retrieval system: that is, books and other materials are classified, indexed, and organized in such a way that anyone who has a grasp of the organizational scheme can retrieve the volume or reference he seeks.

While the conventional library scheme is good—in fact, it is distinguished as a trail-blazing venture toward the organization of knowledge—it is no longer adequate. It is no exaggeration to state that our inability to retrieve existing information is the Achilles' heel of our technological progress. Because of this inability, research is frequently replicated at considerable cost. Some of these repeat performances are deliberate in the sense that the research is known to have been done, but it cannot be located or identified; to be more precise, the cost of finding the existing data is likely to be greater than that of duplicating the experiment. Similarly, some research is repeated inadvertently, because a search of the literature to determine whether such research has been reported may be more costly than the experiment itself.

For these and other reasons there is now under way a series of efforts to improve our hitherto simple but inadequate means of information retrieval. Such research in information retrieval is likely to have an impact on all record-keeping and, in turn, a continuing impact on required office skills.

RELATION TO OFFICE EMPLOYMENT

A major turning point in United States history was reached in 1956 when the number of white-collar workers, for the first time, exceeded the number of blue-collar workers. While it is true that white-collar jobs include categories other than clerical jobs, the turning point has considerable significance for office employment.

CHART I

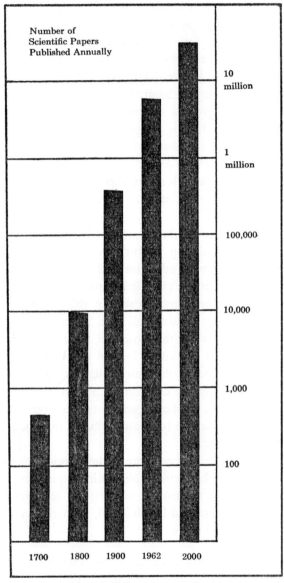

Number of
Scientific Papers
Published Annually

10 million	
1 million	
100,000	
10,000	
1,000	
100	

1700   1800   1900   1962   2000

The number of individual scientific papers published annually has grown sharply since the year 1700. That is, this number of papers has doubled every fifteen years; it has increased by a factor of 10 every 50 years. For example, 10,000 were published in 1800; 120,000 were published in 1900; over 3 million were published last year. There is every reasonable expectation that this historic rate of increase will hold through the year 2000. If so, over sixty million scientific papers will be published in that year. Even aside from scientific literature, every employee in American industry produces an average of some 25,000 pieces of paperwork per year, at an annual clerical cost of $100 billion. The information retreval problem and the scope of our naton's need for a solution will expand together astronomically in coming years.

CHART II

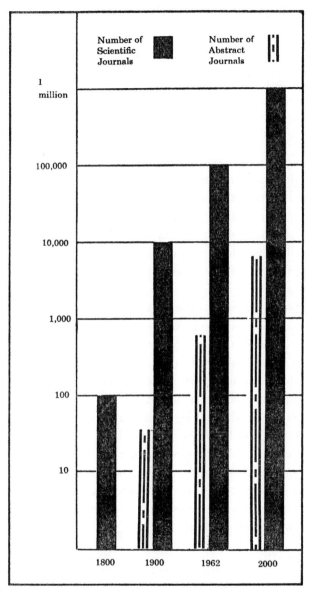

It became evident even before the mid-19th century that a scientist could not possibly read and keep conversant with all the journals relevant even to his own field of specialization. So a new publication, the abstract journal, appeared on the scene. But as the number of journals has continued to mount, so has the number of abstract journals, following precisely the same law of expansion, doubling every 15 years, climbing to 15 by 1900, to 300 today, and an estimated 2,000 by the year 2000.

The 1963 *Manpower Report of the President* provides this description of the phenomenon:

At the turn of the century there were less than half as many white-collar workers as blue-collar workers. By 1950 the employment of white-collar workers had nearly caught up to that of blue-collar ones, and 6 years later the trends crossed. In 1956, for the first time in our history, professional, managerial, clerical and sales employees outnumbered employees in manual occupations.[6]

This crucial turning point came at a time when the computer was barely beginning to appear on the business scene. It is probably not accidental that the rapid subsequent rise of the computer coincides with a slowing in the rate of increase in office occupations. A study by the Bureau of Labor Statistics indicates that office jobs are still increasing, but that the rate of increase has declined.[7] This is not too surprising, for the computer has taken over many of the routine jobs in the office.

This may go counter to the experience and imagination of most persons, but the typical American never sees the "back office" of an insurance company, a brokerage house, or a bank. This is where the bulk of the clerical jobs used to be; and, here rather than in the front office, is where automation has made the greatest inroads.[8] The mailing of a monthly premium notice, the processing of a regularly recurring payment, the tallying of sales and inventory figures—these are tasks which can be programed much more easily than can the customer complaint about a wrong collar size or a leaky radiator.

The computer has made a major contribution to information retrieval in routine dealings; the breakthrough is yet to come in non-routine activities. To a large extent, the latter involves problems of indexing and reading machines.

6. *Manpower Report of the President*, p. 26. Transmitted to the Congress March, 1963. Washington: Government Printing Office, 1963.

7. Carol A. Barry, "White Collar Employment: I, Trends and Structure," *Monthly Labor Review*, XXCIV (January, 1961), 11–18; "White Collar Employment: II, Characteristics," *Monthly Labor Review*, XXCIV (February, 1961), 139–47.

8. Rose Wiener, "Changing Manpower Requirements in Banking," *Monthly Labor Review*, XXCV (September, 1962), 989–95.

THE PROBLEM OF CHARACTER RECOGNITION

Two related sets of initials are beginning to gain increasing currency because they stand for two approaches to a problem which is in the process of being solved.

MICR stands for Magnetic Ink Character Recognition, the system adopted by a committee of the American Bankers Association. Under the impetus of ABA, a series of deliberately distorted numbers are beginning to march across the bottom edge of most checks. They are close to ordinary arabic numerals in appearance, close enough to be readable at a glance; they are sufficiently distorted to enable a scanning mechanism to distinguish between them with a minimal margin of error:

0312⑈00595⑈

The system adopted by ABA a few years ago is not now generally considered to be the most efficient, but it represented a major step forward in reducing human handling of checks and in substituting machine handling. The MICR system is basically magnetic, analogous to the magnetic tapes that have stored electric impulses on sound recorders, computer inputs, and television recordings.

OCR stands for Optical Character Recognition and is another type of device designed to achieve results similar to those achieved by MICR. OCR is expected to become the most widely used in the field of office automation:

> Machines that can read printed copy and handwritten numbers promise to make a significant and growing contribution to office automation. Although the machines presently in use are few in number, the prospect of their wider utilization has raised questions in the frequent public discussions of the implications of office automation for clerical employment.[9]

The present state of development leaves little doubt that MICR and OCR will see increasing use in the years to come, even though economic factors will determine their influence upon the job market and may impede their acceptance to some extent. There remain many unsolved technical problems in this type of automation; even after

9. *Reading Machines for Data Processing: Their Prospective Employment Effects*, p. 2. Manpower Report No. 7, United States Department of Labor, June, 1963. Washington: Government Printing Office, 1963.

they are solved there will continue to be a lag in the use of these devices and techniques because of the great initial costs involved in switching to radically new systems.

Gains in Productivity

It is important to understand current and pending breakthroughs in office automation, especially when they are viewed in the light of earlier changes in manufacturing—the area to which automation first came and where highly visible effects were produced. The following statements indicate the sweeping changes in productivity which technological advances have already brought to agriculture and certain major industries:

In 1947, to produce 1,000 tons of steel, it took 14,700 man-hours; in 1962, it took only 10,900 man-hours.

In 1947, to produce a typical automobile, we needed 310.5 man-hours; in 1962, the total came to just half, or 153.0 man-hours.

In 1947, some 340 man-hours were needed to produce 1,000 bushels of wheat; by 1962 this was reduced to 120 man-hours.[10]

Gains in productivity can also be expressed in a different way: An average American worked 31.2 weeks in 1947 to earn enough to buy an automobile; in 1962 he worked only 24.5 weeks. To buy a refrigerator in 1947, he had to work 180 hours; in 1962, only 31 hours.

APPLIANCE	COST TO CONSUMER		
	1950	1955	1960
Television...............	$230.90	$199.95	$189.95
Automatic blanket.........	52.95	34.95	29.95
Refrigerator..............	329.95	228.00	199.00
Automatic washer.........	394.95	279.95	249.95
Automatic dryer..........	249.95	189.95	189.95

To indicate changes in productivity in a third way, prices (in variable dollars) of some electrical appliances as given in 1960 by the then president of the General Electric Company to a Congressional committee are presented in the accompanying table.

10. *New York Times,* July 14, 1963, p. E 3.

11. Ralph J. Cordiner, "Statement of Ralph J. Cordiner, Chairman of General Electric Company," *New Views on Automation,* p. 228. Joint Economic Com-

By way of underlining this trend, the product of today tends to be superior to that of some 15 years ago, and the gains in productivity as measured by cost to the consumer are, thus, even greater than they would appear to be on the basis of the statistical evidence. The result of this trend is a need for less work for a comparable output, or possibly for increased production, whether of goods or of services.

Some of the gains are translated into increased leisure. This may take many forms: longer vacations, more holidays, a shorter workweek, and greater unemployment, keeping in mind that leisure and unemployment are two sides of the same coin, different in that leisure is voluntary and pleasant, while unemployment is involuntary and unpleasant.

The cumulative effect of our technical progress, already described, has led some experts to see only good in automation. Comments by Roger Bolz, publisher and editorial director of *Automation* magazine, represent this view:

> Properly applied, it [automation] makes possible desired goods and services through two advantages: more wage dollars plus more for the dollar. Growth in total wages paid (and taxes as well) and total employment attests to this.
>
> .   .   .   .
>
> A hundred years ago the same dire predictions were being made about machines that today are being attributed to automation. Yet in the process of time under the force of economics and demand, technological change has continued on with better results. . . . Certainly the history of industrial growth has not been one of machines creating problems.
>
> .   .   .   .
>
> The educated man in a free enterprise economy can be expected to adapt to mobility. He can be expected to fit easily into numerous jobs in the making. He will be motivated to become a businesssman in his own right and in addition create jobs for others.[12]

---

mittee Report of the United States 86th Congress. Washington: Government Printing Office, 1960.

12. Roger W. Bolz, "Automation and Freedom." Talk before the Delaware Valley Engineering Meeting, Philadelphia, December 6, 1961. See also, Bolz, "Automation in the Sixties—a New Era in U.S. Economics." Testimony before the Subcommittee on Automation and Energy Resources of the Joint Economic Committee of the United States Congress, July 1, 1960.

Adjustments to Technological Change

The degree of optimism expressed by Bolz is not universal. The Secretary of Labor, for instance, has drawn attention to the social problems which accompany technical progress, using agricultural progress as an example:

> For many years, the talents of our society were so bent upon increasing the fertility of our soil and the productivity of our farms that we were heedless of the human consequences of "success." . . . We underestimated the significance and the rate of the technological change which was reordering our agriculture.
>
> Even today, as we look back, there is a tendency to think of the job shift away from the farm as a very old thing. We talk about it in half-century spans, pointing out, for example, that in 1900 one out of every three American workers could be found on a farm while in 1960 only one out of every eighteen could be found there. This is a dangerous habit of mind if it leads us to believe that this change has come at a pace gradual enough to ease its consequences.
>
> The simple fact is that productivity has increased on American farms by 81 per cent in the last 10 years . . . [accompanied by] the largest decrease in farm jobs ever recorded in a 10-year period. . . . Technological progress is not human progress unless our social engineering keeps up with our scientific engineering.[13]

People have frequently underestimated the rate of technological change not only in agriculture but in many segments of the economy. Interpretation and prediction may be further distorted, rather than enhanced, by the biases arising from the interest of the observer, interpreter, or forecaster, as illustrated in a statement on the immortality of the horse. It was drawn from the opening address at the 1910 Annual Meeting of the National Association of Carriage Builders:

> Eighty-five per cent of the horse-drawn vehicle industry of the country is untouched by the automobile. In proof of the foregoing permit me to say that in 1906–7 and coincident with an enormous demand for automobiles, the demand for buggies reached the highest tide of its history. The demand during the present season was a capacity one.
>
> The man who predicts the downfall of the automobile is a fool; the man who denies its great necessity and general adoption for many uses

13. Willard W. Wirtz, "Changing Profile of the Nation's Work Force," *Occupational Outlook Quarterly*, VII (February, 1963), 3–4.

is a bigger fool; and the man who predicts the general annihilation of the horse and his vehicle is the greatest fool of all.[14]

A half-century later, this speaker's myopia may be amusing, but it can serve as a warning as well. The problem of recognizing change, and responding to it, is still with us. It is particularly acute now because the rate of technological progress is such that even our best efforts to develop our "social engineering" to match our "scientific engineering" may prove inadequate.

For vocational education, this is an important consideration:

Technological change has labor force implications not only in terms of displacement and adjustment, but also for those new workers who are or will be preparing for a vocation and who will begin their job hunting sometime in the future.[15]

Vocational education, as it turns out, has meant federal support for training in selected skills, but not necessarily in the most appropriate occupational areas. Notably, there is no provision for office occupations in the Smith-Hughes Act of 1917, and that deficiency has not been corrected subsequently, even though attempts have been made to do so. For example, according to Levitan: "The George Bill (1946), as originally introduced, would also have provided funds for training in office occupations, but lobbies from private secretarial schools succeeded in killing the proposal."[16]

Legislation pending in 1963* looks toward a rectification of this long-standing omission, but the attempt comes at a period when cybernation has crossed the threshold of many offices and the rate of growth in office employment is slowing down.

In contrast, there is the large block of money devoted to training in homemaking skills which, though useful, usually are not related

14. *Business Topics* (Michigan State University, Graduate School of Business Administration), XI (Spring, 1963), 4.

15. Ewan Clague and Leon Greenberg, "Employment," *Automation and Technological Change*, p. 114. American Assembly. Edited by John T. Dunlop. Englewood Cliffs, New Jersey: Prentice-Hall, Inc., 1962.

16. Sar A. Levitan, *Vocational Education and Federal Policy*, p. 3. Kalamazoo, Michigan: W. E. Upjohn Institute for Employment Research, 1963.

[* EDITOR'S NOTE: P.L. 88-210 was enacted in December, 1963, but no funds were appropriated as of November, 1964, and the new programs were still not launched.]

to unemployment. The main focus of such training was the farmwife a half-century ago; and agricultural education, without due regard for current needs, has constituted another major block of vocational education. During the last generation, however, agriculture has undergone the revolutionary changes summarized by Secretary Wirtz, as have homemaking and many other vocations.

The Changing Labor Market

STATISTICAL LIMITATIONS

Vocational education, to be effective, must be related to the labor market. Specifically, it must be planned on the basis of labor-market predictions. Does the fact that mechanization of the farm has cut the agricultural work force by more than 60 per cent since 1910 warn of the possible effects of continuing automation in office and factory? Forecasts have value only to the extent that the data and assumptions on which they are based are valid. However, Clague and Greenberg, after a thorough analysis, state with confidence that:

> It is generally expected that during the next decade the economy will grow at a faster pace than it has in recent years, but that output per man-hour will also increase more rapidly . . . disemployment—decreases in employment associated with increased productivity—in nonagricultural industries might amount to 2,000,000 workers or more per year during the next decade. It is important to restate that these figures do not tell the whole story, but they suggest an order of magnitude. . . .
>
> The figures obtained through this analysis do not necessarily mean that all the disemployed workers become unemployed—some may have quit, retired, or died. On the other hand, the figures do not reflect the disemployment that may arise between plants within an industry, nor the replacement and reshuffling that may occur within plants where technological changes are taking place. The figures do not reflect the disemployment arising out of technological competition—where plants may decrease employment or even shut down because they transfer activities to another modern plant, nor do they reflect the impact of technological substitution where plants or industries lose markets to technologically progressive competitors, to new products and to new materials.[17]

As the need for such meaningful manpower projections becomes more acute, there is increasing realization that many existing statistics are inadequate. For example, John I. Snyder, Jr., president of

17. Clague and Greenberg, *op. cit.* pp. 126–27.

U.S. Industries, flatly disagrees with the forecasts of Clague and Greenberg; he told a Congressional committee that automation destroys 40,000 jobs per week.[18]

Surprising as it may seem, there is no national inventory of unfilled positions, although there is a good deal of information about the numbers, nature, and deployment of the unemployed. If there were such an inventory, the schools could do a better job of counseling and training candidates to fill the positions available.

A Congressional committee took evidence relating to such an inventory and called Ewan Clague, commissioner of the Bureau of Labor Statistics, Department of Labor, as one of its witnesses. In describing the problems involved in establishing such an inventory, he stated:

> There has been a great deal of discussion about whether one can get a picture of vacancies.
> Great Britain had quite a successful statistic of this sort, but it was during World War II, and again during the Korean War, when they required all employers hiring people to put their orders through the local employment offices. . . . So the Government obtained some pretty good figures on vacancies. But even in Britain that has now become less satisfactory, because . . . people do get jobs without going through the employment offices. . . . We have found in our past discussion on this subject it is quite a problem to define a vacancy. I have vacancies in the Bureau of Labor Statistics, but sometimes the administrative officer tells me I cannot fill them because we do not have the money. In other words, a vacancy is hard to describe. We are still going to look into it to see if there could be developed any good way of getting such information, because it would be a valuable statistic. It is a fact that millions of jobs are developed over the years, and in each year . . . but we do not have any measure as to the extent to which they exist before they are actually filled.[19]

The president of the National Bureau of Economic Research, Arthur F. Burns, made a similar point. He noted that the lack of national statistics on actual job vacancies is "a vital missing link in our entire system of economic intelligence." Burns, formerly eco-

18. John D. Pomfret, "Automation Called Major Cause in Loss of 40,000 Jobs a Week," *New York Times*, October 4, 1963, pp. 1, 47.

19. *Employment and Unemployment*, pp. 62–63. Hearings, Subcommittee on Economic Statistics, Joint Economic Committee, 87th Congress, December 18–20, 1961. Washington: Government Printing Office, 1962.

nomic adviser to President Eisenhower, said the deplorable lack of
statistics hampers national efforts to reduce unemployment:

Electronic computers open up exciting possibilities for the future. With
their aid, an unemployed worker expressing his need or preference to an
officer of an employment exchange might be referred in a matter of
hours, if not minutes, to a list of potential employers, outside his community if there are none in his own, who need that type of employee.
Employers could be served in a similar manner.[20]

This lack of information is one complicating factor in the forecasting of occupational trends, now aggravated by the rapid introduction of automation and other technological changes. While the
schools have several years in which to provide education and training, they also must make predictions several years in advance. The
Manpower Development and Training Act usually deals only with
a lead time of weeks or months. Nevertheless, even for such short
periods there are major difficulties in prediction.

A spokesman for the Chamber of Commerce of Greater Pittsburgh suggested some revisions of MDTA in a prepared statement to
a Congressional subcommittee in August, 1963:

One phase that continues to give us trouble is "reasonable expectation
of employment." No businessman can tell you today what his exact detailed labor requirements will be in six months or a year from now, as
he must, in order to justify approval of a retraining course under the limitation of the phrase "reasonable expectation of employment."[21]

No matter how difficult it may be to make adequate forecasts, the
attempt still is necessary because, though not definitive, they must be
the basis for planning for the future. The same need would appear to
exist for a national inventory of job vacancies, despite the probable
inadequacy of such information.

One of the merits of the report by the Panel of Consultants on
Vocational Education[22] is that it dealt with long-term trends and

20. *New York Times*, July 24, 1963, p. 33.

21. Malcolm Hay, "Statement on Behalf of the Chamber of Commerce of
Greater Pittsburgh." Hearings on Amendments to Public Law 87-415. Select
Subcommittee on Labor, Committee on Education and Labor, House of Repre-
sentatives, August 15, 1963.

22. *Education for a Changing World of Work*. United States Department of
Health, Education, and Welfare, Office of Education. Washington: Government
Printing Office, 1963.

future needs. Even so, there were shortcomings in the approach taken by the members of the Panel that disappointed those who had hoped for a bold, new approach which would integrate vocational education into the mainstream of American public education rather than continue separate federal support, special rules, and lower standards for teacher certification.[23]

Although problems of education and training, and their relationship to the labor market, have always been important and difficult ones, the current technological revolution, especially its rapid progress, makes these problems even more significant to the national welfare and the well-being of American citizens.

THE OCCUPATIONAL OUTLOOK

Traditionally, the future has been forecast as a projection of past performance. The results have been inaccurate but bearable largely because most cultures were reasonably stable and the rate of change was relatively slow. Man's skills, machines, and societies have evolved throughout history, but at an accelerating pace, with automation and the technological revolution as the current high point.

Again, according to Bolz, there are too many self-appointed prophets who create a false picture of automation "as an uncontrolled ogre of giant proportions."

> For our own good, we must remove automation technology from the realm of science fiction and reveal it for what it really is—nothing more than down-to-earth continuation of our basic manufacturing tools and methods.[24]

Granted that Jacquard's loom or Watts' flyball governor are early examples of numerical control or self-correcting feedback, it does not follow that a swallow or two make a summer, or that an isolated event or invention signals the start of sweeping change. In an age of outer space, controlled in part by computers, it may be questioned whether this really is down-to-earth continuation, especially when our society has had more than 5 per cent of its labor force unem-

23. George E. Arnstein, "Quo Vadis, Vocational Education?" *Phi Delta Kappan*, XLIV (April, 1963), 326–30.

24. Bolz, "Automation in the Sixties," *op. cit.* (cover page of testimony).

ployed for more than five years.[25] Even if this type of disemploy-
ment turns out to be only short-term, it may justifiably be asked just
how long is the short-term, and when will it end?

By general agreement, the main impact of automation in the office
is yet to come; further inroads in manufacturing may be expected,
leaving nothing but the long-term rise in service industries to take up
the slack caused by displacement and the large number of young
people poised to enter the labor force.

In fact, the employment outlook in service industries is better than
in many other areas, but not entirely bright, for, as Michael points
out, "service activities will also tend to displace workers by becoming
self-service, by becoming cybernated, and by being eliminated."[26]

In terms of vocational education, there is an important distinction
between service workers and service industries. Although a diaper
service is part of a service industry, it uses few service workers, for
it is organized like most other businesses—delivery men, bookkeepers,
switchboard operator, company president, and only a few laundry-
men who shift the soiled diapers from a delivery truck into a steel
vat. In terms of job opportunities many service industries reinforce
the statement that there is "no room (or very little room) at the
bottom of the ladder of occupational skills."[27]

For a comprehensive survey of all job areas, the best source is the
Occupational Outlook Handbook, published by the United States
Department of Labor. The sixth biennial edition of the *Handbook*
was published in December, 1963. It continues a tradition of providing highly useful service to anyone concerned with career planning.

The basic information in the *Handbook* is good, and information
presented in future editions should be even better. The *Handbook*
deserves to be better known, more widely distributed, and more
generally used.

Despite the high regard these successive volumes have earned for
themselves, and despite the improvements which have been made

25. George E. Arnstein, "Dissent on Automation," *International Science and
Technology*, XXIII (November, 1963), 15.

26. Donald N. Michael, *Cybernation: The Silent Conquest*, p. 15. Santa Barbara,
California: Center for the Study of Democratic Institutions, 1962.

27. George E. Arnstein, *No Room at the Bottom: Automation and the Reluctant Learner*, p. vii. Edited by Goodwin Watson. Washington: National Education Association, 1963.

over the years, the 1961 *Occupational Outlook Handbook* (the most recent one available at the time of writing) falls short of some of its self-imposed aims.[28] While this edition of the *Handbook* seeks to explain the changing nature of the labor market, it also tends to take a somewhat optimistic view of the future and tends to overstate the services of the United States Employment Service:

> The U.S. Employment Service and affiliated State employment services form a nationwide organization which plays an important part in our economy. Through 1,800 local offices . . . [it] finds jobs for workers and workers for jobs. . . . The local office tries to do more than merely refer a worker to a job—it tries to match the worker and job so that the requirements of each are satisfied.[29]

There follows an explanation of counseling services, placement assistance, testing, and labor market information. This is not the place to engage in a critique of the United States Employment Service; suffice it to note that its performance frequently falls short of the performance implied in the opening section of the *Handbook*.

Fortunately, efforts are under way to remedy some of its deficiencies. There is the beginning of a teletype network to exchange current information about vacancies, and there are experiments with closed-circuit television to facilitate interviews between employers and applicants who are separated by distance. The new Manpower Administration is seeking through various means—including better exchange of employment information—to arrive at a more rational use of our manpower.

Despite some shortcomings, the *Occupational Outlook Handbook* deserves a place on the desk of every counselor and on the shelf of every high-school and public library. To update the reports of the *Handbook*, the Bureau of Labor Statistics also produces the *Occupational Outlook Quarterly*, a magazine with employment information of major interest and relevance to those who would advise students about the job market.

In the final analysis, the Bureau of Labor Statistics is the primary source for most of our employment forecasts, and its publications

28. *Occupational Outlook Handbook* (1961 edition), United States Department of Labor, Bureau of Labor Statistics, Bulletin No. 1300. Washington: Government Printing Office, 1961.

29. *Ibid.*, p. 8.

deserve greater exposure among schoolmen. Granted that the extrap-
olation of future trends is hazardous and subject to error and cor-
rection, it is even more precarious to rely on past records and past
performance without an awareness of the ferment now going on in
our society.

Educational Implications

It is relatively easy to secure agreement on the need for more education and better education. A whole series of witnesses before a
Congressional committee indicated their interest by volunteering
statements recommending both—even though the topic of the hearing was *New Views on Automation.*[30] The difficulty arises when
there is an attempt to explore the details of the recommendation or
the underlying assumptions.

This same difficulty is at the heart of a split on the issue of the role
of vocational education in the United States today. There is little
opposition to the idea of preparing young and old citizens so that
they will have useful skills in order to become eligible for unfilled
jobs. The major disagreement involves the nature of the skills.

Take the specific example of bricklayers and how to teach them,
used in the report of the Panel of Consultants on Vocational Education. In relation to the education of such workmen, Michael has predicted that "if the building trades were to be automated, it would not
mean inventing machines to do the various tasks now done by men;
rather, buildings would be redesigned so that they could be built by
machines."[31]

In contrast, the report of the Panel resolves an unhappy choice in
teacher preparation as follows:

It is, however, much more effective to employ a bricklayer and teach
him pedagogy than it is to employ a teacher and then train him to be a
bricklayer. This is illustrative of the problems of training teachers for
many vocational subjects.[32]

While admitting that teachers who were first "bricklayers" usually
lack "the liberal education which is so important to the teacher,"[33]

---

30. *New Views on Automation.* Joint Economic Committee Report of the
United States 86th Congress. Washington: Government Printing Office, 1960.

31. Michael, *op. cit.*, p. 5.

32. *Education for a Changing World of Work, op. cit.*, p. 237.

33. *Ibid.*

the Panel seems to overlook to a great extent the increasingly abstract and academic content of many modern occupations. The bricklayer, if he is to remain employed, will continue to read blueprints and diagrams, although he may no longer work with bricks. Plumbers have learned to use plastic pipes instead of the traditional metal pipes, but they continue to need skills in numbers, in reading instructions, and for communicating with their colleagues, apprentices, and supervisors. A good case can thus be made for stressing, as part of the vocational sequence, those skills which are likely to be useful for the longest period of time and over a period of change. Conversely, the manual and manipulative aspects of the occupations may be of lesser importance.

Even a first-rate school for bakers may be headed in the wrong direction, for there is evidence that baked goods are increasingly being produced by "factories" where a chemist devises the formula, an engineer is in charge of the machines, a mechanic or electrician maintains them, and an economist or statistician determines the program. There may be a master baker somewhere at corporate headquarters, but there will be slight demand for men to knead the dough or apply the sugar glaze. Except in a minor way, the operation of the small, individual bakery will not remain economically viable. While bakers still bake, it seems safe to predict that this time-honored craft is headed for a major decline.

For that matter, how many shoemakers still *make* shoes in the United States today? Are there any classes in shoemaking, and does anyone advocate that this skill be added to the vocational curriculum of our schools?

The increasing tendency toward better bookkeeping and the more rational use of men and materials have brought as a concomitant the increased use of records. We live in a paper-oriented society, based on the manipulation of symbols, numbers, and letters, which are important to the automobile mechanic who has to order a part from a catalogue and the television repairman who must keep a time sheet. All of them, sooner or later, must make out an accident report, an income tax return, or an application for workman's compensation.

In addition, there are considerations of the role of a citizen in a democratic society and his need to be informed. This, in turn, calls for education, knowledge, and understanding not likely to be taught best by a bricklayer converted into a teacher. The Panel appears to recognize the problem, but its recommendations seem to skirt it.

Vocational education can be effective only when the student has acquired basic educational skills—reading, oral expression, written expression, and numerical computation are important for all but the most rudimentary form of employment. Vocational education should never conflict with basic education.[34]

A special project of the National Education Association has been concerned with this problem, viewed in the context of the over-all impact of technology and automation on education. In articles and speeches, the staff of the NEA Project on the Educational Implications of Automation has made a point of noting the need for basic skills, for flexibility and adaptability, and for the cultivation of positive attitudes toward lifelong learning:

It may be permissible to conclude that learning should be a lifelong, conscious activity and that failure to educate in terms of new developments can only mean unemployment and social disorientation. Although this is not a new idea, it becomes a new imperative. The current rate of change makes it unlikely that any large number of people in this country can safely rely on the early acquisition of skills and knowledge that will serve them for a lifetime. Moreover, it appears that our nation may have to modify some of its traditional values if it is to be realistically oriented to the society of the future. Relevant here is the traditional emphasis on work versus the values of leisure and of social participation.

Throughout its history, the United States has been a growing country with a dynamic concept of social mobility and self-improvement. Compared to certain older cultures, it has demonstrated a much greater acceptance of change. Nevertheless, our history contains some striking examples of failure to gear ourselves to visible and continuing changes. Today, these could be extremely costly.

In the field of education at least two examples can be found to illustrate this point: *Vocational education* has been slow in adapting to changing needs, operating largely within the boundaries of concepts formulated around the time of World War I. Only recently has it begun to receive even a measure of the attention it sorely needs. *Adult education*, as traditionally carried on, must be broadened and many of its former concerns modified. It must assume a much greater role of updating skills and promoting continued learning. The notion of refresher or extension courses, so well accepted in many professions, must become a routine course of action for people in industry and government and must be applied to

34. *Ibid.*, p. 221.

workers in the lowest as well as in the highest echelons. Further, there is a greater need for better facilities for counseling, guidance, and placement at the adult level.[35]

The rapidity of technical and social change, and the concomitant urgency of educational change based on new attitudes, was also emphasized in the Rockefeller report on education:

In this day of technologies that become antiquated overnight, it is hazardous to predict a favorable future for any narrow occupational category. There will be economic advantage to the individual in acquiring the kind of fundamental training that will enable him to move back and forth over several occupational categories.[36]

The following excerpt from the same report serves as fitting recapitulation of this chapter:

The heart of the matter is that we are moving with headlong speed into a new phase of man's long struggle to control his environment, a phase beside which the industrial revolution may appear a modest alteration in human affairs. Nuclear energy, exploration of outer space, revolutionary studies of brain functioning, important new work in the living cell—all point to changes in our lives so startling as to test to the utmost our adaptive capacities, our stability and our wisdom.[37]

35. *Automation and the Challenge to Education*, pp. 6–7. Edited by Luther H. Evans and George E. Arnstein. Washington: National Education Association, 1962.

36. *The Pursuit of Excellence: Education and the Future of America*, p. 10. Rockefeller Brothers Fund, Inc. Garden City, New York: Doubleday & Co., 1958.

37. *Ibid.*, p. 28.

CHAPTER IV

Vocational Education in the Curriculum
of the Common School

LAURENCE D. HASKEW and INEZ WALLACE TUMLIN

The Chapter's Purpose

The remaining chapters of the yearbook examine the nature and functioning of vocational education. This brief chapter is limited rigorously to only one facet of that examination. It focuses exclusively on the elementary and the secondary school—together referred to as "the common school." It deals only with the curriculum offerings of the common school. Its function is primarily that of analyzing issues.

Authors undertaking an assignment such as this perforce engage in exacting limitation and definition of the subject addressed. Lest readers be misled, these are made explicit at the outset.

First, the subject is limited to the common school's curriculum for children and youth who are regularly enrolled in school. Other sections of the yearbook deal with programs for those who drop out of school, for adults, and for youths possessing high-school diplomas. All such programs have great importance. Many of them are conceived and executed by the same organization which directs the in-school curriculum. Personnel engaged in teaching in-school students are often engaged in these other programs, to the advantage of all. Further, the school frequently engages in community-serving functions apart from direct teaching, thus adding still more complexity—and value—to what is accepted locally as the "school program." This chapter, however, devotes its attention exclusively to the curriculum endeavors for regularly enrolled students in the common school.

Second, although it is vocational education which is under examination, it is vocational education inextricably linked in myriad ways with the totality of common education. Vocational education *in* common education is the topic, not vocational education in some utopia where unlimited time, resources, and talent are available to accomplish everything desirable through an educative enterprise. The intent is to lay down propositions upon which elementary schools and secondary schools as known today can rest their plans for vocational education tomorrow. In those schools, every minute is precious and sought after by highly worthwhile concerns. No attempt is made to abstract vocational education from that *milieu*.

Third, the term "vocational education" is used with a fairly precise inclusive and exclusive meaning by the authors. Included in vocational education will be those curriculum experiences whose *prime* objective (but seldom sole objective) is either one or both of the following: (*a*) To produce desirable dispositions (understandings, attitudes, self-involvements) toward occupational endeavor as an investment of life energy. (*b*) To equip the individual with some set of occupational proficiencies which will enable him or her, upon leaving the common school, to engage in an occupation skilfully.

A third-grade class takes a field trip to a dairy. Is this type of curriculum experience comprehended when "vocational education" is used in this chapter? It is not. Neither of the objectives stated is prime, although both are doubtless present. A ninth-grade English unit is titled "Choosing an Occupation." Is this "vocational education" as defined in this chapter? One does not know. The answer depends upon what concerted, exacting emphasis is placed upon acquiring the knowledge (this is technical in nature) entering into occupational choice. Occupational possibilities to be studied may be used simply as an interest-arousing device; primary emphasis can be upon employing language effectively with only minor attention to the content involved. A high school offers a half-unit course, "Advanced Chemistry: The Work of the Scientist." The odds are high that this curriculum experience is vocational education as we define it, since it offers contact with scientists at work and affords not only training but also promotes recruitment for a career in science.

Fourth, a distinction is made between "vocational education" and occupation-titled curriculum divisions. For example, vocational education may be integrally meshed within divisions bearing quite different titles. Counseling and guidance is a case in point; to attempt to separate out the occupationally centered activities of the guidance program is considered unwise by most authorities in the field, since it is the student who remains the unit. Again, an occupationally titled division may center upon many purposes other than those which are vocational. The typical homemaking course is devoted in large measure to citizenship and personal-adequacy outcomes. In fact, it is difficult to locate any occupationally titled division which substantiates the popular stereotype of "courses which develop only job skills." Practically all of them have important, and measurable, extra-vocational outcomes.

With some limitations now made explicit, the purpose of this chapter can be stated once more. It is to examine what the common school curriculum for children and youth should provide in the way of vocational education.

The Setting

Preceding chapters of this yearbook have documented one salient feature of the setting in which the common school seeks to relate itself properly to vocational education. A revolution of unprecedented magnitude is occurring in the occupational sector of American life. The talents of people are now viewed as instruments of corporate welfare, as tools for advancement of mankind's triumph over nature (including human nature), as resources to be exploited fully, lest the economy collapse. On the other hand, the vocational demands of a nuclear space age open opportunities to the individual and establish barriers for self-realization undreamed of a decade ago. Choice of vocation takes place in a frustrating complexity, conducive to escapism and other forms of mental ill-health. In the midst of unprecedented opportunities *for* work, motivation *to* work is in disturbing ebb among young people. In this occupational setting, the common school charts its future.

The setting is also ideational. With America's typical genius for simultaneously generating thesis and antithesis, 1965 sees what is popularly known as "vocational education" enjoying both the greatest positive repute and the most negative evaluation which that movement has known for a century. Positive repute is well symbolized by the 1963 report of the President's Panel of Consultants on Vocational Education. It and many other important documents make a strong case for imperative expansion and modernization of opportunities for occupational training. Education for work is frequently categorized as a national emergency measure and is seen as the route toward solution of some of the nation's gravest social and economic problems. It is clear that a strong contingent of the influential public holds the view that vocational education in the common school is an imperative with new dimensions of urgency.

At the same time, a tide of negative evaluation is at peak in educational circles, also led by powerful opinion-formers. Negative pressures take two chief forms. First is the contention that vocational education as it has been provided in the common school is relatively ineffective in achieving the occupational results it exists to produce. Growing skepticism is expressed that the results sought *can* or should be achieved with children and youth of common-school ages. Others voice doubt that such results can be achieved as efficiently and expeditiously in school as elsewhere or later. The second negative evaluation arises from championing intellectualism as the newly imperative prime objective of common schooling. Time and energy formerly spent upon the cultivation of knowledge in the academic disciplines and upon the tool skills supportive thereof have been insufficient, it is said. Those who first know and understand and gain "the ability to use their minds" will *do* later; the common school cannot dissipate its precious contacts with young people, among other laudable undertakings, so long as the cause of intellectualism so insufficiently served. That there are counterarguments is obvious, but that is not the point. The point is that in 1965 the educational exponents of intellectualism were in the ascendant, and vocational education was one of their favorite targets. Prescriptions range from deleting it entirely to restricting it to the intellectually deprived student or to reducing it to something vaguely designated as pre-vocational or "general principles." In brief, a divided popular and professional opinion of vocational education in the common school is an influential part of the current setting.

Another part of the setting is a vigorous and well-established vocational-education component in the existing curricula of common education. Almost universally distributed, opportunities for vocational education are available to the vast majority of pupils. Even when defined as participation in courses with occupational titles, vocational education is a prominent part of high-school preparation for a significant number of students. Seldom does one find even a very recent statement of objectives for a school system which fails to include one explicit and separate item focusing upon "practical preparation to get and hold a job." Neither do recent polls of parental judgments of schools reveal any diminution of the high store adults set on vocational preparation. The vocational *motif* remains strong in American culture, and the manifestations of that *motif* in the common school are generally accepted as institutionalized and normative.

Thus we have a setting with three variables, (*a*) a revolutionary recasting of the occupational sector of life with consequent transformations occurring in other life sectors; (*b*) a dichotomous interpretation of the proper role of the common school vis-à-vis vocational education; and (*c*) an ongoing but modifiable corpus of institutionalizations of vocational education within the common school. Interaction among these variables will affect the future role of the common school in regard to vocational education and the future role of vocational education in the common school.

Important Issues

As such interaction is occurring and continues to occur, many issues arise. A few of the more pressing ones are now presented.

DISCRETENESS

Discreteness is a major issue and has two prongs. On the one hand is the question of persistence of the presently accepted dyad, general education *and* vocational education. On the other hand is the issue of how much vocational-education content shall find its way into the curriculum compartments labeled with other names.

Popular supposition is that the "vocational-education issue" revolves around the questions of what occupationally labeled discrete courses shall be offered, how many of them shall be permitted to the individual student as alternates for "general education," and at what school levels these alternative offerings shall be available. The vocational purpose is viewed as something discrete from the general-education purpose of the common school, the time spent on vocational education as taken away from general education. But such supposition is fallacious. In the first place, occupation-labeled courses frequently are prime vehicles for achieving such outcomes as proficiency in communication, ability to handle quantitative relationships, command of problem-solving processes, and many other "prime essentials of schooling." In fact, such achievements for some pupils have proved to be impossible in the absence of occupation-centered methodology. In the second place, occupation-centering is typically used as the magnet which holds pupils in contact with so-called general education. In the third place, some vocational education reinforces much abstract learning by affording opportunities for practical applications, thus helping general education make sense.

Yet, these and similar claims—often substantiated by actual practice in some schools—do not dispose of this first prong of the issue. Still in question is whether vocational education is to persist as an essentially different variety of education, an alternate to another variety commonly called academic. Vocational education had its origin as a discrete endeavor of common schools in a context which lent itself to a distinction between "those who will go on" (a minority) and "those who will go to work" (a majority). This context is fading rapidly; "those who will go on" are already in the majority and "those who will go to work" will find that work (it is said) increasingly in positions demanding essentially the same character of intellectual ability and academic grounding as is demanded of "those who go on." Should all discreteness vanish?

Our discussion thus leads to a consideration of the second prong of the issue of discreteness. In the period between 1920 and 1957 much vocational education became institutionalized within the traditional compartments of the common school program—in units of work at the primary level, in the language arts, in mathematics, in various procedures for individualizing instruction, in the guidance program, and in almost all others. The emphasis upon using the common school to develop certain personal qualities and outlooks comprehended a considerable portion of fundamental preparation for being a worker. In fact, one can document a steady trend toward embodying vocational education as one point of reference in the total curriculum design for the common school. With Sputnik, this trend went into decline and may have reversed itself. The traditional vocational-education flavor is noticeably absent from the "new mathematics," the new physics, or samples of curriculum design emerging from Project English. Many observers report lessened school attention to the development of personal qualities, a shift in emphasis from the learner to what is to be learned. Disciplinary rubrics, formulated by scholars in the disciplines, are replacing student-need-interest rubrics in the organization of textbooks and courses of study. These and similar developments may be temporary phenomena, but they give a new ingredient to the issue of discreteness. While, formerly, diffused content and activities were essential to adequate vocational education, present trends may indicate more and not less discreteness for offerings which undertake to add vocational postures for an appreciable number of graduates of the common school.

EMPHASIZED INCLUSION

A second obvious issue is the extent to which vocational education shall be emphasized as a component of the common school's program. Theoretically, one could raise the question of *whether* vocational education, discrete or integrated, shall be included at all. Pragmatically, this aspect of the issue seems to be settled for decades to come. The vocational *motif* in American life is too strong, the practice of vocational education in the common schools is too prominent and too well embedded in the institutional fabric, and the folk expectations for occupational preparation within common schooling are too well established for there to be any alternative to some provision for vocational education. The issues are concerned with quantity and kind of vocational education.

Strong demands are arising which are counter to the present proportionate prominence of explicit vocational education. One is for greatly increased attention to the development of reading and communication ability. Another is for greater understanding of the disciplines of human knowledge *as disciplines;* disciplinary knowledge itself, it is argued, takes on an occupational as well as an "educated-man" value of imperative importance. A third is for mental discipline, long ago discounted as a dead theory of human learning but now resurrected and increasingly glorified. A fourth is for the common school to send on for further formal education a higher and higher proportion of its graduates. Also, demands for more attention to humanistic education and for overwhelming primacy of the intellectualizing function of the common school are steadily mounting. That these demands necessarily undermine the prominence of explicit vocational education is not granted here; the point is that they are increasingly interpreted as being antivocational education in impact. And, it must be remembered that many of these demands have their origin in the occupational sector of American life as it reflects modern technology and suggests the nature of future economic endeavors. It is shown, for example, that the available jobs demand ever increasing depth in the foundational disciplines; the beginning worker must be able to move up through exercise of intellect or become obsolete almost as soon as he gets started.

To such demands are added a number of contentions. As constantly increasing proportions of common-school youth head toward post-high-school educational institutions, the logistic and financial difficulties of maintaining a wide array of explicit vocational offerings are increasing. Patronage in prospect for explicit vocational education is thought to be insufficient to justify many separate offerings. Whether or not the post-secondary educational institutions are college-like in character, their admission requirements are increasingly similar to those of colleges, and their methods of instruction also rest increasingly upon the possession of mental agility and of college-type tool skills in reading, learning by abstraction, and writing. Accompanying all this is a contention that the ratio between time allocated and content covered in explicit vocational education is wasteful. A typical claim is that three school years devoted to agriculture could be telescoped into one without loss in actual learning and that the time saved could be more profitably spent on science and mathematics.

But the issue is joined by opposite demands and opposing contentions. The demand for job-competence for youth under eighteen years of age is perhaps at its peak as more and more insight is gained into the processes for rehabilitating the disadvantaged and the lost ones in our society. Studies are revealing that more, not fewer, technological skills demanded by modern industry can be mastered by high-school youth; their capacities for training in skills have perhaps been as underexploited as those for traditional academic training. For many years to come, the absolute number of tenth-grade students for whom high-school graduation is the termination of formal education will be increasing; although their proportion in the total secondary-school population is declining, the total school population is rising very rapidly. While the demand for disciplinary knowledge is highly significant, there is concurrent demand for the presence of a desire to work and for skilful beginning job performance; for example, executives who locate new electronic data-processing establishments are still asking first about the capacity of the schools to produce the skilled workers needed. Further, the demand for post-high-school education is not as monolithic as sometimes assumed. A significant and growing proportion of those who continue education do so in their home cities, following a vocational path started in the common school. Many others are immigrants to larger cities where they went to seek employment and found that they had no skills to sell. Many more get their chance at further formal training only because they can earn while they learn, or because they capitalize upon previous vocational training to secure employer support for further education. In brief, at least a significant proportion of the demand for further education is concomitantly a demand for vocational education in high school.

Contentions contrary to those cited for phasing-down vocational education in the common school are likewise prominent. Little previous evidence supports the thesis that more student time put upon "disciplinary" acquisition of knowledge results in corresponding gains in average prowess. If there is inadequacy in the present teaching-learning of disciplines, perhaps it lies in the methodology, approach, and content used and not significantly in the time allotted; providing more time is not getting at the root of the problem. Second, the supportive role of explicit vocational education in achieving intellectual and disciplinary outcomes for some students is overlooked with peril. Third, a high proportion of the student outcomes now achieved by vocational education in the common school are highly valuable ones which have stood the test of time; derogation of them as less important for the health of a total pluralistic society than other outcomes is based upon opinion and not upon the experience of America which wisely incorporates an academic community but also seeks an *educated* citizenry. Finally, while the character and nature of vocational education in the common school face the same imperatives toward change as all other components of that program, the essential problem is qualitative and not quantitative. It is not due to any valid dichotomy between desirable objectives for the common school and the role of vocational education.

Thus, the issue of emphasis is joined, and the suitability of vocationalism as an objective and *motif* of common-school education is laid open to new decision in state and local school systems. This issue, let it be said, does not turn on the question of whether vocational education shall be required of all the clientele of the common school (although some of the literature apparently attacks only this straw-man assumption) but upon whether the opportunity for vocational education shall be universally afforded in the common school.

INSTITUTIONALIZED STRUCTURE

In several respects, vocational education has become an institution within the common school. Stated objectives have reached almost creedal status in their persistence. Ways of looking at students are consistently defined from place to place, from subject to subject, and, indeed, from decade to decade. With the exception of efforts beginning in 1956 to shift the focus of homemaking from the household arts to family life, subject-taxonomy remains fairly stable. The self-images of persons teaching in this field often seem to be that of a vocational educator, not that of a high school (or junior high school) teacher. The bases for curriculum design and actual methodologies are firmly established and authoritative. And the categorizations of fields is almost classic and relatively unyielding—guidance, prevocational exploration and orientation, vocational homemaking, agriculture, trades and industries, distributive education, business education. Obviously, all vocational education in the common school is not confined within these categories, but they do dominate both planning and activation of vocational offerings, and each category has developed a high sense of identity, of proprietorship, and of definition of role, and has an established operational protocol.

This institutionalization is being subjected to the stress of contention and the challenge of new developments. Objectives typically stated as "particularized skill in performing the jobs given to the beginning worker" are being challenged by the contention that there are families of generalized abilities which can be taught in less time and with more profit, or by the contention that orientation and understanding are sufficient, since employers can develop the particularized skills. There are other contentions. In the view of some persons, traditional objectives relating to attitudes, ways of thinking, problem-solving abilities, and communication skills are empty because they are not reflected in actual teaching performance. In brief, the creedal objectives of the institution of vocational education are at issue.

Similarly, institutionalized curriculum-design procedures are being subjected to serious question. The local-community origin of curriculum emphasis is challenged; farming practices and problems of one community furnish inadequate preparatory material for the agricultural occupations upon which most high-school graduates enter, it is pointed out. It is charged that the problems identified for curriculum organization are chiefly of surface character; the significant problems of which these are only symptoms are not dealt with. The methodology includes too much repetitive practice, too many "projects" from which the increments of learning are minor; it relies too much upon the educative effects of sheer work experience. But the fundamental allegation is that the curricula of vocational education are inert under a burden of no longer viable concepts of the worker and his vocation.

Another tension arises from the formal categorizations of vocational education in relation to the exploding occupational world. The "newer" occupations find their way with difficulty into the established repertoires; many of them are neglected because they do not fit traditional lines of separation and, hence, have no sponsor. At the other extreme in popular acclaim, but increasingly crucial in socioeconomic life, are the unglamorous jobs which a large proportion of common-school students do get and use either as steppingstones toward solid citizenship and self-realization or as defeats and parents of desperation (for instance, jobs as filling-station attendants, porters, day laborers, or waitresses). They, too, are largely unsponsored and generally ignored among the traditional categories of agriculture, trades and industries, and so on.

Which occupational fields, if any, should be given a place in the vocational-education programs of the common school is a crucial and continuing problem. Present categorizations often render a decision exceedingly difficult and sometimes allow it to be made by default because of historical distributions of emphasis and support. It is normal institutional behavior to protect one's own category, or to secure its aggrandizement, but such behavior adds gravity to the issue of whether institutionalized vocational education is outmoded for dealing with the demands confronting the common school. And, if the classic categorization is outmoded, should the common school discard the entire apparatus or should it seek only some modifications in it?

Adding to the problems in securing modernization is the traditional institutionalization of vocational education as extraterritorial, as something not entirely of the school's program, particularly at the senior high school level. Rare is the top local school administrator who feels the same obligations toward the curriculum in vocational education that he feels, for example, toward the reading curriculum. Existence of federal and state agencies for financial support and some control, with the resultant evolution of patterns and standards and contract status, lends itself to mutual frustrations in effecting change. The "outside" agencies find it difficult to get local authorities to do more than become willing customers for packaged goods, while local authorities find it difficult to initiate departures from current practice until state or federal programs have been produced. That the alleged rigidity of treaty provisions and the alleged impotence of local authorities are largely mythical is attested by many recent local innovations under local leadership. But the myth is believed and modernization of the status quo is inhibited by that belief.

To summarize, the existing institutionalizations of vocational education evolved from successful performance in an era which is now largely at an end. Institutional obsolescence is increasingly apparent as the common school enters a new era. This obsolescence may be no more serious than that of all other institutionalized forms of response to educational needs, but it *is* serious. The issue, so far as the common school program is concerned, is whether the task is one of modernization through transformation or one of almost complete discarding and starting anew.

OBJECTIVES AND CONTENT

The discussion of the three issues already treated has indicated puzzling choices among objectives and content for vocational education in the common school. They may be summarized as follows:

In *objectives*, at least three choices, not mutually exclusive, exist:

1) To make the prime objectives of vocational education coterminous with the intellectual training and personal-development objectives of the common school. The "vocational" modifier of education designates only a vehicle to be used for some students, an extra extension of fundamental learning through illustration and application. It represents a different approach for acquiring basic command of the disciplines of communication, social science, mathematics, natural science, and the arts; for the development of abstract reasoning abilities and other intellectual skills; for the cultivation of constructive command of self-relations and other relations. Achievement of occupational understandings, work abilities, and job placement are incidental; acquisition of knowledge, intellectual training, and development of prowess in cerebration are central.

2) To make occupational orientation for all and portal preparation for some the peculiar contribution of vocational education to a total common-school program. While reinforcement of other "central" common-school learnings will be sought, vocational education is, first, a vertical departmentalization of the common-school curriculum. Just as English is a department with prime responsibility for achieving the objectives of communication, vocational education is a department (in effect a socioeconomic science) to carry the major burden of developing intellectual command of the occupational manifestations of American culture. Then as a second obligation, vocational education furnishes a limited specialization for some students. The assumption is that the common school can and should provide a small number of alternative specializations for its students, one of which is a portal preparation for occupational performance. While "portal" remains undefined, presumably it would consist primarily of preparation to engage in continuing education to develop vocational skill and be limited to one or two Carnegie units in credit value.

3) To make the objectives of vocational education primarily those of job-training for the emergent labor market, open to large numbers of students as an alternative to the academic specialization routes in the junior and senior high schools. It is assumed that explicit and realistic job training in depth is possible and feasible for numerous teen-agers and is as valuable for them and for society as preparation

for academic pursuits. Under this conception, vocational education would spread out horizontally to cover most of what is required for occupational success under a rough approximation of "what is good for the worker and the employer is good for the country." The full range of employment opportunities for teen-agers would be covered, from the lowest to the highest, and in effect job-preparation would be one track in a multitrack common school.

In *content*, the choices can likewise emanate from three different frames for selection:

1) Content which is essentially focused upon the basic concepts inherent in academic disciplines, aimed at intellectualization of abstract principles and generalizations which, in turn, will produce "the behavior of the educated man." For example, occupational performance would be viewed as inductive material from which to build basic concepts of communication, or as one utilization of the concept of "sets" in mathematics, and so on.

2) Descriptive content drawn from the social sciences pertinent to an understanding of the dynamics of occupational culture, from the behavioral sciences pertinent to understanding one's self and others as workers and as members of groups, and from the results of modern occupational analysis pertinent to identifying emergent job-trends and basic skills required. For specialization, there would be added content suitable for actual training in broad categories of work abilities and learning abilities.

3) Content which is dominantly oriented toward job-performance. This may be derived from modern analysis of the dynamics of job-evolution and worker-progression, rather than from stilted job descriptions. It may focus on life-off-the-job as well as life-on-the-job. But, the prime criteria proposed for selection are (*a*) the performance ability essential to success, as judged by the employer and by the employee himself, and (*b*) the knowledge, understanding, and ability necessary to the worker's continued progress and adequacy in a dynamic occupational world. These criteria almost dictate considerable reliance upon practice as the means for acquiring the content selected, since actual performance is the referent.

Ancillary to these choices are other concerns. Which rationale is vocational education in the common school to follow—the inclusive (to each according to his ability) or the selective (to those who can meet or exceed arbitrary standards)? Is it to be as rigorous (though perhaps in different dimensions) in its demands upon students as are the other components of the school program? If discrete offerings continue, perhaps the most serious of all concerns is whether the traditional orientation of the teachers of occupational courses toward the student as a whole person is to be transmuted into an academic orientation toward a subject. For many, this is the fundamental issue regarding objectives and content for vocational education, since it cuts to the heart of the larger issue of what is to be the crucial role of the emerging common school.

OCCUPATIONAL SELECTION

The common school is community-based. Traditionally, its selection of the occupational fields for which it offers specialized preparation is likewise community-oriented. But almost every common school now serves a region far beyond the geographical borders of its district, serves people who are perpetually on the move, and serves an age notably unlike the age which shaped its present community. Re-examination of the repertoire of occupational offerings is inevitable and raises many issues. Some of these have become apparent in preceding delineations, but four deserve explicit presentation.

The first is the extent to which the common school is to base its selections upon local economic life rather than upon nonlocal occupational opportunities for students. Activities connected with vocational offerings can be of great benefit to local agriculture but of questionable value as occupational training in agriculture for students who will soon emigrate, largely to urban centers.

A second issue lies in the influence to be accorded quantitative supply-demand criteria in selecting the limited number of occupational fields which the common school may include among its offerings. Closely related to the question of specificity in occupational training is that of whether, for example, to cater to the historically stable high demand for typists or to the quantitatively small but crucial future demand for engineering aides. The typical selection procedure has been to survey local employment prospects and to decide to offer what will serve the greatest number. Yet, the very factors which cause quantitatively impressive local demand also tend to create local training opportunities other than those of the common school and thus raise the question of what does constitute the most statesmanlike husbanding of the common school's resources for providing occupational training.

The third issue springing from the localization of planning for occupational training is an old one. To what extent shall the common school be a service agency for local employers, in effect performing worker-training for those employers at public expense? The community school, by tradition and advocacy, is concerned with the economic health of the community in which it exists; it is one agency which the people of the community use to promote a more vigorous economy. The whole community has a stake in the competitive success of its dairy industry, its appliance manufacturer, its home office for an insurance company, its retail stores. Hence, the whole community benefits by what the common school can do to provide employers with trained personnel. Further, the common school is presumably rendering valuable direct service to its students when it makes them immediately employable because of their specific training. But, do these public benefits, local in application, warrant continuation of such arrangements? Is there a larger public which should benefit from occupational training for labor markets that are nonlocal, or even nonexistent at the present time? Does concentration upon employers' needs result in neglect of those students with low aptitudes and motivations and, in some instances, of those who could and should rise beyond the ceiling of the surrounding economic enterprise? The role of the common school in occupational training is, quite obviously, small in comparison to the roles to be assumed by other components of a tremendous enterprise in vocational education. In its choice of occupational fields, it determines how strategic that role shall be.

Another issue involved in occupational selection is not geographic in origin. Inevitably, when one discusses occupational training in the common school, there is a tendency to treat the amount of such training as a finite and almost predetermined quantity. Thus, it makes considerable practical difference whether certain subjects continue to be placed in the curriculum as occupational subjects. Tangibly, shall the subjects of homemaking, typewriting, descriptive drawing, industrial arts, and a few others continue to be conceived, designed, and allocated as occupational subjects? On the one side is the fear that they will be lost completely if they are not so considered. On the other hand is the contention, especially viable for homemaking, that we are dealing with a universal and important set of learnings needed by all people. Certainly, the postwar trends in homemaking programs toward analytical study of family life, child nurture, and applications of the behavioral sciences to individual and social maintenance are difficult to characterize as occupational training. The question of whether the common school has a mandate to deal with similarly crucial matters not yet catalogued under academic disciplines is pertinent. Under the aegis of vocational education, it is doing so for at least a considerable number of students. Out from under that aegis, modern homemaking might completely vanish when subjected to the onslaught of preparation for college life rather than for family and personal-social life (although, to increasing degree, success in the former seems to depend upon success in the latter). But, if homemaking remains occupational in placement, will it necessarily cling to training in sewing and cooking and household finance to the disadvantage of content potentially more useful and, at the same time, automatically exclude other subjects from the occupational repertoire of the common school? Adding to the perplexity is the question of whether the manifold services now offered to adults as the result of having "vocational" homemaking in the common school could or would be continued if the vocational label is removed.

Although not so sweeping, similar issues arise in connection with typewriting—hardly more "occupational" now than was handwriting a few generations ago—and with several other subjects whose great spread of utility make them increasingly foundational rather than specialized in nature. Another category comprehends a considerable array of subjects which, at least traditionally, require a long period of calendar time to bring the students to the level of occupational proficiency—shorthand, mechanical and architectural drafting, woodworking, agriculture. Three years of woodworking, for example, can be said under the prevailing finite-quantity conception to squeeze out three other subjects which could be handled satisfactorily in one year each. Thus, the issues surrounding the common school's selection of occupations become weighty ones. And, because of their complexity, they add to sentiment that the best selection may be none at all.

An Emerging Rationale

For years to come, the actual place and nature of vocational education in the common-school curriculum will manifest working resolutions of issues delineated in the preceding sections. These resolutions will be varied, evolving, and seldom terminal. They will be made by people and agencies through a series of decisions for both the immediate and the long-range future. But is it possible to derive any rational or any tentative hypotheses which may be helpful to those who attempt to make their resolutions constructive ones? The authors now present a series of propositions and their implications which may be helpful.

The first proposition is that the common-school curriculum itself has entered an era of marked transformation. In such an era, the opportunity for creative syntheses and fresh departures becomes much greater. The focus of attention, it appears, can be upon conscious invention and experimentation. Tradition, authority, and institutional lore will undergo challenges which may reduce their relative weights. The implication is that issue-resolution concerning vocational education can be bolder, more creative, less hidebound by established doctrine than in the immediate past.

A second proposition is that the common-school program will address itself far more completely than before to a common core of disciplinary content and intellectual prowess. The nature of this core has been indicated in preceding discussions; the pertinent feature at this point is its increasing universality. Every offering will face an increased demand to contribute to that core; expectations for such contributions will be raised in quantity and quality. This does not mean that other contributions become negligible nor necessarily that they will be relegated to second-class status. What it does mean is that an intellectual imperative confronts all curriculum components privileged to belong to the common school. Meaning may go one step farther. Offerings which do not embrace this imperative may belong elsewhere than in the common school.

Implications of this proposition for vocational education are legion. The content of separated courses will need to focus more largely upon the acquisition of competence in speaking, writing, reading, handling mathematical concepts, and upon developing and applying concepts in the natural sciences, for example. In methodology, *memoriter* what-to-do must be supplemented by why-we-do and why-it-works. The development of inductive reasoning, analytical mental skills, and methods of attack will be objectives consciously sought from all curriculum organization and teaching procedures. To handle such responsibilities successfully, vocational-education supervisors and teachers with new dimensions in academic background may be required. This, in turn, will affect collegiate and in-service teacher education; the "vocational major" of sixty or seventy semester hours in a baccalaureate-degree program may have to be telescoped sharply to provide time for at least that much in genuine academic foundations for the teacher of occupational courses. The practical effect of the intellectual imperative may be to furnish a criterion for inclusion or exclusion of a given occupational offering; for instance, the criterion would dictate that, if the course can be taught, with available manpower, in a given locality by no better than a craftsman with a flair for instruction and for good relations with youngsters, it does not belong in the common school. Also, the common discipline-intellectual cause will argue for close *rapprochement* among all teachers, erasing separated status of those whose specialization is vocational education and of those whose specialization is academic. Outcomes of all offerings, regardless of labels, will be tested more rigorously; occupational guidance, for example, will be examined in terms of what mental and attitudinal equipment it produces in students, not in terms of what motions are gone through or what commendable objectives are stated. Thus, all who become involved as common-school educators will become involved to an increasing degree in planning the achievement of intellectual outcomes, and this will demand requisite ranges of ability, disposition, and dedication.

The third proposition is that impending transformation of the common school is toward realistic acceptance of talent utilization as an outcome to be achieved, not merely verbalized as an objective. This means concrete implementation through curricula, organizational structures, methodological differentiations, student-centered services, and educational technologies. It also means that the vocational *motif*, rather than vanishing from the common school, gains in stature since America, by "talent utilization," refers to the vocational application of talent. But, as has been noted earlier, the vocational *motif* in the common school may differ considerably from the present one. It seems likely to shift from primary attention to arranged education *for* work to arranged education *to* work.

Again, implications are legion. *To* work now becomes an integral part of the common core for everyone, notably for those formerly somewhat disdainful of occupationally labeled courses or curricula. The complex of attitudes, value adherences, and life meanings which either constitute or destroy purposefulness in life must be got at, not left to chance. Self-assessment and thoughtful long-range relation of the young person to the world of work become important concerns of all teachers and program-builders for the common school. Those with specialized preparation in vocational education should have valuable contributions to make. It is clear, however, that their contributions will be better utilized in the framework of a common core than in a segment of schooling open only to a relatively few students who decide "to take the vocational route." In brief, talent utilization, as a thematic concept for the role of the common school, calls for a new definition of vocational education as a pervasive component of that part of schooling devoted to production of a student's life posture.

More tangible implications can be derived from the proposition that the common school will be transformed in the direction of talent utilization. Instead of being considered a disaster, early employment of some students may well be considered a valuable and integral portion of common education. Change of the curriculum vehicle from the classroom to the filling station may not be as difficult as it was once considered; going to work may become one of the planned differentiations for talent discovery, development, and utilization. As is being demonstrated increasingly, such differentiation can continue considerably beyond mere required formal class work as an adjunct to being permitted to earn money before a legal quitting age; it can provide an efficient curriculum for many students. Presumably, many of the staff specialists for this variety of education can be drawn from those with training in vocational education, but it is common-school education to which they will be devoting themselves. Similarly, dedication to talent utilization may dictate in-school differentiations in the vehicles used to achieve the common core's desired outcomes. Among junior and senior high school students there will apparently always be many whose latent powers go undiscovered and undeveloped when the standard disciplinary approach represents their sole opportunity. The thought of work-preparation may furnish necessary motivation for some; procedure from projects to concepts may fit the learning styles of others. Thus, occupationally titled courses joined with talent-utilizing guidance may take their places along with English and foreign language as core curriculum offerings for capable students; outcomes sought will be largely identical but the vehicles will differ.

A fourth proposition is that the transformation will be toward a common school which is a preparatory rather than a finishing school. That is, it prepares for further education on the part of almost every pupil and is oriented in striking degree toward readiness rather than specialization. In the occupational area, to be specific, it looks toward later completion of job competence and lifelong continuation education in keeping with a constantly revolutionized world of work. That this transformation will occur overnight is hardly possible; that it will tend to transpire is a reasonable forecast.

Implications for vocational education may be quite significant if this proposition is accepted. As pointed out earlier, the potentiality of all students to acquire further education will also require additional program development. Although the further education may be technical or even merely training in character, academic skills and competencies will be involved to an increasing degree. This may say something quite important about what is to be taught in a course labeled woodworking, for example, or about the prominence and nature of related training in distributive education. Carried to its ultimate, this transformation could shift most employee-training to post-high-school agencies, since development of capacity for further education will have first call upon the common-school's time, staff, and instructional energy.

The fifth proposition is that the common school will have its frames of reference transformed. The local community will become a site, not an origin, of the school. The frame of reference—for objectives, for scales of value for curriculum alternatives, for content and its organization, for allocations of precious time, and for expectations—will be chiefly the American socioeconomic-cultural enterprise. More specifically, present trends indicate that local tradition and need will not hold off the accumulated national backlog of knowledge which should be added to the curriculum of the common school. Standards of expectation for the performance of all school pupils, whatever the field, seem destined to increase sharply over many present local norms. The common-school student will be viewed as a mobile and crucial component of a national pool of manpower, still free to stay at home but equally free to go where he is needed or where he sees opportunity arising without locally induced educational handicaps. Attempts to meet individual employment and national manpower needs with occupational training will be increasingly the concern of national and regional arrangements supplementary to the common school and only incidentally dependent upon location as a point of reference.

As the frame of reference shifts, vocational education in the common school faces challenging opportunities. What can be done in existing offerings to make the new frame of reference acceptable? What can be dispensed with? What can be used with greater long-range profit? Can teaching conform to the new expectations for student performance? More fundamentally, can bases for the selection and organization of occupational offerings be evolved which will be consonant with national reality and less restricted by local history, previous institutionalized categories, and established proprietorships? Answers to these and similar questions are the concern of those known as vocational educators, to be sure, but now become more than ever the concern of those who make the fundamental definitions of the common school.

The final proposition to be offered is this: The shape of actual transformation in the common school can be affected distinctively by initiative from within. Although reference thus far has been chiefly to forces playing upon the common school, it remains true that this school also remains capable of a measure of self-direction. Impacts such as those cited in this chapter have resulted in organic fluidity and alertness. This could be precedent to the development of leadership relations. And leadership can introduce conscious directions for change. It is not, at present, foreordained that twentieth-century classicism shall dominate the transformation of the common school, or that the disciplinary revival shall furnish the sole organizing center for the common-school program. Other alternatives await the exercise of initiative toward internal leadership.

Three examples of implied opportunity must suffice. First, the common school might be able to do something constructive for those students, perhaps increasing in number and certainly increasing in strategic importance, variously known as the disadvantaged or culturally deprived. Little in the intellectual-disciplinary entente seems very promising for these youth; the same might be said for the traditional vocational-education approach. But somewhere there may lie a program based upon the needs and promptings of such young people —and vocational educators have much experience in beginning with flesh-and-blood human beings in education—which can be a promising venture area for the common school. That the American people will define the common school to include such venturing if they have the chance, there is little doubt.

Second, America has many high schools organized to such extent around occupational motivations that they are known as vocational high schools. It is doubtful that their continued existence is threatened seriously by transformation of the common school, in spite of glib references to their early demise. Survival is not the problem. The real challenge, already being met in marked degree by some such schools, is to demonstrate all-around excellence in achieving the core outcomes of common-school education. If vocation-centering is an efficient device for total education for able students, some of these schools can perhaps establish that fact. Vigorous efforts to refine and demonstrate the role of the selective vocational high school in providing high-quality total education might have decided influence upon the future shape of the common-school system.

The third example has had former reference. The common-school curriculum seems to be headed toward a rationale for organization in which subjects will give the materials necessary for meeting life problems, mental discipline will provide the competence for arranging those materials to be of use, and cultivated intellectual skills will assure the acquisition and application of more materials when needed. Synthesis of these components is conceived to be chiefly automatic, requiring little if any practice except that which "life" affords. However, the possibility remains that a counterapproach can find living room as a part of the impending core curriculum, an approach which starts with synthesis around live problems of pervading importance. Certainly, most citizens are still deeply concerned with what young people can and will *do* as the result of schooling. And furthermore, American people are much concerned with constructive implementation of the family as a basic unit of civilized living. The opportunity for creative leadership confronting homemaking is great, although there are numerous barriers. With initiative and dynamic reconstitution, this subject might have much to do with the shape of the transformation to come.

In this section it has been necessary to appear didactic and prophetic in order to visualize elements of a rationale which is, so far, more nebulous than planetary. What we have made appear as imminent and inevitable are, in actuality, only probabilities. Even the probabilities are not endorsed as what "should be" but are presented as natural phenomena to which vocational education can seek to adjust—or from the effects of which it can seek to escape—as it finds its place in the common school. The transformation is envisioned chiefly as a gradual process in which the momentum generated by history is acted upon by the forces of current culture and by the intelligent planning of those responsible for the program of the common school. The succeeding chapter deals with the initial phases of such planning.

CHAPTER V

Vocational Education in the Secondary School

JOHN PATRICK WALSH and WILLIAM SELDEN
WITH THE ASSISTANCE OF OTHERS

Introduction

The focal point of the program of vocational education is the instruction that is given in a curriculum designed to meet the employment objective of an occupational area. To the degree that such instruction is given for occupations in which there is reasonable expectation of employment and to the degree that it contributes to the labor-force requirements and economic growth of the area served, the program can be considered a valuable asset to the community and a contribution to national welfare and security. To the degree that the converse is true, it can be a liability.

It is the purpose of this chapter to review the program-planning aspects of vocational education and to provide a limited description of the several areas of occupational preparation that are usually considered as the categories of vocational education. Because of the importance of the teaching function and the unique characteristics of vocational teaching, an effort has been made to portray the role of teaching in vocational-education areas.

Program-planning

Program-planning for vocational education looks in two directions at once: the occupational areas to be included in the over-all program must be determined; then other plans must be made for structuring specific curricula for the several occupational areas. For the one purpose, determinations are based on manpower requirements and on labor-market information; for the other, they are based on occupational analysis and the programing of learning units.

This inherent duality requires the utilization of many individuals and a wide range of services in order to achieve viable goals in each of the ventures.

DETERMINING THE SCOPE OF OCCUPATIONAL PREPARATION

A balanced program of vocational education considers not only present manpower requirements and labor supply but also probable future requirements and projected supply—hence population mobility must be taken into account. Therefore, planning begins with a basic survey of the labor market to determine occupational categories, levels of employment in the several categories, prognosis for changing requirements within the categories, prognosis for emerging occupational categories, and an analysis of employment trends. To be effective, the survey must include the entire constellation of occupations, accounting for all employment, actual and potential.

An examination of the determined demands in relation to the sources of manpower available for replacement and expansion purposes projected over a range of years—a requirements-and-resources analysis—defines the training problem. Subtracting the training potential of the private sector, the result indicates the scope of the program to be provided through public vocational education.

Arousing the community to a degree of concern for the manpower posture of the community is the first step in the development of an active manpower policy. An active manpower policy contributes to the economic growth of the community by increasing the quality and improving the adaptability of manpower and by providing the mechanisms needed for effective matching of qualified workers with jobs. In turn, economic growth helps provide the expansion of employment opportunities needed for an expanding population.

An active manpower policy for matching jobs and workers envisions the interplay of a variety of labor-market practices of which vocational education is of prime importance. Educational institutions, various placement organizations, and other public and private institutions all play roles.

All action elements of such a policy contribute to the planning and functioning of programs for vocational education. The following basic needs and activities are involved:

1) *Information.* Labor-market information must be available, including details on type of occupational demand and available-skills supply, both current and prospective. For maximum reliability and value, the information should be drawn from, and with the co-operation of, all parts of the employer, labor, and educational community.

2) *Guidance and counseling.* Effective guidance and counseling service is needed to translate statistical information into job opportunity information of value to those seeking career guidance. Such services should be started in elementary schools and should guide youngsters toward career decisions in vocations requiring training in accord with their aptitudes and aspirations.

3) *Early warning of change.* An early-warning system, freely contributed to by employers, is needed to advise of impending employment shifts, changing occupational requirements, and needs for new categories of workers resulting from planned product changes, major technological innovations, or long-range expansion. Such a system can provide the necessary lead time for the initiation of necessary training programs.

4) *Research.* Major and continuing research efforts are needed to gain increased understanding of key factors affecting functioning of the labor market and to make more available and to improve the accuracy of information on current and projected occupational requirements.

5) *Education.* Current jobs and, increasingly, those of the future cannot be filled adequately by workers lacking minimum basic education. Each individual should be given a thorough general education as a base for acquiring necessary specific occupational skills.

6) *Vocational education (training and retraining).* A balanced program of vocational education is required to provide the range of skills needed in a competitive labor market. To bridge the gap between workers with unneeded skills and job requirements, retraining must be provided in both public and private sectors.

7) *Apprenticeship.* To assure a continuing supply of highly skilled craftsmen, apprenticeship programs should be initiated and supported by business and industry. Vocational programs are needed to provide pre-apprentice education and related instruction for apprentices.

8) *Placement.* Good placement services can speed the matching of jobs and workers. Such services, (including recruiting, testing, assessing, and counseling on the basis of specific job vacancies and trained work-seekers) complete the cycle of transition from school to work.

The preceding enumeration of needs and activities makes it evident that the planning of a vocational-education program involves major segments of the community and the state agencies which provide services in the areas of employment security and vocational education. Thus, the program that eventually evolves becomes a program "of the people, by the people, and for the people." Labor, management, civic, and municipal groups become deeply involved in an assessment of manpower requirements and resources. Out of the public-spirited churning comes the determination of the occupational areas for which vocational education and training must be provided, either through the vocational school or through a co-operative venture involving the facilities, knowledge, and skills of the commercial and industrial community.

PLANNING THE CURRICULUM

Having determined the occupational areas for which instruction is to be provided, whether in business, industry, agriculture, health services, marketing, homemaking, or other field, the task at hand is one of curriculum construction: the assembling of units of instruction into courses and the combining of courses into a sequential curriculum. These curricula must meet the skill and knowledge requirements of the occupational objective as well as the graduation requirements for the high-school diploma or certificate of completion prescribed for the program. Here again the knowledge and skills of the school administrator and the curriculum experts *must* be supplemented with the advice and assistance of representatives of the business-industry community who have access to a wealth of knowledge growing out of their personal involvement in the occupational area as employers, managers, and workers.

Knowledge acquired of what a worker must know and what he must be able to do, supplemented by advice from occupational advisory groups, will provide the raw materials and ingredients for the several courses that will make up the occupational skill and knowledge development program. The involvement of the business-industry representatives provides additional insight into the equipment and paraphernalia needed to provide effective instruction. And for a bonus, their very involvement insures a clientele for placement purposes—a clientele that feels that the program belongs to it.

Curriculum development is a continuing process requiring an evaluation of the efficiency and effectiveness of the program. The major criteria for evaluation are success in the placement of the graduates and their ability to hold jobs and move ahead in their fields. Again, the advisory groups continue to be an asset in assisting in the evaluation. Too, the former students, now job-holders, become a source of information useful in adjusting the curriculum to meet evolving needs.

Regarding the program in vocational education, there are some principles to be observed.

1) Vocational education should occur as close to the time of application as possible. On the secondary level, vocational courses should be concentrated in eleventh and twelfth grades.
2) There must be sufficient concentration of work in each area to enable the student to develop sufficient competence to hold an entry job in a given occupation upon the completion of the curriculum.
3) A well-planned vocational program integrates vocational education and general education. The vocational development should be built on a sound base of general education.
4) Some diversity of curriculum offerings is needed to provide for individual needs and to give flexibility to the program.
5) All aspects of an occupational area cannot be included in the curriculum. Those skills which form the core of the occupation and which are necessary for entry into the occupation should be taught.
6) Vocational instruction must be geared to the times, preparing the individual to enter the world of work of today and tomorrow.

Areas of Occupational Preparation

Occupations representing a cross section of the world of work below the professional level are served by vocational-education programs. The uninitiated are often led to develop a limited conception of the range of the program because their attention is focused on the several categories of training eligible for aid under the provisions of the federal acts. Because vocational education is dedicated to preparation for the world of work, it follows that the range of programs could conceivably run the gamut of entry occupations listed in that section of the *Dictionary of Occupational Titles*.[1]

Actually, there is a natural division of occupational categories based on the world of work and the sectors of the economy concerned with producing, processing, facilitating, distributing, utilizing, or consuming the goods and services making up our gross national product (GNP). However, there does exist a flexibility or a

1. Federal Security Agency, Bureau of Employment Security, *Dictionary of Occupational Titles*, pp. ix–xviii. Washington: Government Printing Office, 1949.

fluidity which makes possible the inclusion of emerging or evolving occupations resulting from divisions, amalgams, innovations, or pure genesis in a changing world of work.

A rapid review of occupations and employment by the economist usually begins by using two basic categories—agricultural and non-farm. A further refinement provides a distribution of goods-producing and service-producing categories. For further refinement, one must move to the major categories found in the *Dictionary of Occupational Titles*.

Major areas of occupations and the vocational-education service providing occupational preparation for them can best be arrayed as follows:

Basic production (manufacturing, agriculture), construction, and related services. Through trade and industrial education, technical education, agricultural education.

Marketing, sales, distribution, and related services. Through distributive education.

Facilitating functions (business communication, information and data storage and retrieval, fiscal accounting, and related services). Through business education or office education.

Personal and public service. Through trade and industrial education and health-occupations education.

Home and family services and related wage-earning occupations. Through home economics or homemaking education.

TRADE AND INDUSTRIAL EDUCATION[2]

A major objective of trade and industrial education is the orderly development of occupational skills, technical knowledge, safety attitudes, work attitudes, and practices required to *enter* employment at a productive level with the necessary educational background to move ahead within the occupation and its related areas. This objective is achieved through a variety of programs designed to meet the training needs of potential workers—programs that range from the simple to the complex, that serve youth destined for employment in jobs ranging from the single skilled to the highly skilled, from the maintenance-worker to the technician classification.

Program parameters.—The operational arena for trade and industrial-education programs is undoubtedly the broadest of all vocation-

2. Prepared by John P. Walsh.

al-education categories. The delineation of the area provided in the regulations of the Office of Education indicates its global dimensions:

(*a*) Any industrial pursuit, skilled or semiskilled trade, craft, or occupation which directly functions in the designing, producing, processing, assembling, maintaining, servicing, or repairing of any product or commodity.

(*b*) Other occupations which are usually considered technical and in which workers such as nurses, laboratory assistants, draftsmen, and technicians are employed and which are not classified as agricultural, distributive, and other business, professional or homemaking.

(*c*) Service occupations which are trade and industrial in nature.[3]

Thus it can be seen that the curriculum for trade and industrial education includes programs for manufacturing, construction, mechanical service, personal service, public service, health service, and technical and fisheries occupations.

Preparation for entry-level jobs takes place through full-time preparatory programs involving a combination of shop or laboratory practice and academic subjects designed to meet secondary-school graduation requirements; through co-operative programs combining academic preparation in the school and supervised skill development on the job; through specialized occupational curricula in trade schools or vocational-technical schools; or through occupationally oriented curricula in community or junior colleges. Whatever the organizational pattern of the institution, the major focus of the curriculum and the major thrust of the instruction are directed toward occupational preparation.

The programs are characterized by curricula which include courses, content, and instructional materials derived through occupational and content analyses, with the assistance of advisory groups drawn from the occupational sector that will ultimately employ the individuals to be trained. Similarly, the instructional personnel, the product of specially designed vocational teacher-training programs, are drawn from the ranks of successful practitioners of the occupation that they will teach. Finally, the instruction, designed to produce learning products sought after by employers, is provided in special-

3. U.S. Department of Health, Education, and Welfare, Office of Education, *Administration of Vocational Education*, pp. 16–17, Vocational Education Bulletin, General Series, No. 1. Washington: Government Printing Office, 1958.

ized facilities, such as shops, laboratories, construction sites, and manufacturing facilities which are readily recognizable as a part or replica of the actual operational arena in which the trainee will ultimately be employed.

Current practice in offering trade and industrial courses does not provide a clear-cut indication of the type of institution utilized or of grade-level placement. Although a larger number of comprehensive high schools than vocational-technical schools or junior colleges *offer* such courses, by far the majority of *students enrolled* in such courses are registered in separate vocational facilities, thus perhaps indicating the limitation on range of offerings in the comprehensive high schools.

Challenges and issues.—By all observable dimensions and current projections the conclusion can readily be reached that "what is past is prologue." All evidence on resources and requirements promises a positive upward slope for an already burgeoning program. However, such a prognosis for growth is not without the warning that certain challenges and issues must be dealt with decisively.

The basic challenge—keeping pace with a growing economy and a changing technology—rests most heavily on trade and industrial educators, not only because of the breadth and depth of the program but because many of the areas they serve are keys to future technological change and future occupational fluidity. Attendant to the basic challenge, indeed emerging from it, are the following requirements which relate directly to almost all occupational categories:

Increasing skill and knowledge requirements
Changing occupational patterns and specific job content
Changing work-life patterns and retraining requirements
Providing for emerging skill requirements and evolving job practices resulting from fractionating or amalgamation

Thus, some of the needs and issues become clear, while others remain somewhat obscured. Among the less obscure are the following:

Providing the range of program within a given community, area, or region to adequately meet the needs of the individual student and the business-industry community with its personnel requirements. Program-planning must be broadened to meet the occupational-preparation requirements of the range of individual talent, including the slow-learner and potential dropout, minority groups, the disadvantaged, the student of average ability, and the talented. Similarly, program offerings must serve those who will become the single-skilled operatives as well as those who will become the craftsmen and technicians; the helpers as well as the supervisors; the detailers as well as the designers; the doers of deeds as well as the planners.

Providing sufficient breadth and depth to the training programs to generate the flexibility needed by individuals who must withstand the trauma of job changing and changing occupational requirements.

Providing preparatory programs for new and emerging occupations that are suffering the fluidity of genesis. Similarly, providing the instructional staff for such unstable occupational areas.

Providing flexible facilities to meet the requirements of changing-needs patterns of the future—facilities designed to serve a wider range of individuals in changing occupational fields.

Providing broad-gauged leadership and administrative ability needed to build a balanced program attuned to the times and geared to the trade and industrial occupational needs of the area served by the program, the school, or the system.

HOME-ECONOMICS EDUCATION AT THE SECONDARY LEVEL[4]

Home-economics education may be "vocational" in one of two senses. First, it may prepare students for the vocation of homemaking through the development of those understandings, abilities, and attitudes which contribute toward effectiveness in the homemaking role. Second—and this is an emerging trend—it may prepare them for wage-earning. This latter purpose may be achieved in three ways: (a) by preparing girls for entering those service occupations that are related to home economics; (b) by helping girls learn to carry the dual role of homemaker and wage-earner with success and satisfaction; and (c) by helping students achieve employability—through the improvement of personal appearance, through developing skill in human relations and in the management of resources, and through the development of those attitudes desired by employers.

At the present time, approximately 1,600,000 students are enrolled in local-state-federal programs of vocational home economics.[5] The vast majority of these students is enrolled in programs at the second-

4. Prepared by Elizabeth J. Simpson, Associate Professor of Home Economics, College of Education, University of Illinois, Urbana, Illinois.

5. *Education for a Changing World of Work*, p. 5. Summary Report of the Panel of Consultants on Vocational Education requested by the President of the United States. Washington, D.C.: Government Printing Office, 1962.

ary level. The principal aim of home economics at this level is to help individuals and families "improve the quality of their family living through efficient development and utilization of all human and material resources."[6]

Basic to all that is taught in home economics is belief in the importance of family life. The family has long been recognized as the basic unit of society, "the foundation on which all other groupings have been built or from which they have developed."[7] It is the preserver of the human values which give meaning and dignity to life. In the Family Service Association Bulletin, *What Makes for Strong Family Life*, it is stated that:

The family is almost as old as man himself, and families have been faced with threats to well-being from within and from without ever since our ancestors first arrived on earth. To a highly successful degree the family has met these challenges and changes. This constitutes a remarkable testimonial to the strength and adaptability of people and the soundness of the family as an institution. . . .

The family is the fountainhead of the personality and character of every individual. What the family is today—and will be tomorrow—determines, more than anything else, what life is like for us and will be like for our descendants.[8]

The family is a dynamic unit with potential for growth, development, and change. Home-economics-education programs geared to the homemaking purpose are based on the conviction that family life may be improved through education. These programs include the study of many phases of family living:

Home management and family economics
Family and social relationships, and personal development
Child development, care and guidance
Food and nutrition
Housing and home furnishings
Clothing and textiles
Home care of the sick and the aged
Art related to the home

6. "Home Economics Education: Facts You Should Know," p. 4. Washington: American Vocational Association, 1960.

7. Claude Burton Hutchison, "Home Economics—Education for Living," *Journal of Home Economics*, XLI (September, 1945), 353–56.

8. *What Makes for Strong Family Life*, p. 5. New York: Family Service Association of America, 1958.

Patterns of offerings in home economics at the secondary level exhibit great variety. In general, courses are either composite in nature, including within any one year the five or so major areas of the field, or they are specialized, usually with each of the two semesters devoted to one of the major areas. There appears to be a definite trend toward programs that provide both the composite course, usually in the first year or two, and the specialized course, generally in the later years. Enrichment in the home-economics-education program may be provided through the organization, Future Homemakers of America, and through programs of home experience and home visitation.

Program emphases in the '60's.—The conditions and needs of society and of families within the society constitute one important basis for curriculum decisions in home economics. Among the conditions that affect today's home-economics program are:

The increasing urbanization of families
The lessened self-sufficiency of the family unit and concomitant dependency on outside agencies
Increased mobility of individuals and families
Developments in the mass media of communication
The increasingly skilful use of propaganda
The complex roles of family members today
The high divorce rate
The lengthening life span
The high rates of juvenile delinquency and mental illness
The establishment of families in larger numbers and at younger ages
The high and increasing proportion of women who combine homemaking and wage-earning
The decrease in the proportion of jobs for unskilled workers
The increase in service occupations
Technological advances
The lack of security in our national life
The rapidly changing world scene
Expanding knowledge in all areas

Space does not permit a discussion of each of these conditions and of their implications for the home-economics-education program. In general, what is implied is need for increased emphasis in home-economics programs in the areas of human relationships and personal development, child development and guidance, and home management, including consumer education. A result of increased attention to these areas is more emphasis on the cognitive aspects of preparation for homemaking and less on the manipulative or performance aspects.

Following is a brief discussion of some of the trends in each of the major subject areas of home economics at the secondary level. The impact of the changes in society and in family life are apparent.

Home management.—Home management, as the term is used in the field of home economics today refers to ". . . the decision-making aspect of the comprehensive job of homemaking. It is the conscious planning, controlling, and guiding of the family resources in order to achieve the kind of home life that is satisfying to the family and to society."[9]

Home management is an area of increasing emphasis in home economics today. Present-day conditions in family life, particularly the increase in the number of women assuming the demanding role of the homemaker-wage-earner, suggest educational needs in this area. As Wood, Hill, and Amidon point out:

> The problems in home management become more acute as technological advances, and changing social and economic forces affect the functioning of the home. Diverse activities force upon family members new responsibilities and many decisions that were not a part of family life in a less complex world.[10]

The principles of home management may be integrated in all areas of home economics. In addition, there is a trend toward specialized units of study and semester courses in home management. Here the principles of management are emphasized with applications made to homemaking problems in such areas as food and nutrition, clothing and textiles, housing and home furnishings, and family relationships.

Family economics.—Another area receiving increased attention in the home-economics curriculum is family economics. The change of the home from primarily a producing to a consuming unit underlies the new emphasis.

Family economics is generally considered a major aspect of home management and, as such, may be included in the specialized units of study and semester courses provided in this area. It may also be inte-

---

9. Mildred W. Wood, Alberta Hall, and Edna Amidon, *Management Problems of Homemakers Employed Outside the Home*, p. xii. Washington: United States Department of Health, Education, and Welfare, 1961.

10. *Ibid.*, "Highlights," front cover.

grated in all areas of home economics. In particular, consumer buying of goods and services has applications in the areas of food and
nutrition, clothing and textiles, and housing and home furnishings.

In the area of family economics, increasing attention is being given
to the influences of personal values and goals upon the use of money.
Ethical considerations related to selection and consumption of goods
are also considered.

Family and social relationships and personal development.—In the
modern home-economics program, family and social relationships
and personal development are areas of increased emphasis. Offerings
are geared to the needs of today's families which, in large measure,
result from the changing conditions of life in particular:

Early dating and marriage
Employment outside the home of a large and increasing proportion of
women
Greater complexity and flexibility in family roles
Wide variation in family structure
A larger proportion of aging family members
The changing relationships of teen-agers and adults, including the
emergence of a distinct teen culture

A study of human relationships may run like a thread through all
other subject areas of home economics. Special courses in family and
social relationships and personal development may be offered on a
semester or yearly basis for both girls and boys. Specialized units in
these areas may be included in composite courses in the early years
of the secondary-school home-economics program.

Child development, care, and guidance.—Child development, care,
and guidance receive increased attention in a home-economics program based on the needs of today's families. More time in the program is provided through longer units of study and through semester
courses. Laboratory experiences with children are frequently provided.

The modern home-economics department provides facilities for
laboratory work with children. In larger school units, a full-time
nursery school may be in operation with a specially trained teacher
in charge. She may co-operate with home-economics personnel in
providing opportunities for secondary-school students and adults to

learn through guided observations and through actually caring for and guiding the children under her supervision.

In other situations "play schools" may be set up. They are planned by the secondary-school students and the home-economics teacher. Children are brought into the classroom for a specified period of time, usually a few hours a day, for a period of a few weeks. In this situation, also, students learn through guided observations and through working with and caring for the children. To facilitate the operation of a play school, flexible home-economics classrooms are necessary. Such equipment as small tables and chairs, play materials, hooks for wraps, and child-size bathroom facilities are desirable.

Ideally, child development is taught in such a way as not only to prepare students for parenthood but also to develop increased self-understanding. Study in this area is an important part of the preparation of both girls and boys for establishing and maintaining a home.

Frequently, year-long coeducational courses in *family living* are provided. Two areas which are organized in most such courses are family relationships and child development.

Food and nutrition.—Emphases in today's home-economics program, in the area of food and nutrition, are placed upon meeting the nutritional needs of family members, the scientific principles related to food preparation, management of resources in providing for the family's food needs, and consumer-buying of foods. Attention is also given to the use of modern prepared-food products and to the cultural aspects of food.

There appears to be an emerging trend toward reducing the time spent in preparation of foods that supply mainly calories and little else of nutritional value. There is much emphasis on nutrition as it relates to appearance and physical and mental well-being.

Food and nutrition are taught in specialized units of study in composite courses and in semester courses. Actual class time spent in preparing foods has been reduced in favor of increased time for the management and relationship aspects of food and nutrition and of homemaking, in general.

Housing and home furnishings.—Housing is said to be the biggest single item of expense for the average American family. It has been estimated that 24,000,000 families are buying houses. Of these, 8,000,000 have bought their houses since the second World War.

With expanded credit the rate is accelerated each year. Ninety-five per cent of all purchases of houses are financed through mortgages.[11]

These are only a few of the facts that emphasize the importance of providing education in the area of housing and home furnishings. Increasing attention is being given this aspect of home economics at the secondary level. Units of study in composite courses and semester courses in the Junior and Senior years focus on housing and home furnishings. Study in this area is frequently provided in coeducational family-living courses.

Integrated in housing and home furnishings units and courses are: family economics, family relationships, home safety, and principles of art. The sociological and psychological aspects of housing are also incorporated, particularly in the semester-long courses.

Clothing and textiles.—Realistic choices in the home-economics program must be made in terms of the practices and needs of families. As has been pointed out, today's family is primarily a consuming rather than a producing unit. In the clothing area, there is increased need for understanding how to make wise selections of personal and family clothing in terms of economic, aesthetic, and social factors and in terms of goals, values, and standards. Technological advances have resulted in the development of new textiles, and keeping informed about these as a basis for wise selections poses a problem for the homemaker. Thus, the selection of clothing and textiles and, in addition, care of clothing and textiles, are emphasized in a modern home-economics program.

Construction of clothing remains in the program but has been de-emphasized. Only the basics of clothing construction can be a part of a home-economics program geared to the needs of today's family. An exception might be made in programs that provide for the election of a semester course in clothing and textiles; even in such programs, it would seem that more emphasis should be given to the selection, use, and care of clothing and textiles rather than to their production.

Home care of the sick and aged.—The place of home care of the sick as a part of the home-economics program may vary according to whether or not it is included elsewhere in the total school program.

11. Marjorie Savage and Hilda Geuther, "Teaching Housing in Senior High Schools: II," *Illinois Teacher of Home Economics,* V, No. 8 (April, 1962), 343.

Some schools provide for its inclusion in the program of health and physical fitness. To a certain extent, some aspects may be incorporated in the study of food and nutrition, family relationships, child development, and housing and home furnishings. In some situations, specialized units of study may be desirable in view of inadequacies of the school program and community need.

The lengthening life span has resulted in an increasing proportion of older family members. This fact has implications for the teaching of all aspects of home economics. Whereas, there would seem to be no need for special units of study on aging and care of the aging, particularly pertinent instruction might be provided in appropriate units.

Art related to the home.—This is one of the so-called "thread areas" that is related to many aspects of homemaking, particularly clothing and textiles, home furnishings, and foods. Teaching in this area is likely to be more effective when co-ordinated with the art-education program of the school.

Recent trends in home-economics education at the secondary level. —Trends in home-economics education at the secondary level include:

1) Growth and development of junior high school home-economics programs, usually composite in nature
2) More emphasis on the management and relationship areas of home economics at all levels
3) Longer units of study, particularly in the later high-school years, in which semester-long units to provide for greater depth in study are becoming more common
4) Increased attention to individual differences in ability, with special courses for fast learners or college-bound students and sections for slow-learners in some areas
5) Increased rigor in home-economics education
6) More structuring and organization of the subject matter of home economics, particularly of the basic concepts and broad generalizations of the field
7) Increased emphasis on development of the ability to think in home-economics classes
8) Increasing attention to the possibilities of providing education for wage-earning as well as homemaking in home-economics programs at the secondary level

Perhaps two of these trends—development of the ability to think and the increased attention to education for wage-earning—merit some special attention.

1) "Teaching students to think"[12] is not a new educational objective. But, certainly in recent years, it has been given increased attention in educational research, in the general literature of the field, and in classroom practice.

How has home economics responded to the increased emphasis on this educational objective? First, there appear to be strenuous efforts in teacher-education programs, at both the preservice and in-service levels, to prepare home-economics teachers to work more effectively with their students in developing reading lists and themes for educational conferences, and in attempts toward curriculum development taken by cities and states.

There are several aspects of and approaches to teaching for development of the ability to think. Those to which home economics at the secondary level appears to have given major attention in recent years include (a) semantics, (b) problem-solving, (c) drawing warranted conclusions in the form of principles and generalizations, and (d) making and supporting value judgments.

In addition to several large organized research projects devoted to investigation of how people think and how they may be helped to think in more productive ways, exciting experimentation on a smaller scale is occurring in many secondary-school classrooms, including home-economics classrooms. Several recent reference books and pamphlets on education for thinking, a few with applications to home economics, have proved invaluable guides for teachers attempting to develop in children the ability to think.

2) An issue[13] in home-economics education is: What responsibility, if any, should home-economics education at the secondary level assume for preparing students for wage-earning occupations as well as for the vocation of homemaking?

Although this question is only now emerging as an active issue, it is really not an entirely new concern. In 1940, Spafford wrote:

12. This section adapted from: Elizabeth J. Simpson, "Selected Issues and Problems in Secondary Education—How Are They Being Met?" *Journal of Home Economics*, LV (January, 1963), 11.

13. *Ibid.*, pp. 11–12.

An examination of curriculum materials of vocational programs shows little attention being given to employment aspects, either guidance into or education for wage-earning vocations. The school may do several things along these lines without interfering with the achievement of its home-making purposes.[14]

She continued by suggesting several possibilities. In 1942 she wrote:

The finding of one's relation to and place in the vocational world and preparing for it is the fifth major purpose of importance to home economics. Students in home economics should come to know themselves better—their assets and liabilities for employment—as well as the job demands of many different occupations. The field has much to offer in increasing the general employability and job satisfaction of all young people. Many types of occupations grow out of home economics, some of a semi-skilled type, others of a highly professional nature.[15]

Among those factors that have combined to bring this whole question into increasingly sharp focus are (*a*) the employment of large numbers of women outside the home and the likelihood that this situation will continue; (*b*) the sharply dropping proportion of jobs for unskilled workers; (*c*) the high proportion of unmotivated young people who drop out of school; (*d*) the increase in service occupations, many of them directly or indirectly related to home economics.

There are a number of positions that might be taken in relation to the issue stated in the first paragraph of this section. One position would be that preparation for homemaking should be the only concern of home-economics education. Those who hold this view would still recommend that the program be made more realistic than it sometimes is through a recognition of the nature of the dual responsibilities carried by a large proportion of women. They would, accordingly, place more emphasis on management and relationship in order to help girls learn how to combine these responsibilities with success and satisfaction.

Others would like to see increased attention given in the home-

14. Ivol Spafford, *A Functioning Program of Home Economics*, pp. 249–50. New York: John Wiley & Sons, 1940.

15. Ivol Spafford, *Fundamentals in Teaching Home Economics*, p. 4. New York: John Wiley & Sons, 1942.

economics program in the secondary school to education which is more directly related to wage-earning. Such efforts might include the following:

(*a*) Application of basic facts, principles, and generalizations developed in class to employment situations as well as to homemaking.

(*b*) A genuine effort to help students see the possibilities for home-economics-related occupations requiring varying levels of training or education. This would apply not only in so-called "career units" of study but also, from time to time as such possibilities might be made evident, through class or community activities.

(*c*) Direct teaching for development of those personal traits and habits that make for employability. (One teacher who does this surveyed the employers of the community to discover the desired traits and habits they thought most lacking in the young women that they employed. She gives special emphasis to these without sacrificing the homemaking values in the program. In fact, these values are enhanced, since the traits and habits important in employment are also important in homemaking.)

(*d*) Co-operation with those in other areas of vocational education, including guidance, in developing and maintaining meaningful work-study programs, especially for slow-learning and unmotivated students. To be sure, this is being done to a limited extent. What is suggested is much more extensive development of this type of program—through *co-operative* efforts.

(*e*) Experiments with this approach in units of study and with groups of students where a pre-employment emphasis might add a new dimension to motivate, provide a sense of reality, and perhaps provide for the development of some skills that make for greater employability.

Things are changing so rapidly! This, of course, must be the watchword in planning any educational program. In educating for wage-earning, the teacher will necessarily be alert to the employment situation locally, state-wide, and nationally. She will avoid placing a narrow emphasis on training for a specific job. Her key words will be flexibility, adaptability, and mobility.

It seems most likely that preparation for homemaking will continue to be the central focus in home-economics education at the secondary level. But it also seems likely that increasing attention to preparation for wage-earning will be given. Explorations in this area are in progress, but at the present time the direction the program will take in achieving this vocational purpose is still uncertain.

DISTRIBUTIVE EDUCATION[16]

The term "distributive education" identifies a program of instruction for students in the eleventh and twelfth grades of high school. The student alternates classroom study of the principles of marketing and distribution with paid employment in retail, wholesale, and service business establishments.

While in school the student studies such basic courses as English, history, mathematics, and science. In addition, he is enrolled for a course in distributive education in which he studies the principles of business operation, product information, and salesmanship. These three areas could be expanded into three or more courses. Business operation covers store location, organization, personnel, store maintenance, merchandising, advertising, and selling. Product information covers materials, construction, operation, manufacture, care, selling price, price lines, and customer benefits. Salesmanship deals with customer identification, sales training, sales personality, merchandise knowledge, sales approach, sales techniques, sales systems, aids to selling, sales rating, compensation, selling as a career, and securing a selling job.

Students who are enrolled in distributive education, work in all types of entry jobs. They are salespeople, stock boys, order clerks, cashiers, waitresses, wrappers, display helpers, delivery boys, and service-station attendants. Places of employment include grocery stores, hardware stores, wholesale pharmaceutical establishments, restaurants, service stations, and motels. The students work primarily in sales and sales-supporting jobs in all departments except office and maintenance.

The field of distribution is represented by a complex of large and small businesses. The average person is well aware of large retailers, such as Marshall Field and Company; the May Company; Sears, Roebuck and Company; and J. C. Penney. He knows, too, that the small hardware store, the service station, or the beauty salon is of equal importance to him as a consumer. The suppliers, such as the manufacturers, wholesalers, and distributors, are necessary parts of the complex system of distribution. They sell to the retailer, and the retailer serves the ultimate consumer.

16. Prepared by William B. Logan, Professor of Education, Ohio State University, Columbus, Ohio.

Challenges and issues.—Four major challenges confront America in providing occupational preparation for the youth in our schools who will enter the fields of distribution and marketing:

1) Changing occupational picture

Distribution is rapidly becoming the most important segment in our economy. Before this century, our economy was based largely on production; providing the necessities of existence required nearly all of our effort. Now we are able to produce more than we consume. Automation has made it easier to produce what we need and want.

With all the productive effort that is now available, we must find more efficient and less costly ways and means of distributing the goods and services. This is a problem for research and education.

We need more people in distribution and marketing today than ever before in the history of our country. A projection by the United States Department of Labor indicates that sales is one of the three fields which will show the greatest increase in number of people employed during the next ten years.

2) Change within distribution itself

At the turn of the century, and as late as the 1920's, the general store served most of the needs of the community, and a wholesaler in a near-by city supplied most of the merchant's needs. Use of the automobile was limited, family life was relatively simple, and most family expenditures were for the essentials of life. All of this has changed radically. (The wide ownership of automobiles enables the family to purchase goods over a broad geographical area.) Large numbers of women work outside the home, thus expanding the market for prepared foods. Increased incomes of families permit the purchase of more and more luxury items as well as a greater variety of the "necessities" of life. This increased income permits the purchase of more services than ever before.

Distribution has changed as a result of greater markets, a more highly educated and more discerning consumer, and keener competition for the consumer's dollar. Fifteen years ago a product was manufactured and then turned over to a sales manager to be sold. Now, manufacturers have a vice-president in charge of marketing. This person has the responsibility for the complete business process. He determines what consumers want, gives instructions to production on what to produce, designs the packaging of the item, establishes sales plans, and market the product.

Major changes have occurred in the handling of the product on the wholesale and retail levels. Stores have increased in size, the number of specialty stores has increased, shopping centers have been developed in all sizes of communities—with multiple units in large cities—the number of service establishments has increased, and the number of hours which stores are open has increased. As a result of these changes, the duties and responsibilities of the salesman, delivery clerk, department head, floor supervisor, and manager have all changed. Because this change has led to increased specialization, virtually all low-level jobs have been eliminated.

Although many stores have increased in size, the number of small stores, concentrated in shopping centers as well as in downtown areas, has increased. In small stores each employee usually performs all the jobs. Such an arrangement forces the employee to have a complete knowledge of all phases of the operation as well as of the policies and the procedures for handling and selling the merchandise.

Another change in distribution has been the increase in the number of products and services available to consumers and the increase in the complexity of these products and services.

3) Change needed in the high-school curriculum

The high school has an obligation to prepare its graduates for employment as well as for higher education. Instead of facing up to this task, most high schools have organized their curricula primarily to prepare their graduates for college. A relatively small percentage of the high schools include salesmanship as a part of the curriculum, and fewer include distributive education in their vocational-education offerings. This is true despite the fact that only three out of every seven high-school students enter college, and only two graduate. Because a very large number of youth enter the field of distribution directly from high school, more attention should be given in school to the job-preparation of this important group of the population.

Every major study of the high-school curriculum by educational groups has recognized the need for job-preparation. Distributive education requires the active support of an alert school administration, the resourcefulness of guidance personnel, and the initiative and perseverance of a skilful teacher. A distributive-education program, to be successful, is not just "put in" a high school. The successful program is the one in which administrators, teachers, and other school personnel co-operate.

The distributive-education class cannot be the same as any other class, such as the English class or the history class. Because of the nature of the subject matter to be studied and of the students enrolled, there should be more types of activity than are typically found in the academic class. The students in distributive education must study subjects directly related to distributive work and many of these require special types of classroom activity.

4) Needed change in the administration of distributive education

Since its inception in 1937, distributive education has been primarily a program in which boys and girls are enrolled for one or two years during their eleventh or twelfth years of high school. In order to be in the program, the student is required to work a minimum of fifteen hours a week.

The greatest need is added depth. Distributive education is a discipline because of the wide variety and complexity of the substantive information it provides the student. There should be a curriculum of studies leading to graduation in the discipline.

In light of the present-day situation, the on-the-job requirement of fifteen hours needs to be reconsidered. Many students are denied distributive-education classes because of age and other limitations. Also, many high schools are located in areas where there is a dearth of placement opportunities. The students in those schools, therefore, will continue to be denied distributive-education opportunities as long as the fifteen-hour requirement is retained.

Opportunities for research and exploration are also greatly limited by the fifteen-hour requirement. This does not mean that this requirement should be eliminated in the case of all students. It means that, in order to have a broader and more effective program of distributive education, there should be not only some classes that might adhere to the present requirement but also some which would permit the use of the project method in place of work experience.

Trends and new directions.—Broader concepts of distributive education have emerged and are emerging; additional programs are being organized; and there is a definite trend toward co-operation of distributive education with other agencies.

1) Broader concept of distributive education

Distributive education was originally conceived as the training of salespeople for work in stores. The first major breakthrough was the recognition that wholesaling had proper training stations for students. To wholesaling has been added a succession of various service establishments, specialty stores, outside selling, and, finally, marketing departments in manufacturing establishments. Following the recognition of various types of enterprises was the identification of the various functions within a place of business, and, finally, the training of the students for careers in distribution.

2) Increased number of distributive programs being organized

The number of distributive-education programs is steadily increasing in both the large metropolitan centers and in the medium-sized communities of the United States. For example, in Chicago a few years ago there were five programs. By 1962, the number had increased to 34. In Ohio there were 52 programs in the 1961–62 school year. In 1962, 21 programs were added for a total of 73 programs.

Nationally there has been a steadily increasing rate of growth. The past five years have witnessed an increase of more than 50 per cent—from 1,271 programs to 1,914. Almost two-thirds of this growth has taken place in the last two years, during which 413 new programs were added.

3) Co-operation of distributive education with other services

Numerous examples of co-operation between distributive education and other services are to be found. In small communities, in which neither distributive education nor business education could operate successfully alone, a working relationship has been established between the two programs. One state now has eight of these programs. It is planned to introduce others during the next few years.

Plans are under way in two states for the development of co-operative programs involving distributive-education co-ordinators and vocational-agriculture teachers. In rural areas which had previously had no distributive education, it has been made available through traveling distributive-education instructors, each of whom teaches in the schools of an area. Other arrangements to bring distributive education to small high schools have also been found to be feasible.

4) Career concept

The entry job in distribution is not an end in itself. Higher salaries, prestige, and the possibility of travel motivate the student to study and work hard in order to advance on the job. Interesting careers await the persons who are willing to prepare for them. The ability and initiative inherent in the person establish the terminal point in his education in distribution. Teachers as well as students are aware of the career possibilities in distributive education. Much of this awareness can be attributed to the influence of the increasing number and activity of the Distributive Education Clubs of America.

5) Expansion of distributive education for special needs

Currently there is much interest in rural and urban youth who are identified as disadvantaged or less able. Several states are developing programs to meet the needs of the blind, the dropouts, and the less able. There are scores of simple jobs in distribution for which most of these youth could be prepared. Programs for them require great amounts of research and all the ingenuity of skilful teachers.

AGRICULTURAL EDUCATION[17]

The Smith-Hughes Act of 1917 contains the basic provisions that have served to shape the direction of vocational education in agriculture for nearly five decades. Section 10 of the Act states that ". . . such education shall be that which is under public supervision and control; that the controlling purpose of such education shall be to fit for useful employment; that such education shall be of less than college grade and be designed to meet the needs of persons over fourteen years of age who have entered upon or who are preparing to enter upon the work of the farm or of the farm home." Since the beginning of vocational education in agriculture, the guiding aim has been to "train present and prospective farmers for proficiency in farming."

17. Prepared by A. W. Tenney, Director, Agricultural Education Branch, Office of Education, Department of Health, Education, and Welfare, Washington, D.C.

Vocational education is administered and supported co-operatively by local school districts, the state, and the national government. After the local board of education has qualified for state and federal aid, it exercises direct control of and supervision over the program. The program offered must meet certain standards as to facilities, programs, and qualifications of instructors as prescribed in the state plan, which is prepared by the state board for vocational education and approved by the United States Office of Education. The state department of education checks the local departments for compliance with standards, distributes reimbursement funds according to law, and assists in the improvement of instruction.

Educational opportunity in agriculture has traditionally been provided through three types of programs—programs for day-school students, for young farmers, and for adult farmers. Instruction for the day-school student is provided as a part of the regular curriculum in high school. A student is enrolled for three to four years in vocational agriculture and studies the subjects offered in farm production, management, marketing, and farm mechanics.

In general, the instructional program emphasizes the exploratory phase during the first year, with increasing specialization and depth as the student progresses through the program. The principles of biological science as applied to crop and livestock production are stressed throughout, as are economic principles and record-keeping. The student constructs a supervised "farming program" either on his home farm or on a farm provided by the school, or, in some cases, he may be placed for farm-work experience on a selected farm in the community. The planning is done co-operatively by the student, the teacher, and the parents. The teacher of vocational agriculture makes regular visits to the students' farms and helps them apply classroom instruction to home-farm conditions.

The course of study is designed to provide the maximum of vocational training that is consistent with the completion of such academic subjects as science, mathematics, English, and history, which are necessary if the student wishes to continue his education in college.

High-school students of vocational agriculture may, and quite generally do, become members of the Future Farmers of America. In this organization they have opportunities to learn how to express themselves, to develop leadership qualities, to co-operate with fellow students and others of the community in worthy undertakings, and to assume their responsibilities as citizens.

A second type of instruction conducted by teachers of vocational agriculture is for young farmers who are endeavoring to establish themselves. Classes are scheduled during the slack work periods of the year or in the evenings. Many groups meet on a monthly basis the year round. Instruction is based upon the needs and interests of the students. In many communities the group organizes a young-farmer association, which provides a vehicle for leadership-training and social activity.

The third type of program organized and conducted by teachers of vocational agriculture provides systematic instruction for established farmers. The nature of the instruction usually is determined by the problems and desires of the farmers. Classes are regularly scheduled for ten or more meetings. The instruction usually deals with management aspects of farming with emphasis on means of making the most effective use of capital investment, labor, and other resources. Such classes serve to bring the latest research findings of experiment stations and other institutions direct to farmers, thus narrowing the gap between research and application.

Since the inception of vocational-agricultural education in 1917, it has enjoyed continued growth and development with rapid expansion following World War II. In a single year in the early 1960's, there were about 10,000 schools offering vocational agriculture in programs qualifying for reimbursement under provisions of the National Vocational Education Acts. These schools employed approximately 11,000 teachers of vocational agriculture. The enrolment in day-school classes was 474,118, which is approximately half of all farm boys of 14–17 years of age. In addition, there was an enrolment of 78,977 in young-farmer classes, and 269,569 in classes for adult farmers, making a total enrolment of 822,664 persons in vocational-agriculture classes.

Many factors have contributed to the farmers' abilities to produce to an extent that makes our country the envy of the world in this mast basic industry. Study after study, however, has shown the superiority in farming by students of vocational agriculture over those who have not had such training.

Vocational agriculture is a component of general education, tending to strengthen the whole educational process. It complements the instruction in other subjects by providing opportunities for practical application. The strong emphasis on work experience, "learning by doing," should be maintained as the core of the program. The value attained through this practical experience, such as good work habits, decision-making ability, and responsibility are lifetime assets. In addition, much value is derived from the strong leadership capabilities which students acquire through their participation in activities of the Future Farmers of America organization. The FFA has helped many young men attain positions of prominence in their farm and civic organizations and in government. Through their supervision of farming programs and other activities, teachers of vocational agriculture work closely with students and their parents over a period of years. These associations permit the teachers to contribute effectively as counselors in the personal and career development of their students.

Agriculture has changed and is continuing to change rapidly. No longer does the term "agriculture" refer only to the occupation of producing crops and livestock. Agriculture now includes hundreds of closely associated occupations. It is comprised of two major components: the farming or production segment and the nonfarming segment, which includes the off-farm functions of agriculture. In recent years the number of persons engaged in agriculture has remained fairly constant, the decrease in the farming segment has been balanced by a rise in nonfarm-agricultural employment. Approximately six million persons are actually engaged in productive farming. Another estimated sixteen million are engaged in off-farm agricultural occupations, such as marketing, providing supplies, processing, and servicing. Others are employed in such fields as agricultural research and education. Many of the nonfarm-agricultural occupations require persons with a background of training and experience in farming. It is important that instructional programs in agriculture prepare a sufficient number of competent people for these agricultural occupations.

Never before have so many people been dependent upon so few farmers; never was it so important that farmers be well educated and efficient. The applications of science, technology, and management, and the use of modern machinery and equipment, have transformed farming into a highly specialized and complex business. Agriculture is one of the primary areas of scientific research and discovery. About 250 million dollars are now spent annually for this purpose. The immense accumulation of research findings would be of little value to America if not communicated to the farmer and put to use on the farms. Public schools have had and should continue to have an important role in helping farmers understand and use the information made available by research. There must be ever greater competence on the part of those who will farm if they are to be successful in attaining an economic status comparable to that of persons engaged in other occupations. This will require a quality program for high-school students and a greatly expanded program through the public schools for upgrading young farmers and adult farmers.

Vocational education in agriculture is increasingly necessary to train competent farm operators and workers, a need that is not being fully met today. This program of vocational education must also serve the vast number of persons who will enter or are now employed in the nonfarm-agricultural occupations for which training in agriculture is essential. This will require continual restructuring of programs to provide pre-entry and on-the-job training for a wide variety of agricultural occupations.

Since agriculture embraces the two major components, farming and nonfarm-agricultural occupations, a two-track agricultural-education program seems necessary. Programs should be designed to meet as nearly as possible the needs of the individual students preparing for or engaged in the various agricultural occupations. The nonfarm-agricultural occupations may require preparation in two or more distinct segments of vocational education. The production and sale of ornamental plants are examples of agricultural occupations which require specialized preparation in agriculture combined with sales and business training. The basic instruction for these kinds of occupations may be given by the high school, but it seems likely that the specialized training will need to be offered through post-high-school vocational programs. Systematic educational programs from one to two years in length are urgently needed for the training of agricultural technicians at the post-high-school level.

Owing to the development of agricultural technology, an abundance of food and fiber can now be produced on fewer acres of cropland. This situation makes possible the use of the unused acres for a wide range of recreational, aesthetic, and economic purposes. This conversion of land will supply the growing demand for outdoor recreation areas and wildlife promotion and will offer additional income and employment opportunities for many farm people. It is likely that many operators will combine farming with a recreation business and will need education in both areas.

Vocational agriculture in high school contributes significantly to agricultural-college preparation for professional occupations. The vocational-agriculture program is an important source of students for the agricultural colleges. In many colleges of agriculture, students who were formerly enrolled in vocational-agriculture classes in high school are in the majority. Research indicates that students with this type of high-school training perform in college equally as well as, or better than, students who took the usual college-preparatory courses.

These facts assume greater importance when it is realized that the colleges of agriculture are graduating only one-half the number of trained professional workers required in agriculture.

While it always has been necessary for some farm youth to migrate to the cities, it would seem desirable to retain at least enough young men with farm background, experience, and training to supply the needs of agriculture. A strengthened program of agricultural education, coupled with intelligent guidance, will accomplish this. The entire world looks to the United States for agricultural leadership. It must be our concern that a reasonable share of our most capable farm youth be encouraged and educated to remain in agriculture, so that we may provide this leadership. Such leadership can be maintained by keeping production high in this country and by providing commodity and technical assistance abroad.

Challenges.—In view of the challenges that face agriculture, vocational education in agriculture should be extended and improved in the years ahead:

1) Vocational-agriculture courses should be continually modernized in keeping with technological changes. Principles of farm science and management need greater emphasis. A broad educational program to include supervised work experience and to continue leadership and citizenship training is essential.
2) The high-school program should serve a larger clientele since it must provide basic training for farming and for a wide range of nonfarm-agricultural occupations for which training in farming is essential.

3) A greatly expanded program is needed for young farmers who are striving to become established in farming and for adult farmers who need to increase their proficiency. Less than 10 per cent of this group is now being served by the public schools.

4) A similar program for the upgrading of employed workers in nonfarm-agricultural occupations is urgently needed.

5) A program of education in agricultural technology is needed for high-school graduates to further prepare them for employment in agricultural industries and businesses. Such programs should be staffed with highly trained agricultural personnel. Programs should be provided in secondary schools, community colleges, or area schools.

6) Co-operative programs involving two or more segments of vocational education should be attempted, possibly in the Senior year of high school but definitely in post-high-school training.

7) Enrolment in programs for training teachers of vocational agriculture should be increased in order to overcome the current shortage of qualified teachers. Special training should be made available for those teachers needed for the nonfarm-agricultural-technology programs.

8) Provisions should be made for pilot and experimental programs at national, state, and local levels. There is need, also, for more opportunities for teacher-trainers and supervisors of vocational agriculture to extend their competencies in professional leadership.

9) Provision should be made to continue and to further develop leadership and citizenship training through a youth organization for those who will enter an agricultural occupation.

10) There is a need to further develop programs of vocational education in agriculture on an area basis so that all persons who need such training may have an opportunity to control.

BUSINESS EDUCATION[18]

The classification of clerical and kindred occupations has been the fastest growing area of employment since 1900 and presently designates the second-largest occupational group in the nation. Workers in this classification number approximately 10.5 million (2.6 million secretaries, stenographers, and typists, and 7.9 million other clerical employees), or 15 per cent of the total number of persons employed in the United States. Between 1900 and 1950 the number of employees in this classification increased 725 per cent, and between 1950 and 1960, 32 per cent. It is estimated that by 1975 more than 14 million will be employed in clerical work, which will represent an increase of approximately 45 per cent between 1960 and 1975.

18. Prepared by William Selden.

Office work (classified as administrative-clerical) is the second-largest occupation in the military service. More than 20 per cent of the enlisted men and probably 80 per cent of the officers perform work so classified. Young men who have acquired an occupational skill in a business-education program have an excellent opportunity to receive an office assignment in the military service. Transcending the military service, but of equal importance to the defense of America, is the missile industry, in which 20 to 25 per cent of the employees are office workers.

One of the goals of business education should be that of meeting the manpower needs of the nation. Instruction in vocational-business subjects should develop the maximum potential of those preparing for or engaged in clerical occupations in both our economic life and our defense activities. For this reason, it is desirable to conduct surveys of business offices and to do follow-up studies of graduates of the business courses. Research of this type helps determine the adequacy of instruction received by business pupils and indicates the type of retraining programs needed.

There is a large turnover in the clerical and kindred occupations group. Female workers, who represent approximately 70 per cent of the group, usually work only a short period of time before they marry and leave the labor market to rear a family. Because of this turnover, 20 to 25 per cent of the high-school population should be enrolled in the business curriculum to meet the manpower needs of business offices. The comparatively small male portion of clerical workers (approximately 30 per cent) use initial jobs as stepping-stones to better positions. For the ambitious, hard-working, able young man, there is ample opportunity for advancement in the business office. Therefore, more boys should be encouraged to enrol in the business curriculum. Counselors and teachers must accept the challenges to meet the demand for trained and highly proficient employees, especially in the stenographic and data-processing areas.

Curriculum.—There is a place in the vocational-business program to provide for the varied needs of all pupils—the above average, the average, and the marginal. For example, an above-average pupil might prepare to become a stenographer; an average pupil might prepare to become a bookkeeper; and a marginal pupil might prepare to become a file clerk. There are opportunities for advancement on all levels—the file clerk, for instance, may eventually become a filing supervisor.

This points up the need for separate and distinct programs for different types of pupils who are interested in the broad area of business education. These programs will be referred to as supplementary (academic-business), occupational, and basic skills (general clerical); however, they may not represent respectively programs for the above-average, average, and marginal pupils already mentioned. For instance, an above-average pupil who wants to enter office employment rather than go to college would take the occupational rather than the supplementary curriculum.

1) Supplementary (academic-business)

The supplementary program is intended for pupils who are above average in ability and have indicated an interest in attending college. Its objective is to provide vocational training for the college-bound pupil who is in the upper 20 per cent of his class academically. In this program, pupils enrolled in the academic curriculum would take a limited amount of business-education work. Some suggested plans for offering a supplementary program in business classes in two separate and distinct areas to pupils for a limited period of time (two units of work in Plans A and B and three units of work in Plans C and D) follow:

Plan	Organization	Stenographic	Data-Processing and Bookkeeping
A..........	Grade 11—one unit Grade 12—one unit	Typewriting Shorthand	Bookkeeping Data-processing
B..........	Grade 12—two units	Typewriting Shorthand	Bookkeeping Data-processing
C..........	Grade 10—one unit Grade 11—one unit Grade 12—one unit	Bookkeeping Typewriting Shorthand	Bookkeeping Data-processing Business organization and management
D..........	Grade 11—one unit Grade 12—two units	Typewriting Shorthand Office practice	Bookkeeping Data-processing Business organization and management

The public secondary schools of New York City are operating Plan B in the stenographic area successfully. The textbooks and materials in these accelerated courses in typewriting and shorthand are the same as those used in the two-year course. However, because of the scholastic ability, maturity, and higher motivation of the pupils, they proceed approximately twice as fast as the regular eleventh- and twelfth-grade business classes. As indicated, this program requires business teachers to make adaptations, to upgrade content, to telescope two years of instruction into one, and to organize a course in such subjects as data-processing.

Perhaps a course in data-processing should be a survey or a principles course. Topics that can be covered in such a course might include the history and language of, present and emerging jobs in, different types of hardware used in, and the effect on our economy of dataprocessing. Rather than purchase or rent equipment, an occasional trip could be made to data-processing installations. Sample forms and audio-visual aids are a necessity in this course.

Although the program that has been outlined may not provide the complete education that is desired, it will give some vocational skill to a prospective college student. We cannot blind ourselves to the fact that approximately half of those who start college do not finish. Those who drop out of college should have some vocational skill to enable them to earn a livelihood. Those who remain in college can use, in part-time jobs, the competencies they have learned in business classes. Such training is practical for many boys and girls who want to attend college but who must support or partially support themselves while doing so.

A possible adjunct to this program would be the addition of subjects providing for advanced placement in the business curriculum. These subjects would be over and beyond the "personal use" and accelerated courses that presently are being offered. A goodly number of high-school graduates take business administration in college. It appears reasonable that they should be permitted to earn college credit while attending high school by taking collegiate courses in business and passing examinations in them, as do students in academic subjects. Examples of courses that might be offered include accounting, business law, and insurance.

2) Occupational

The program described in this section is, for the most part, the current program of business education. It is intended for pupils of at least average ability who will spend one-third to one-half of their time in Grades X, XI, and XII taking vocational-business subjects. Since this program is vocationally oriented, it should be developed in accordance with the needs of the pupils and the employment area. This program should be flexible enough to permit pupils to elect subjects other than those in vocational business.

Suggested programs for pupils majoring in the two more commonly offered business sequences are:

Grade	Stenographic	Bookkeeping
10..........	Business mathematics* General business	Business mathematics* General business*
11..........	Bookkeeping I Shorthand I Typewriting I	Bookkeeping I Principles of selling Typewriting I
12..........	Business English* Business law* Office practice Shorthand II Typewriting II	Bookkeeping II Business law* Data-processing Office practice

* Subjects allied to those that are vocational and provide added knowledge and skills.

In addition to offering these two more commonly offered business sequences, consideration should be given to developing a sequence in office management for prospective office managers and those who have aspiration for higher-echelon jobs in business and industry. It is probable that this sequence should be offered in larger high schools and in areas that have an employment potential for a goodly number of office personnel.

This sequence should be designed basically for pupils who do not plan to attend college, who have leadership potential, who are above average in ability, and whose career objective is the position of office manager. A high-school graduate of this program would not, of course, receive a job as office manager or assistant office manager immediately upon graduation from high school. He would have to accept an entry-level job and work up to the position of office manager. After gaining maturity and experience, one with this type of background should be ready to assume greater responsibilities.

In Grades X and XI, these pupils might take the same subject matter as that taken by students in the bookkeeping sequence. On the twelfth-grade level, business law might be offered to provide the additional knowledge and skill that a prospective office employee should possess. The other subjects of a vocational nature that might be offered in this sequence are business management, systems and procedures, forms design and control (one semester), and data-processing (one semester).

Because of the educational background of business teachers, there would be no problem in offering a course in business management. Books designed for the high-school level are available for this course; and although schools do not offer an office-management sequence, a course in business management is offered by high schools in a few states.

The material now available for a systems-and-procedures course was designed for collegiate instruction; however, since this course is being proposed for high-level-ability twelfth-grade pupils, it should be possible to adapt present textbooks for their use. The main problem is the lack of business teachers who have taken work or have had experience in this area. Systems and procedures consist of the making of plans to accomplish what needs to be done by the most economical method in terms of money and time. Work in the broad area of systems and procedures includes the analysis of what is being done, charting of procedures to be followed, making time and motion studies, studying work flow and layout, and developing the design and control of forms. The last phase is so important that a separate one-semester course is recommended.

Forms design and control and data-processing are each semester courses. Forms design and control probably should be offered in the first semester and data-processing in the second semester, since the former leads into the latter. The content matter of both courses would be basic, since, as in the case of a course in systems and procedures, the background of the teachers would be limited.

3) Basic skills (general clerical)

The basic-skills program is intended for pupils of marginal ability who may not necessarily qualify for high-school graduation. Conant[19] states that "vocational courses should be provided in grades 11 and 12 . . . however, for slow learners and prospective dropouts

19. James B. Conant, *Slums and Suburbs,* p. 44. New York: McGraw-Hill Book Co., Inc., 1961.

these courses ought to begin earlier." These pupils would spend approximately half of their time in Grades X, XI, and XII taking business subjects. It might be desirable for this group of low-ability pupils to take at least one business subject in Grade IX, such as general business, which is sometimes referred to as junior business training. This subject, if taught as originally introduced in the curriculum, would include certain vocational skills, such as filing and telephone usage.

Because of the difficulty of the subject, pupils in this group would be advised not to take shorthand, and it is questionable if all of these pupils should elect bookkeeping. It is desirable, especially in large schools, to include subjects that are tailor-made for this group. A suggested curriculum follows:

Grade	Subjects
X	Business mathematics Clerical practice Consumer education
XI	Principles of selling Record-keeping Typewriting I
XII	Bookkeeping* Business law* Office practice Retailing* Typewriting II

* Elect one.

Clerical practice suggested for Grade X would include instruction in handwriting and spelling plus business forms, such as purchase requisitions and invoices, and might include work on filing, payrolls, and credit.

Also, consideration should be given to the implementation of work-experience programs specifically organized for this group. Work experience appears to be a coming program for possible "dropout" pupils, who might conceivably participate in a carefully organized work-experience program as early as the ninth or tenth grade. This program designed for potential "early-leavers" should be considered as an integral portion of the total public school education program. Present child labor laws make the administration of this program somewhat difficult. Education, government, and industry need to work as a team in an effort to resolve this problem.

The Department of Commercial and Distributive Education of the School District of Philadelphia has developed a business curriculum for potential dropouts who, for the most part, are pupils of marginal ability. Business educators from many states have visited Philadelphia to observe this program.

Much has been written about the large number of unemployed youth today. Conant refers to this group as "social dynamite." He also states in this publication that he is "not nearly so concerned about the plight of suburban parents whose offsprings are having difficulty finding places in prestige colleges as . . . about the plight of parents in the slums whose children either drop out or graduate from school without prospects of either further education or employment."[20]

A widely quoted magazine article presented a picture of this growing national problem by stating:

Unemployment among young people under 21 constitutes, in the words of Secretary of Labor Arthur Goldberg, "one of the most disturbing aspects of our entire unemployment picture." At the moment, there are an estimated 1,000,000 jobless young people between 16 and 25. A majority of these are high-school dropouts who have little or no training to qualify them for any but the most menial jobs. The problem will even get bleaker. Some 2,500,000 of the 10,800,000 students now enrolled in the ninth through twelfth grades will leave school before graduation. Authorities estimate that, within the next few years, the number of dropouts will reach 7,500,000.

Says a high-school psychologist, "I sometimes think it's the fault of the whole educational system. Much too much importance is put on classical book learning and on subjects that will not in any way be useful to the student unless he goes to college. A great many youngsters are bored stupid by the usual courses in high school. Why force them to study things that don't mean anything to them? I think a truly dynamic system would appeal to and help both the non-academic and academic types. The teenagers who aren't interested in book learning should be detected in grammar school and given a completely different kind of education in high school. . . ."[21]

Conclusion.—The citizenry of a community pays taxes and votes bonds for the support of a school system; therefore, it will evaluate

20. *Ibid.*, p. 2.
21. Chandler Brossard, "Teen-ager without a Job," *Look*, February 27, 1962, pp. 31–32.

rather critically the product of the school. Pupils who can be most readily evaluated are the graduates of the business curriculum. This group works for businessmen who are in a position to make this appraisal, especially during the first year or two after graduation. It is somewhat more difficult to evaluate the academic pupils as many of them matriculate in college. This points up the fact that the business-education department must keep currently informed about the business offices and must prepare pupils who are equipped to meet the challenge of constantly changing technological developments.

EMERGING OCCUPATIONAL AREAS[22]

Changing work patterns, adjusting occupational categories, and evolving team concepts to cope with new processes, practices, techniques, and systems have resulted in the emergence of new or modified areas of vocational education. Most notable have been the burgeoning programs for the technical and the health-service occupations and for other assisting or subprofessional groups. While it is true that programs were developed to meet needs in some of these areas during the early years of vocational education, usually as a part of trade and industrial education, it was only during the decade of the 50's that such programs exhibited growth and thrust that made them recognized as specialized categories.

Health-services education.—The evolving team concept in the health-service areas has not only resulted in the recognition of certain assisting groups as identifiable occupational categories but has brought into the occupational matrix a new series of subprofessional practitioners who require specific vocational preparation, either on an institutional base or through the co-operative activities of school and health agencies.

The nursing-services area provides a fine example. Not too long ago there existed only one recognizable category of nurse—the RN, the professional. Today the rosters of our hospitals, clinics, and nursing homes are replete with categories which run the gamut from administrators to aides—all identified as part of the nursing-services area and charged with a descending order of duties and responsibilities requiring a variety of training programs. The categories below the professional nurse—the subprofessionals, technicians, practical

22. Prepared by John P. Walsh.

nurses, nurses aides, and the like—fall within the area of training responsibility of the vocational-education program.

Today, we find programs in our vocational schools for practical nurses, nurses aides, operating-room technicians, occupational and physical therapy aides, medical assistants, dental assistants, orderlies, dietary aides, and laboratory assistants. There will be many more as the nation's programs for health care become more sophisticated, more highly specialized, and more diversified.

The most notable characteristics of vocational-education programs in the health-service areas are:

1) Licensure requirements for the assisting groups most clearly associated with the professional, that is, for the practical nurse
2) Curricula designed to meet state board requirements or standards set by the "parent" profession
3) The integration of the supervised learning process in the classroom, the laboratory, and the ultimate employment arena—the hospital ward, the dental office, the clinics, and so forth
4) The utilization of occupational professionals—professional nurses, dietitians, therapists, dentists, doctors, and so forth
5) The utilization of "patient-centered" teaching as the core of the instructional technique

Technical education.—One true indicator of the dimension of the growth of our technology has been the increase of the incidence of technical-worker categories on the payrolls of our business-industry community. In fact, the technician has become the symbol of technology in transition. To meet the demand for technical workers in a wide range of industries, there has emerged a series of occupation-centered curricula designed to prepare such workers through preparatory programs in vocational-technical high schools and junior colleges.

Technical-education programs are designed to prepare students for employment in business, industry, and government in a range of activities which include research and development, manufacturing, maintenance, operation, and construction. Provision is made for the development of technical workers, technical specialists, and manufacturing or engineering technicians in a variety of specialty and technology areas.

Technical curricula are based on skill requirements and technical and practical knowledge requirements closely coupled with basic education in mathematics and science. Instruction is usually offered in broad occupational areas of technology, such as electrical, mechanical, electronic, chemical, aeronautical, production, instrumentation, civil, data-processing, and computer programing.

The broad technology programs are designed to prepare individuals to enter a cluster of occupations in the sphere of technology. The built-in flexibility—a hallmark of the program—is a plus factor in preparing for the work world of tomorrow. As new technical jobs emerge, they tend to fall readily into the broad technologies and their carefully designed curricula. Even so, there is a need to provide separate courses for certain technical specialties evolving in the missile and aero-space field or in other similarly sophisticated sectors of the world of technical work.

Other areas.—As our standard of living continues to move upward in our quest for the "better life,"the demands for services will spawn new categories of subprofessional workers in a multitude of occupational areas as yet unborn. The team concept will invade the social service, municipal service, recreation, and education fields. The computer can be depended upon to bring about new work areas as information retrieval speeds up our social, scientific, manpower, and human research and provides us with new concepts for and new approaches to improving the welfare of the individual in the expanding environment of the space age.

Vocational education, the manpower-development function, can be depended upon to provide the preparation for the subprofessional occupation of tomorrow.

Teaching in Vocational-Education Areas[23]

The quality of any educational program is directly related to the quality of instruction. In vocational education, the first measure of quality is the level of competence of its shop, laboratory, and classroom teachers.[24] Some of the competencies of vocational-education

23. Prepared by Mary S. Resh, Special Assistant to the Director, Office of Manpower, Automation, and Training, United States Department of Labor. Formerly Program Specialist, Trade and Industrial Education Branch, Office of Education, United States Department of Health, Education, and Welfare.

24. Shop teachers provide instruction in the manipulative skills and practical processes of an occupation. In some schools, shop teachers also provide the required related instruction as an integral part of the shop program.

Laboratory teachers provide instruction in the skills and processes of an occu-

teachers are the same as those required of all teachers, but the objectives, occupational structure, and operational patterns of vocational education call for a host of specialized abilities and understandings as well.[25]

Because the primary purpose of vocational education is to prepare individuals for employment or advancement in an occupation, the instructional program is based on the requirements and practices of an occupation, and teachers must be equipped by practical experience and professional training to provide students with the occupational skills, knowledge, attitudes, and appreciations they need to fulfil their aims. These students may be in-school youth or out-of-school youth and adults who are not employed and who need training to enter an occupation; in-school youth who work part time and who need technical instruction related to their occupation in addition to general-education courses required for high-school graduation; or full-time employed youth and adults who need supplementary training in order to upgrade their skills and knowledge for job security or advancement. To meet the diversified educational and training needs of these individuals and groups of individuals, teachers in the vocational areas must be not only occupationally competent but expert in the use of distinctive teaching methods. Teachers must be skilled in "how to teach" students with vocational goals as well as in "what to teach" these potential workers. Teachers must have not only a general understanding of the learning process but an understanding of how people learn in a vocational environment. Teachers must know not only the general principles and methods of teaching but also the most effective methods of developing the skills and employment potential of youth and the skills and employment potential of adults.

Teachers must know not only the differences and similarities in shop, laboratory, and classroom instruction but also the most appro-

---

pation that is more technical in nature than are goods and service-producing occupations.

Classroom teachers include those who provide instruction related to an occupation, such as applied science or applied mathematics; those who provide special, related instruction to students in co-operative training programs; or those who teach the general education courses required for graduation.

25. John P. Walsh, "Teacher Competencies in Trade and Industrial Education." Office of Education, Division of Vocational Education, Bulletin 285, Trade and Industrial Series, No 69. Washington: United States Department of Health, Education, and Welfare, 1960.

priate teaching techniques for certain situations in each area. Teachers must be qualified to provide not only group instruction but individual instruction.

DEVELOPING THE CURRICULUM AND DETERMINING COURSE CONTENT

A shop or a laboratory teacher plays a key role in developing the curriculum and determining the course content for his training program. For this role, he needs a basic understanding of procedures in curriculum development and revision, the ability to analyze what the worker does in the practice of the occupation, what the worker needs to know in order to practice his occupation, what is desirable or advantageous for him to know, and what attitudes he should possess in order to build and maintain good working relationships. The instructor who was recruited from the ranks of skilled workers in his occupation has the background and experience for this important responsibility. He also enlists the co-operation of employers in determining what is expected of an employee at the level of employment for which the instruction is to be given.

DEVELOPING INSTRUCTIONAL MATERIALS

To meet the training objectives of a vocational-education program, instructors need a wide range of instructional materials to guide students in their practical work and study assignments. Textbooks per se are but a small part of the instructional materials required in occupational-training programs. Textbooks generally lend themselves better to laboratory and classroom instruction than to shop training, and both basic and supplemental texts are used effectively in the more formal aspects of the program. However, textbooks have not been written for many occupational-training areas, and, frequently, available texts soon become obsolete through technological change. Moreover, vocational-education programs require a variety of instructional materials especially designed for use in individual teaching; hence, in addition to textbooks and other published information suitable for group instruction, teachers need to provide job-instruction and operation units for skill training on an individual basis, lesson sheets or study guides for technical instruction, and information units to implement the job-instruction units and study guides.

Many vocational-education teachers are required to develop their own instructional materials. This involves writing, illustrating, editing, and duplicating written instructional materials and constructing model mock-ups and other aids. In some instances, available instructional materials are purchased for teachers, in which case they adapt or modify them to meet their particular teaching needs.

Because skill development depends to a great extent on how successfully the student visualizes, understands, and practices the techniques, processes, and operations involved in the performance of a particular job, the field of occupational instruction is ideally suited for the use of visual materials. Films, slides, illustrations, charts, mock-ups, and scale models are examples of the visual aids which vocational-education teachers must know how to use effectively. Of equal or even greater importance is the teacher's ability to create and to develop the kind of teaching aids that will enhance and strengthen his own program.

ESTABLISHING THE SAFETY CONCEPT

Developing student attitudes toward safe practices and safety consciousness in job performance is an important facet of the vocational-education program, be it agricultural, business, distributive, home economics, trade and industrial, or technical education. Safety in the use of tools and the operation of equipment is emphasized throughout the instructional program. It is taught by precept and example, by demonstration and practice, by close supervision, by lectures and visual aids, and by special techniques used successfully in business and industry to promote and maintain safety.

COUNSELING TRAINEES

Teaching in vocational-education areas involves more than good instruction. The nature and physical setting of vocational education fosters a close relationship between teacher and student, and, consequently, the student is likely to share his job, educational, and personal problems with the teacher. Thus, the vocational teacher has opportunities and responsibilities for counseling. This does not imply that vocational teachers are always trained counselors or that their counseling activities are a substitute for professional guidance services. It does mean that the vocational teacher who knows his students intimately—their strengths and weaknesses, their aspirations and frustrations—is in a unique position to provide the information and inspiration that will help them achieve their vocational objectives. Moreover, teacher-counseling frequently continues in connection with the student's job placement and follow-up. The vocational teacher who has helped guide a student into and through an occupational-training program helps guide him into employment upon the completion of training. Finding the right job for the right worker, placing him in the job, and maintaining contact with him and the employer to evaluate progress and to provide additional assistance if needed, these are important parts of the vocational teacher's follow-up responsibilities. Often these responsibilities must be carried out after school hours and on Saturdays.

STRENGTHENING INSTRUCTION THROUGH PRODUCTION

One of the motivational forces in vocational education stems from the use of production or service jobs as vehicles of shop instruction. Real jobs in vocational shop-training should not be confused with projects in industrial-arts classes which are usually avocational and exploratory in purpose and nature. A "live" job can be an excellent teaching-learning medium and is used in preference to a pseudo-job or exercise work. However, care must be exercised in the selection and utilization of live jobs. Teachers must choose the kinds of jobs that fit into the occupational curriculum and enhance the learning process. Administrative policies may also have a bearing on the use of real jobs or certain types of real jobs. Most important of all, however, is the teacher's rsponsibility to see that real jobs do not replace instruction with production.

Lack of adequate materials and tools may place some limitations on the use of actual jobs, but vocational teachers are frequently able to overcome this handicap by enlisting the interest of local industries or businesses in contributing some of the materials and tools needed for this phase of the instructional program.

TEACHING IN VOCATIONAL-EDUCATION AREAS

To stimulate student interest and desire to succeed, the competent vocational teacher knows how to use, and uses, a variety of techniques. The teacher must be sensitive to teaching-learning situations in the shop, in the laboratory, in the classroom, and in the part-time student's place of employment. He must be able to easily adapt or modify instructional content and methods to the particular needs of a group of students or of an individual student.

The importance of individualized instruction in vocational education cannot be overemphasized, and a student's progress in school and later in employment is frequently due to the special and numerous benefits derived from this type of instruction. While used effectively in all areas of vocational education, individual instruction is preeminently suited to co-operative training programs—teachers and co-ordinators in distributive and industrial co-operative training programs must be masters of this technique.

Like all teachers, shop and laboratory instructors must be adept in the use of verbal presentations, but verbal presentations alone will not develop competent workers. The teacher must be able to demonstrate a variety of skills on an individual and group basis; he must be skilful in the use of individual and group conferences; he must know how to develop the student's appreciation of good workmanship and safe work habits.

The teacher must also be at home in his environment. A knowledge of the paraphernalia of vocational instruction—tools, machines, equipment, and supplies—is essential to teaching success in vocational education. In an instructional area filled with hardware, the instructor must be able to "run the shop or business" and at the same time carry out his major responsibility for teaching. Thus, he must be competent in the management of students.

Because vocational students may not be as highly motivated toward classroom instruction as they are toward shop and laboratory work, classroom teachers must be especially creative and imaginative in order to stimulate and maintain student interest in related and general-education courses. Teachers of science and mathematics courses must use every opportunity to relate their instruction and to apply the principles involved to the student's shop work. Social-science teachers must use every opportunity to show that subjects like history, civics, and economics have many implications for the job-bound student and for his responsibilities in adult citizenship. Some schools offer a social-studies course of particular interest to vocational students, such as a course in labor legislation; other schools include a unit on the labor movement in their regular social-science curriculum. English teachers, too, must seek and find ways to make literature and poetry have more meaning to students than a required credit toward graduation. Vocational-education programs do not deal with intangibles, and every part of the program must contribute something useful to the student's occupational and personal goals. Perhaps this, more than any other factor, binds shop, laboratory, and classroom teachers together into an integrated and co-ordinated whole working for a common cause.

Summary

It becomes crystal clear that the requirements of vocational education for the future will be such as to give top priority to program flexibility. Not only must there be continuing adjustment and readjustment made within the separate curriculum areas but, also, there will need to be a redefinition of some curriculum areas themselves.

Strong interrelationships must be developed between the closely related practical-arts areas and the vocationally oriented curriculum areas, but beyond this, in keeping with evolving occupational requirements, there must be an evolving interrelationship between specific vocational-curriculum categories in order to meet the job requirements of the future. Already, we are seeing close co-ordination of such vocational instruction as agriculture and distributive education, trade and industrial education. Such interplay between what had been tightly compartmentalized areas of instruction is necessary to cope with a world of work that does not always recognize or work in such restricted areas. Planning for the vocational-education programs of tomorrow must take into account the ways in which the capabilities of the several segments of vocational education interlace their contributions to match the man of tomorrow to the job of tomorrow.

Similarly, instructional techniques, devices, and media must reflect the progress that has been made both technologically and socially in bringing to bear all of the effectiveness of instructional personnel in order to improve the efficiency of the instructional process. To the degree that instructional-materials development keeps pace with vocational-education facility and equipment development, there will exist the professional competence needed to meet the challenge of the future.

CHAPTER VI

Vocational and Educational Guidance

FRANKLIN J. KELLER

What Vocational Guidance Does

THE CHILD AND THE WORLD

At the 1961 convention of the American Association of School Administrators, John Ciardi gave a notable talk on what a poem should *do*. Not what a good poem *is*, but what it *does*—to the reader. An exquisite, tender, thoughtful, and psychologically sound presentation. Subsequently, I have thought that the whole problem of the development of the individual with relation to vocational choice might be presented in two poems, one by Walt Whitman, an affectionate understanding of the ways in which a child becomes an adult through his experiences; the other, by Kahlil Gibran, a keen appreciation of the interplay between the individual and his occupation.

THERE WAS A CHILD WENT FORTH

There was a child went forth every day,
And the first object he look'd upon, that object he became,
And that object became part of him for the day or a certain part of
    the day
Of for many years or stretching cycles of years.
The early lilacs became part of this child,
And the grass and white and red morning glories, and white and red
    clover, and the song of the phoebe-bird,
And the third-month lambs and the sow's pink-faint litter, and the mare's
    foal and the cow's calf,
And the noisy brood of the barnyard by the mire of the pond-side,
And the fish suspending themselves so curiously below there, and the
    beautiful curious liquid.
And the water-plants with their graceful flat heads, all became part of
    him.
The field-sprouts of Fourth-month and Fifth-month became part of him,

Winter-grain sprouts and those of the light-yellow corn, and the esculent roots of the garden,

And the apple trees cover'd with blossoms and the fruit afterward, and woodberries, and the commonest weeds by the road,

And the old drunkard staggering home from the outhouse of the tavern whence he had lately risen,

And the school mistress that pass'd on her way to the school,

And the friendly boys that pass'd, and the quarrelsome boys,

And the tidy and fresh-cheek'd girls, and the barefoot Negro boy and girl,

And all the changes of city and country wherever he went,

His own parents, he that had father'd him and she that had conceiv'd him in her womb and birth'd him,

They gave this child more themselves than that,

They gave him afterward every day, they became part of him.

The mother at home quietly placing the dishes on the supper table,

The mother with mild words, clean her cap and gown, a wholesome odor falling off her person and clothes as she walks by,

The father, strong, self-sufficient, manly, mean, angered, unjust,

The blow, the quick loud word, the tight bargain, the crafty lure,

The family usages, the language, the company, the furniture, the yearning, and swelling heart,

Affection that will not be gainsay'd, the sense of what is real, the thought if after all it should prove unreal,

The doubts of daytime and the doubts of nighttime, the curious whether and how,

Whether that which appears so is so, or is it all flashes and specks?

Men and women crowding fast in the streets, if they are not flashes and specks what are they?

The streets themselves and the facades of houses, and goods in the windows,

Vehicles, teams, the heavy-plank'd wharves, the huge crossing at the ferries,

The village on the highland seen from afar at sunset, the river between.

Shadows, aureola and mist, the light falling on roofs and gables of white or brown two miles off,

The schooner near by sleepily dropping down the tide, the little boat slack-tow'd astern,

The hurrying, tumbling waves, quick-broken crests, slapping,

The strata of color'd clouds, the long bar of maroon-tint away solitary by itself, the spread of purity it lies motionless in,

The horizon's edge, the flying sea-crow, the fragrance of salt marsh and shore mud,

These became part of that child who went forth every day, and who now goes, and will always go forth every day.

WALT WHITMAN

ON WORK*

Then a ploughman said, Speak to us of Work.

And he answered, saying:

You work that you may keep pace with the earth and the soul of the earth.

For to be idle is to become a stranger unto the seasons, and to step out of life's procession, that marches in majesty and proud submission toward the infinite.

When you work you are a flute through whose heart the whispering of the hours turns to music.

Which of you would be a reed, dumb and silent, when all else sings together in unison?

Always you have been told that work is a curse and labour a misfortune.

But I say to you that when you work you fulfil a part of earth's furthest dream, assigned to you when that dream was born,

And in keeping yourself with labour you are in truth loving life,

And to love life through labour is to be intimate with life's inmost secret.

But if you in your pain call birth an affliction and the support of the flesh a curse written upon your brow, then I answer that naught but the sweat of your brow shall wash away that which is written.

You have been told that life is darkness, and in your weariness you echo what was said by the weary.

And I say that life is indeed darkness save when there is urge,

And all urge is blind save when there is knowledge,

And all knowledge is vain save where there is work,

And all work is empty save where there is love;

And when you work you bind yourself to yourself; and to one another, and to God.

And what is it to work with love?

It is to weave the cloth with threads drawn from your heart, even as if your beloved were to wear that cloth.

It is to build a house with affection, even as if your beloved were to dwell in that house.

It is to sow seeds with tenderness and reap the harvest with joy, even as if your beloved were to eat the fruit.

It is to charge all things you fashion with a breath of your own spirit,

And to know that all the blessed dead are standing about you and watching.

Often have I heard you say, as if speaking in sleep, "He who works in
marble and finds the shape of his own soul in the stone, is nobler than
he who ploughs the soil.
And he who seizes the rainbow to lay it on a cloth in the likeness of man,
is more than he who makes the sandals of our feet."
But I say, not in sleep but in the over-wakefulness of noontide, that the
wind speaks not more sweetly to the giant oaks than to the least of
all the blades of grass;
And he alone is great who turns the voice of the wind into a song made
sweeter by his own loving.
Work is love made visible.
And if you cannot work with love but only with distaste, it is better that
you should leave your work and sit at the gate of the temple and take
alms of those who work with joy.
For if you bake bread with indifference, you bake a bitter bread that
feeds but half man's hunger.
And if you grudge the crushing of the grapes, your grudge distils a poi-
son in the wine.
And if you sing though as angels, and love not the singing, you muffle
man's ears to the voices of the day and the voices of the night.

KAHLIL GIBRAN

VOCATIONAL GUIDANCE IS A LIFETIME PROCESS

Vocational education, like education, is a lifelong process and,
like education, is not something that takes place only in the school.
In discussing the distinction between education and schooling, Herskovitz wrote as follows:

> Most persons of Euroamerican culture tend to regard educaton as sy-
> nonymous with schooling. Few anthropologists who have discussed the
> training given boys and girls in nonliterate societies, and stressed the care
> taken by parents to make available to their children the cultural resources
> of their society, have not subsequently been confronted with statements
> such as "The X tribe has no system of education." What is meant by such
> a statement is almost always revealed to be something quite different—
> that the people in question have no *schools*. The significance of the dis-
> tinction between "schooling" and "education" is to be grasped when it is
> pointed out that while every people must train their young, the cultures
> in which any substantial part of this training is carried on outside the
> household are few indeed.[1]

1. Melville J. Herskovitz, *Man and His Works*, p. 311. New York: Alfred A.
Knopf, 1952.

When life is simply hunting and fishing, all that one needs to know is transmitted through imitation. Only later, as hunting and fishing develop into domestic economy, into commercialism and industrialism, and finally into complex technology, are the essentials of living abstracted, compacted, and too often, formalized, into what becomes "school." But if it is a good school, it is still good living. And education remains life.

What is a "good" school? It begins with kindergarten, which incidentally has more in common with the vocational school than any other part of the educational system. Froebel's insight was uncanny. (He cluttered up his pedagogy with a good deal of futile symbolism, but fundamentally he was sound.) Let the children play, but help them to play well. Release their energy, but channel it. Above all, give them an opportunity to create. And so, in the kindergartens of today, not only do we have games and singing but also construction, building, making things. When the children "play" house, they make the house, they furnish it, and they operate it. It is a child's world, but it is patterned after an adult model. And the children put a great deal of "work" into it.

The teacher does not have to interest them. There may be a few who do not respond, forerunners of adults who cannot or will not work, but by and large the children react with enthusiasm. Why then must we teach what the organism cannot learn, cannot identify with itself? Why must play become drudgery rather than wholesome, happy work? What immediate interests can be tapped? What abiding interests can be conjured up? What purposes can be developed?

The answer lies in the engagement of children in activities to their liking, with gradual but insistent development of these activities into occupations that reproduce on the child's level the occupations of adults. These occupations will not be money-producing, in fact many of them will be humane and contributory, but they will represent life at its best. It is exceedingly important that adults conceive of their occupation as service to others, rather than as mere bread-getting. Therefore, this early training in "industry" must necessarily be on so high a plane that it sets the standard for the remainder of the child's life.

The "occupation" of the child carries with it faint adumbrations of "What I want to be"—"What I want to do." The academicians express great horror at the early choice of an occupation: "The child knows nothing about the world and very little about himself." But regardless of its usefulness, children do, sooner or later, express preferences—choices voiced with varying degrees of earnestness; choices based on backgrounds that vary from zero to considerable. The academicians again, as with the doctrine of interest, strongly emphasize the individual in their writings. At the same time the fear of too early choice of occupation has received expression in frequent recommendations that vocational education begin only after high school—as if interest, purpose, drive, imagination, all lay dormant in the child until he had absorbed this thing known as general education. Some children know what they want to do as soon as they can talk. The expression of desire, no matter if they change their minds about the object, is the signal to seize the opportunity to "educate." Wisdom and intensity vary with the child and, in any one child, vary with age. Moreover, economic and social conditions change—we remember periods when all boys wanted to be locomotive engineers, then chauffeurs, then airplane pilots, then radio mechanics. But whatever the particular goal may be, it is incumbent upon the school to make the drive move along the lines of both individual and social development.

It is interesting to note the relationship of children's motives to the part that craftsmanship plays in the motivation of the adult:

... it seems to be neither the perfected talent nor the automatic habit that has driving power, but the imperfect talent and the habit-in-the-making. The child who is *just learning* to speak, to walk, or to dress, is, in fact, likely to engage in these activities for their own sake, precisely as does the adult who has an *unfinished* task in hand. ... The active motive subsides when its goal is reached, or, in the case of a motor skill, when it has become at last automatic. ... Now, in the case of the permanent interests of personality the situation is the same. A man whose motive is to acquire learning or to perfect his craft can never be satisfied that he has reached the end of his quest, for his problems are never completely solved, his skill is never perfect. Lasting interests are recurrent sources of discontent, and from their incompleteness they derive their forward impetus.[2]

That is the point—"a man whose motive is to acquire learning, or to perfect his craft, can never be satisfied that he has reached the end

2. Gordon W. Allport, *Personality: A Psychological Interpretation*, pp. 204-5. New York: Henry Holt & Co., 1937.

of his quest, for his problems are never solved, his skill is never perfect." The quest for perfection is lifelong.

[Moreover, in a democracy there must] be equality of opportunity. There must be free association, a common goal. People must work together. They must believe in each other's work because they feel they are serving others and others are serving them. They must be common sharers in the task of making life livable. Vocational education assumes and works upon the principle that every individual is worthy of preparation for an occupation and that every occupation is worthy of the individual who persues it, whether it be manual, intellectual, or emotional, thus arriving at the "dignity of labor" by action rather than by preachment.

It is notable that striving toward a common end through association takes place after as well as during working hours. Eavesdrop on any discussion during a social gathering of vocal men and women and what do you hear? Talk about their work and their fellow workers, reminiscences, prognostications, and a good measure of criticism. Workers live their work at all hours. They dream about it. An occupation is the most occupying of all human activities. When it is freely shared with others, it is the most democratic.[3]

AN OVERVIEW OF PRESENT PRACTICE

Some good counselors say that there is so such thing as vocational guidance, there is just *guidance*—for life. Others say that *all* guidance is vocational guidance because education contributes to success and happiness in a vocation. However guidance may be conceived, let us, on the basis of observation, opinion, and experience, point to those procedures that reveal vocational aptitudes, to those techniques that lead pupils to choose schools and vocations in which they will develop their highest potentialities, and to those personalities (administrators, teachers, *and* counselors) who will inspire these youngsters to formulate high ideals and enable them to embody those ideals in their own lives.

This process goes on from the lowest to the highest grades, even in the elementary school, as we have shown. This guidance with reference to occupation must concern the whole school system. Otherwise, how will children in elementary and junior high school know what high school they wish to enter, unless well before graduation they have learned much about occupations and about their own

3. Franklin J. Keller, *Principles of Vocational Education: The Primacy of the Person*, p. 6. Boston: D. C. Heath & Co., 1948.

interests and desires? And when they gain new experience, develop new ideas, and change their minds, how will they know "what to do" unless a counselor is handy and alert at every point along the line? Despite this, some vocational schools have no guidance program at all and assert that they do not need it. Others want it, but plead poverty and lack of staff. Some conduct guidance on an occasional, semi-emergency, disciplinary basis, rather than as a vital school function.

Some schools operate superb programs, and it is these programs that are worthy of emulation.

What follows is predicated upon observation, deduction, and, latterly, upon conviction. On the whole, the vocational-education process suffers more from inadequate guidance than it does from competing academic education. For lack of guidance, at every level of ability from backward, dull, reluctant learners (whatever ugly or glamorous name is given them) to the brilliant, potential engineer, many vocationally talented pupils are lost. Let us then list some of the salient features of general guidance and education.

1) Generally, teachers in elementary and junior high schools (excluding some industrial-arts teachers) have had no experience in trades taught in vocational schools, do not understand them, and convey to their pupils no respect for them.

2) In vocational schools the same complaint is prevalent regarding counselors. Women constitute the vast majority of teachers and counselors in elementary and junior high schools, and a considerable majority in senior high schools, and they do not have the opportunity to learn to respect hard masculine work, no matter how skilful they are. In any case, the child suffers. (This is probably the most general complaint voiced in vocational schools. We write in full knowledge and with appreciation and reverence of three superb women counselors who were successively head of our guidance department in Metropolitan Vocational High School. We were just lucky.)

3) Throughout history the so-called intellectual occupations have been respected, but the manual trades have been looked down upon. This is a fact that affects the whole vocational-education situation, and will be expanded upon later. It must be noted here because it permeates the guidance process.

4) Expressed tersely, the same idea may be conveyed in the words of John Gardner, "Can we be equal and excellent too?"

5) Note that the faculties of vocational schools literally go out and beat the highways (the better the school, the more thorough the beating) for the highest intelligences available and then accept only 40, 50, or 60 per cent of those who apply. Where do the others, supposedly yearning for vocational education, go? They go to academic high schools or special schools for dull pupils, to attend spasmodically, and drop out at sixteen.

6) In connection with Community Talent Search (now Higher Horizons), New York City Junior High School No. 43 planned discussions of higher education for the eighth-year homeroom periods. Before long the guidance department succumbed to the almost universal demand of these brighter pupils that they learn about vocations, thus bringing the counselors back to what they had supposedly learned about the importance of occupational information.

7) At this point it should be indicated that no vocational educator believes for one moment that vocational interests and abilities can be isolated from all other characteristics, aptitudes, and achievements, and thus used to determine success in vocational education and in occupations. On the contrary, he knows the importance of spelling, reading, arithmetic, personality, and so on. In fact, much of the public and many of the academic teachers do not know that vocational schools are dealing with these subjects just as effectively, in some cases more effectively, than they could be dealt with anywhere else.

The Phases of Vocational Guidance

GUIDANCE PRECEDING ADMISSION TO VOCATIONAL HIGH SCHOOL

Guidance preceding admison to the vocational high school is usually a junior high school problem and is of momentous importance for secondary vocational schools. The outstanding complaint of these secondary schools is that "the junior high schools use us as a dumping ground. We get all those pupils who are no good in academic work." As set forth in the section on "Vocational Guidance is a Lifetime Process," most of the phases of vocational guidance are pertinent to all the schools that prepare for senior high school. Especially important in the junior high school are industrial arts, exploratory courses, testing, cumulative records, and occupational information.

INDUSTRIAL ARTS, TRYOUTS, EXPLORATORY COURSES

There is plenty of evidence that, in recent years, industrial arts and other exploratory courses have diminished in both number and quality in the junior high schools. One explanation is that the cry for more science and mathematics has caused them to replace the very kind of tryouts, orientation, and other efforts directed toward the adjustment for adolescents that gave rise to the establishment of the junior high schools in the first place. Such a change cheats the youngsters out of their right to reveal their vocational preferences and to learn what they like or do not like about work, and makes it impossible for vocational schools and comprehensive high schools to reach and develop the boys and girls for whom these schools have been organized.

In some communities where these phases of guidance are lacking, the vocational and comprehensive high schools have set up such courses in the tenth year (or in the ninth when it exists) with considerable success in orienting the pupils for the eleventh and twelfth years. This is a phase of vocational guidance that is essential somewhere in the seventh, eighth, ninth, or tenth years, but preferably as early as possible.

When an exploratory course is given in a vocational or comprehensive high school, it is more likely to be a sample of a course in a particular trade than true industrial arts. It is, then, really a "tryout." In any case, whether called industrial arts or exploratory work, it should give the pupil an opportunity to "try out" his own aptitudes and abilities with a view to selecting the kind of work he would like to do in the future.

One other comment is necessary. Where industrial arts still exists in junior high schools, it has often become so "generalized" that both principal and teacher speak of it as general education for cultural development!

ADMISSION TO VOCATIONAL HIGH SCHOOLS

The only pupils whom the vocational high school can admit are those who apply. Those who apply are the ones who have earnestly, sincerely, and wisely determined that they want such training as is given in a vocational school, plus those who are told by counselors that they cannot and will not succeed in an academic high school (the slow, the reluctant, the delinquent, the nondescript). The vocational schools always hope that the total number of applicants will exceed the capacity of the building and that, by close scrutiny of the record cards, by intensive interviews, and by various tests, the "cream of the crop" may be admitted. In such a situation the leftovers are compelled to enter academic schools, which must always find or make room for them.

That vocational schools should not be "dumping grounds" is obvious, reasonable, and incontrovertible. That the unfortunate, rejected pupils should be sacrificed to this practice is indefensible. That the possibility, and often the reality, of this situation, should exist, is an educational lapse that must lie heavily in the minds and on the hearts of the local superintendent of schools and the members of the board of education. Where the pupil's school record and entire personality are being scrutinized by the vocational school with reference to admission, the organization doing the scrutinizing should be centralized, and its objective should be to give every pupil an appropriate education. And here is where the double-purpose, comprehensive, and area high schools come in, which alone can assure every child an adequate education.

THE CUMULATIVE RECORD

In name, the most impersonal of all instruments in the guidance program, the cumulative record card can become as exciting as a documentary film, the history of a pulsing, living, human being. Yet it is not the form or even the substance that makes it vital, but the use to which it is put. It is not simply a listing of subject ratings or a device for bookkeeping. In significance, any one item, any one characteristic, for instance, may outweigh everything else in the record. It enables a teacher, principal, counselor, doctor, or nurse to pick up the student's life, from birth to the crucial present moment, and hopefully project it into the future. Here is a boy who came into this secondary school as a child and who in a few moments will be leaving as a young man. Any judgment passed upon such a person is bound to differ from that accorded a mere name of a boy in a particular class on a certain date who wants to change his shop because he cannot get along with his teacher, or who wants to be accelerated because he has done the whole term's work in half the usual time.

The substance of the cumulative record has been discussed often and needs no repetition here. Literally everything should go into it. But what is more important is the spirit of the record. The primary characteristic of the usual cumulative record is its inactivity, its resting in the file. It is also closely guarded so that the student will never see it. It is too far away from those who know the student for them to use it conveniently. And, in short, it has no conspicuous utility except at term-end for promotion purposes. There are no inducements to make it live. The remedy is simple. A few fundamental practices, well publicized to the students and the staff, bring the cumulative record into the foreground of the staff's atention along with the student whose story it tells.

1. *Take the cumulative record out of the central file,* and give it to the adviser who is primarily and continuously responsible for the student throughout his school life. The adviser is responsible for the entry of all ratings and other data. He is thoroughly familiar with the card for it usually remains in his possession for four years. It can become his pride as well as his responsibility.

2. *Let the student see his record.* Let him, too, feel that he is making history. Let him take it to the counselor, to his teachers, to the principal, whenever he has a request for an adjustment or has an honor bestowed upon him, or has been delinquent. Let him know that his card is his passport. If he loses it or destroys it, or lets it be destroyed, he will be like a person in a foreign country without his credentials.

The only answer to any objections to this procedure is that it works. Over a period of eight years (this statement was originally written in 1948) with probably 8,000 cards involved, we know of one that was destroyed and another that was lost in Metropolitan Vocational High School. In both instances the cards were reconstructed from original data. The extreme of solicitude occurred when a boy from the Maritime School, while leaving the training ship, accidentally dropped his card into the East River and promptly dived in after it. He retrieved a very soggy card, but he still had his passport.

Some schoolmen question the desirability of letting students see the results of general intelligence and other tests. So far as we can discover, only good effects result from friendly, co-operative consultation with a student regarding his whole personality in terms of its full development for a useful life, especially in its vocational phases.

3. *The principal, head counselor, and other administrators should demand the card along with the student,* whenever making any decision regarding the welfare of the student. The principal will not see a boy without his card. The principal makes his entry in red ink, reading it aloud as he writes. He takes every opportunity to dignify the record in the eyes of the young person. If any pertinent data are missing, he sends the record back to the adviser for completion. He writes notes of commendation to those advisers who keep especially good records. He nearly always has a few cards on his desk, pending decision, and regards them as respectfully as if they were the boys and girls themselves.

Again may we say, for the pupil, the cumulative record is an all-time story. It follows him to the end of his school career and, even then, lies dormant only until he decides to go to school again. So, it is the alpha and omega of guidance and comes first in our category. In vocational schools the substance of the records is generally adequate. However, it is a rare school in which these records attain the intimacy and vitality such as is described in these paragraphs.

TESTING

Tests given.—The importance of discovering the vocationally talented makes the question of testing a serious one. Some schools give an extensive battery of tests to all applicants. Some give no tests at all. Some give only intelligence tests with various "cut-off" points and give no aptitude tests. Some depend entirely upon test records from sending schools, but such tests are generally of academic achievement (usually in junior high schools). Some schools give standard aptitude, achievement, and general intelligence tests. Some devise their own tests, others go down the list to the point where they have enough to fill existing vacancies. Others temper the testing standard with judgments derived from the school records and interviews. Many others believe that test results are usually misleading. About half the vocational schools give some kind of tests, with strong emphasis on general intelligence tests and achievement tests in language and arithmetic. The other half give no tests. Schools which must admit all applicants may need no tests for selection, but may use them later for internal guidance purposes or, they may find that exploratory courses, intensive interviewing, and keen observation provide more valid results than tests.

Diversity of tests and procedures, even failure to give any tests at all, may indicate keen judgment as to local needs, but they also reveal lack of knowledge of useful progress in testing research. Critical comments, however, must be offered cautiously. The schools are anxious to admit pupils who show high mechanical ability. They also want general intelligence, mathematical ability, reading ability, scientific ability. They want students who are interested in mechanical and technical occupations. Human beings are complex, and the needs of the schools are complex. The schools have their problems to which, for the most part, they are devoting themselves loyally. However, a consideration of current vocational-school participation in tests, causes one to ask questions.

A treasure of talent and a wealth of tests.—There is no dearth of talent among American children nor of tests devised for its discovery. We shall note only a few of the well known. They do not differ much in character, although they vary in ease of administration, time consumed, validity, and cost. They include many tests of traits which are loosely related to vocational aptitude but which are essential to occupational success. In many jobs, personality is all-important, and thus there are the *Minnesota Personality Scale*, the *Minnesota Multiphasic Personality Inventory*, and the *Bernreuter Personality Inventory*. There are also tests for specific measurable qualities, as for example in musical ability, the *Seashore Measures of Musical Talent* and the *Kwalwasser-Dykema Tests,* and in art, the *Graves Design Judgment Test* and the *Meier Art Test.*

Certainly we need no proof that vocational talent is abundantly available in these United States. But no concerted, intensive, effective development and training exists to carry out fully the American obligation to provide equal opportunity to all.

Note the *Mental Measurements Yearbook.* Its fifth edition[4] covers

4. *The Fifth Mental Measurements Yearbook.* Edited by Oscar K. Buros. Highland Park, New Jersey: Gryphon Press, 1959.

a seven-year period—1952 through 1958, and lists 957 tests, most of them described and reviewed. These tests are concerned with knowledge, achievement, character, personality, intelligence, and aptitudes, all of which in some degree determine the success and happiness of the individual doing his part of the world's work. But let us confine ourselves to those listed under vocations and under business education, industrial arts, and multiaptitude batteries. Vocations are classified under clerical (11 tests), interests (157), manual dexterity (3), mechanical ability (17), miscellaneous (16), and specific vocations (50). Under business education are listed 25 tests; under industrial arts, 4; under multiaptitude batteries, 15. We hesitate to confine ourselves to these obviously vocational classifications, especially in view of technological developments. The newer kind of technical job calls for sensitivity, such as is revealed in sensory-motor tests; the *Yearbook* describes 25 tests of hearing, vision, and motor abilities.

Of course, the *Strong Vocational Interest Blank* literally put "interest" on the psychological and guidance map. And the *Kuder Preference Record* has run a close second. Assuming the high validity of these tests and supposing that both of them, or even one, were given periodically to all pupils in the later elementary and junior high school grades, might this procedure have a strong effect upon the pupils' choices of occupation and selections of high-school courses? The fundamental query is whether or not the schools are using all the available techniques to promote valid choices by all the pupils. The claim for the Kuder test is that "over one million two hundred and fifty thousand students are given these tests." Are the results used effectively? It is important for one to realize that he likes to work outdoors with animals and growing things, or is so persuasive that he would like to meet with people and to promote projects of selling, or is mechanical-minded and would like to work with machinery and books.

Mechanical ability and manual dexterity seem to trouble the reviewers, especially as to competent validation. The well-known *Minnesota Paper Form Board* is still used to a considerable extent, as is the *Bennett Test of Mechanical Comprehension*. Perhaps as reliable as any are the *Mechanical Reasoning* and *Spatial Relations Tests* in the various multiaptitude tests. To what extent ability to perform manual and mechanical operations can be tested through paper or verbal operations remains an unsolved problem. It leads to our comment on exploration, which appears in succeeding paragraphs.

Clerical aptitudes are comparatively easy to test. *The Minnesota Clerical Test* is still outstanding in this area.

Beyond these are various tests for specific vocations, usually not for aptitude so much as for skills and knowledge that have already been learned.

The case against tests.—The principal or director of a vocational school or the superintendent of the school system often says something like this: "If 500 boys request admission to my school, I can assume that they are motivated by the desire to get training in a trade of their own selection, or they have been advised by counselors and teachers to attend a vocational school because they have done poorly in their academic subjects, or have behaved badly, or both; or the pupils realize their own shortcomings, and do not know what they want to do. If I have room for only 250, I am more likely to get good workers by eliminating the academic failures and the 'bad actors' through tests of general intelligence, of reading and arithmetic. The boys of higher intelligence will almost certainly have wanted vocational education and will probably have chosen the right trade."

Under these circumstances and according to his lights, the principal is right, but the principle is wrong. Vocational education should be just as open to all pupils who are adapted to it as academic education is open to all those who want it and are adapted to it. To bring this about, the vocational school should, in the first place, be big enough to hold all vocational pupils. In the second place, *all* elementary and junior high school pupils should be tested for interest and aptitude in vocations, without the prejudicial advice of counselors and teachers who know nothing about vocations. It is interest and aptitude before the youngster has had any vocational instruction that counts.

There are other ways out, but only in special cases would they be practical:

a) Industrial arts should be a major subject for all junior high school pupils. It should be taught by a highly competent adviser. He should use methods closely allied to those in the trades (instead of the "ash-tray-and-roller-towel" ploy), and would see that every good worker sought admission to vocational school. There would be other guidance factors, but special aptitude tests would not be necessary. Of course, if there could be two or three or four different kinds of shops with competent teachers, the exploratory process would be stepped up considerably.

b) If such junior high school shops cannot be set up, then every effort should be made to get as many pupils as possible into the vocational school where they would, for periods of two or three months, attend each of several exploratory shops. Of course, this plan has the great weakness of not attracting all those boys who should be attracted.

In other words, the case against tests is, in reality, very weak. Even if all the other phases of the entire guidance program (which we are about to discuss) are strong and effective, valid standard tests should be used *pari passu* for repeated evaluation.

ORIENTATION

The whole problem of orientation is presented most effectively, and in considerable detail, in a previous yearbook of the National Society for the Study of Education. Suffice it here to quote the five summarizing statements:

1. To guide the student in becoming acquainted with the new institution in order that he may adjust himself happily in the new environment through participating effectively in its life, and that he may utilize its opportunities for furthering his growth.

2. To guide the student in a reconsideration of his goals and purposes in relation to increased self-knowledge, and in the perspective of his new opportunities for well-balanced growth.

3. To guide the student toward a growing awareness of the wider social scene and of his place therein.

4. To contribute to the development of increased skill in self-direction through improved skill in adjusting intelligently to the new environment and through experience in utilizing new opportunities.

5. To provide opportunities for school officials (administrators, guidance workers, and other teachers) to become better acquainted with new students and more aware of their growth needs, in order that the school environment may be made more responsive to these needs.[5]

5. Margaret E. Bennett, "The Orientation of Students in Educational Institutions," in *Guidance in Educational Institutions*, pp. 175–95. Thirty-seventh Yearbook of the National Society for the Study of Education, Part I. Chicago: University of Chicago Press, 1938.

HEALTH

In some schools there is a slowly developing interest in and action toward consideration of a healthy physique, not only for its inherent advantage to the individual but with relation to his or her future occupation. The health of the child is primarily the responsibility of the parents, and when in those many instances of parental neglect the school must step in, its task should be one of elementary diagnosis followed by referral to other public agencies. However, when physical defects become occupational handicaps or physical advantages (such as highly discriminating vision or finely adjusted muscular coordination), the vocational-guidance program should be prepared to help the possessors to realize these liabilities or assets in choosing an occupation.

PERSONAL AND SOCIAL ADJUSTMENT

Inherent in all vocational-guidance service is a study of the individual's personality as he adapts himself to all the other personalities with whom he must live and work. This is of such extreme importance that, as has already been noted, there is a tendency in the personnel literature to make it the sole objective of guidance. This literature is sound in its exposition, as far as it goes, and since it is easily available, there is no need to labor the point here. The vocational aspect is discussed in a previous NSSE yearbook.[6]

PLACEMENT

Through an advisory board or commission, the vocational school maintains contact with industry, business, or the professions. The audition, examination, or inspection of students acquaints employers, and other workers as individuals and in association, with the workers of tomorrow. Commission members who have assisted in the formulation of courses and curricula leading to placement in their own vocations feel a proprietary interest in the product. Thus, the early stages of placement occur long before the final act of accepting a job —in some cases upon admission to the school.

6. Robert Hoppock and Nathan Luloff, "Vocational Guidance," *Vocational Education*, p. 92. Forty-second Yearbook of the National Society for the Study of Education, Part I. Chicago: University of Chicago Press, 1943.

Whether printers, architects, garment designers, artists, physicians, or welders, competent teachers of vocations maintain their old occupational associations and acquire new ones in order that they may assist in finding opportunities for their graduates. It is only when teachers keep in close contact with the realities of life that their teaching is vivid and their products useful.

An effective vocational-guidance program, through individual counseling, through lessons in occupational information, and through continued emphasis upon the importance of individuality, stimulates students to make their plans for employment long before graduation and leads them to use their own initiative and not to depend upon others for help to any greater extent than the circumstances warrant. This is the normal, salutary procedure which should not be weakened by unnecessary help and direction. It is only when the young person is on his own and facing up to the realities of life, with its disappointments and bitternesses, that he appreciates the successes that come his way.

This in no way diminishes the importance of the organized placement office. Organized, systematic solicitation of job opportunities; carefully planned, scientific analysis of individual abilities; and finally, the conjunction of opportunity and individual can be effected only by those who devote themselves assiduously to these specialized tasks.

FOLLOW-UP

Follow-up constitutes a kind of continuous placement or replacement, with all its attendant problems. Adjustment to occupation is not accomplished by entrance upon the first job for which a graduate qualifies. The young man who begins as an apprentice in a skilled trade has many steps to take before he reaches the level of the full-fledged craftsman. His advancement may be smooth or exceedingly rough. Some employers establish sound personnel policy, others have none at all. Should he experience the latter, and get caught up in a maze of conflicting policies and unsympathetic supervisors, the counsel of the school can be of great value.

Ideally, the school requests and receives periodic reports from all its graduates, who have been so strongly imbued with the importance of sending in this information that they rarely forget to do so. A staff of co-ordinators visits their employers to acquire general information useful not only in counseling the young people but also in enriching the fund of knowledge and wisdom of the counselors. A co-ordinator makes such adjustments as he can for each individual and adds the data to the store of information already existing in the school. The school sets up in its guidance program a consultation office for graduates, conducted in the evening, where former students can be counseled in ways of securing advancement, of finding other and better jobs, on subjects and places for further study, and on relationships with fellow workers. In other words, with exceedingly valuable data at hand, the school helps its graduates solve the problem of facing up to reality. Recently, much has been made of longitudinal studies. This type of investigation, if carefully focused upon the combination of type of pupil, kind of curriculum, and character of job, could do much for the validation of present practices or for their improvement.[7]

THE HOMEROOM, TEACHING OCCUPATIONAL INFORMATION, THE ADVISORY SYSTEM, AND A CLOSE ADULT FRIEND FOR EVERY PUPIL

The homeroom and the advisory system.—Whatever ideals and whatever techniques a guidance program may offer, its heart is a person who cares and accepts responsibility for the continuous adjustment of the student to school and the social life. The familiar grade adviser, when he follows a class through all four years, is an approach to the problem, but when his family reaches 150, 200, 400, even 700, as it often does, the opportunity for understanding and intimacy disappears. Daily immediacy is a primary condition of human adjustment.

In the advisory system which we describe here, the entering student meets his adviser in a homeroom period every weekday morning during the entire three or four years. The adviser is his surrogate parent, his teacher-friend who listens to his woes, rejoices in his good fortune, punishes his transgressions, fights his battles, and only incidentally marks his attendance.

The advisory group is heterogeneous as to intelligence, grade, age,

7. These sections on placement and follow-up are drawn largely from Keller, *op. cit.*

achievement. Its components are as unlike as the members of a family, and as unified. The older members are big brothers and sisters. The young ones are taken in with solicitude and kindness. The group aims to be the "best section in the school." The adviser backs his charges against all comers, and assures their effectiveness by helping each individual to surpass himself.

The adviser's duties are heavy and responsible ones. The cumulative records of his students are in his possession, and he maintains them. He receives reports on studies and reports from all other teachers. He counsels with individuals during at least one assigned period a week. He conducts the homeroom activities. He sees that all the services of the school—curricular, extracurricular, and personal—function for each individual in his section. He is overworked, but he is usually a happy counselor and friend. Incidentally, his effectiveness as a counselor is not conditioned by the subject he teaches during the remainder of the day. He may be a teacher of English, mathematics, or music or automobile mechanics, but in relation to the members of the home section the adviser is primarily a friendly and concerned man or woman.

The essence of the homeroom period lies in the spirit and activity of the adviser. Homeroom lessons are lessons in personal adjustment; they may take any form that the group elects, and, to the extent that they are student-managed, they are good lessons. One period a week is devoted to discussion of the report on student activities by the section president, who is a delegate to the student council. The section, as an "election district" or "county," contributes to the spirit and unity of the entire school. Under inspired leadership, the homeroom really becomes a home, where the problems of adolescence are threshed out with candor and satisfaction.

Occupational information.—The adviser, with the help of a counselor, instructs his group in occupational information. It might be said that in a vocational school, where for the most part pupils have made a choice of vocation, information regarding other occupations is not necessary, but rapidly changing technologies, even world movements in trade, require that every prospective worker be alert to these changes. Certainly such information is of great importance to junior high school pupils. The whole problem is presented with great competence and in considerable detail in a book by Robert Hoppock.[8]

A close adult friend for every pupil.—The comprehensive high school is a social system in which all the adolescents of a community spend nearly half their waking hours. Boys and girls should find in it as much friendliness, justice, and security as they do in their homes. When they comment upon their schools, they are much less concerned about the nature of the curriculum or the modernity of the building or the college degrees of the staff than they are about the friendliness of the teachers, the companionship of fellow students, and the "justice" of the administration. The satisfied pupil tells you, "This is a pleasant place. Many of the boys and girls have become my friends. I like the teachers. They are always just in their marks and punishments. Everyone is treated alike. Whenever I am in trouble I know my adviser will get me out of it. He understands me and will fight for me if necessary. He praises me for everything I do well. This is a friendly school."

The principal's dream is a school in which every pupil talks this way. The key element in realizing even an approach to such a dream is a sponsor (adviser, homeroom teacher), who, as an adult friend, meets the same pupil every day during his stay in school. The shocking weakness of most high schools is that they provide no such friend. In 67 of the 77 schools visited during the study of comprehensive high schools, no teacher or counselor or administrator was held responsible for the continuous educational progress of a small group of 20 or 30 boys or girls from the Freshman to the Senior year.

Several of the 67 schools tried the continuous homeroom idea but have abandoned it because the "teachers felt the responsibility is too great a burden, the record-keeping is too onerous, the obligation for teaching subjects outside their specialty is unfair." This, too, is shocking. What do we mean when we say, "We must teach children, not subjects?" And what do we have in mind when we talk about the dignity of the person and then leave him floundering among 2,000 pupils and 100 teachers, none of whom could possibly know him as a person? A "counselor" with a constantly changing group of 100 or 500 cannot know any one of them in any real sense.

8. Robert Hoppock, *Occupational Information: Where To Get It and How To Use It in Counseling and Teaching.* New York: McGraw-Hill Book Co., 1957.

Experience is the important word for both guidance and the development of skill. The vocational school not only offers full-time courses for high-school boys and girls but also fosters part-time employment (co-operative courses), apprenticeship courses (part-time in co-operation with management and unions), extension courses for out-of-school youth and adults, and evening courses for all who work during the day. At least 50 per cent of the schools operate co-operative courses, usually in the second half of the twelfth year, and sometimes during the entire Senior year. One school allows pupils full-time employment during the second half of the last year but requires them to come to evening school to complete their academic work if they desire a regular high-school diploma. Apprentice courses are usual where industry will co-operate; evening courses are offered in most schools. In addition, liberal-arts colleges may insist on part-time work: the co-operative courses of Antioch College, for example, are outstanding. The new book by Wilson and Lyons, *Work-Study College Programs*,[9] tells the complete story.

The Administration of Vocational Guidance

Today it is generally recognized that "guidance" cannot be plastered on top of a traditionally organized vocational or academic school, that it requires competent operation, expert and painstaking supervision, and lively stimulation and support from the superintendent and the board of education. This section will be devoted to a consideration of these needs.

THE COUNSELORS MUST BE TEACHER-TRAINED, WORK-EXPERIENCED, AND OCCUPATION-MINDED

The authors of a recently published text have stressed the distinction between teacher and counselor.

Much progress should be made in the direction of accepting the fact that teaching need not be a prerequisite to becoming a counselor. It may be heresy to include this point, but the time has come to recognize that a *master teacher* is one type of specialist, and a *master counselor* another.

9. James W. Wilson and Edward H. Lyons, *Work-Study College Programs: Appraisal and Report of the Study of Cooperative Education.* New York: Harper & Bros., 1961.

Each has its own particular professional, technical, and personal require-ments, and experience as one is *not* absolutely necessary in order to be-come the other! The key concept here is not whether a person has taught children, but whether he is the type of person who can relate well to both children and adults and who is competent to deal with them in an educational setting.[10]

This is heresy; it is in complete disagreement with experience in the field of vocations. Everything in the work of the counselor points to a need for knowledge and understanding of the work of the teacher and of the work of the worker. Nor is the other extreme tenable: "Guidance is just good teaching." Certainly the counselor should be a master counselor, but he becomes that only because he combines the best in the jobs of teaching, counseling, and the work of the world. Moreover, this "best" avoids that sense of "profes-sionalization," which minimizes the services of teachers in the occu-pational phases of guidance, and unduly exalts the counselors' services as psychologists (which even teachers should be, to a reasonable extent), and even as psychiatrists. Some of the best counselors I have ever known had been excellent shop teachers who knew about trades and knew about boys—a combination that is irresistible!

Whatever his background, the counselor will have to deal with the deadly sins of supersensitivity to status and social class and of worship of the diploma elite in vocations and vocational guidance. These sins crop up in five familiar forms:

1. White-collar work is superior to manual work.
2. Self-employment is superior to employment by others.
3. Clean occupations are superior to dirty ones.
4. The importance of business occupations depends upon the size of the business; but this is not true of agricultural occupations.
5. Personal service is degrading, and it is better to be employed by an enterprise than to be employed in the same work by a person.[11]

10. Walter F. Johnson, Buford Stefflre, and Roy A. Edelfelt, *Pupil Personnel and Guidance Services*, p. 337. New York: McGraw Hill Book Co., 1961.

11. Theodore Caplow, *The Sociology of Work*, p. 42. Minneapolis: University of Minnesota Press, 1954. This book should be compulsory reading and study for every counselor, teacher, and administrator. Similarly with Lawrence G. Thomas, *The Occupational Structure and Education*. Englewood Cliffs, New Jersey: Prentice-Hall, Inc., 1956.

This kind of thinking is an ancient evil. And while it is rampant in our lives and in our schools, it is something that a dedicated educator should abhor.

THE TEACHER AS COUNSELOR

Now and again the statement is heard: "No special vocational-guidance program is necessary in a good school, for every teacher is a counselor." This statement contains a modicum of truth: every teacher can be and often is a counselor—but usually in an unplanned and an ineffective way. On the other hand, unless teachers co-operate wholeheartedly with counselors and administrators, and especially with other teachers in the capacity of advisers, the guidance program can be only partly effective. One of the advantages of the advisory system is that nearly every subject teacher is also an adviser, appreciates the problems of the adviser, and can therefore be expected to co-operate with all other advisers.

The competent instructor, no matter what the subject, makes every effort to reach students as individuals and, even in large classes, succeeds to a considerable extent in doing so. Individual instruction and solicitude for the young person at all times makes of the teacher a most important adjunct of the guidance program.

Then again, the teacher whose classes provide discussions, require the use of judgment, and elicit information, especially about occupations, is performing one of the functions of a good counselor. The planning and teaching of occupational information is of itself one of the principal functions of guidance, often performed by a trained counselor. However, there is every reason why this type of information should also be disseminated by instructors of all subjects, for it is a poor subject that does not have some occupational implication.

Finally, the teacher's personality is always, for better or for worse, a guidance factor. The friendly, interested, glowing man or woman inspires worshipers, who want to be "just like him" or "just like her." His words are carefully weighed by the students and are often translated into action. Students crowd around him before and after sessions for a chance to ask questions and be beamed upon. The value of such guidance cannot be measured, but anyone who has the good fortune to sit at the feet of a real mentor has a very keen sense of being "guided."

To all this must be added the tremendously important fact that shop teachers, science and mathematics teachers who have come up with industry, any teachers, men or women, teaching whatever subject, who have experienced the world and who love people, make good counselors and are treasures in their schools. The vocational schools have many of them, but not nearly enough, and the vocational school that has anything approaching its full need of such counselors is very, very rare. It has difficulties. Some teachers will appeal to high heaven—too much work! Some will declare incompetence! Some will hint at its illegality, believe it or not! But the great majority, men and women, devoted to the world of young people, will work at it, will love it: and, years afterward, Johnny will return to school, looking healthy, happy, and well-fixed in life, proclaiming that he came back, "especially to see that wonderful man, Mr. Maier, my adviser." The system works.

THE HOMEROOM AND THE ADVISORY SYSTEM

The homeroom and the advisory system were described at some length in the preceding section. Such a system must be set up by the administration. It is not easy to do. Teachers usually think it is too much work. Counselors often belittle the ability of teachers to "become close adult friends" of the pupils. Actually, the working combination of homeroom teacher and counselor is ideal, for their cooperation is a tremendous boon to the pupils. Moreover, it is one of the ways of meeting the evils of "professionalization."

. . . to do our job properly in the fields of education in which we operate, it would appear to be . . . appropriate to think of personnel work as part of that larger and, yet, in some ways more defined professional area of teaching. Within this broad area, personnel workers have developed a number of specialities. At least one of these specialities, namely, the field of student health service, has professional status. . . . Another, the field of counseling, seems to be well on its way toward the achievement of this goal. . . .

Specialization and professionalization are not necessarily synonymous. Certainly, there are entire fields of operations within the area of personnel work which rightfully need never be held to the restrictive criteria which would characterize a profession entitled to legal definition and support. Suffice it to say that if the next quarter-century sees our schools and colleges and universities staffed with personnel workers with minimum requisites of education in human understanding and appreciation, the personnel movement will have progressed immeasurably toward its goals of educational and human service. With this accomplished, the arguments about professions, professionalization, and professional associations will vanish as the mist in the light of a blazing sun of achievement.[12]

Of course, at all times the counselor must be a close student of personality. In this same yearbook, Wrenn[13] speaks highly of Gardner Murphy's contribution to the theory of personality. I must confirm this judgment. Once you have read the 998 pages of Murphy's book, and then, on a second reading, have studied them, you will really know as much about personality as can be gleaned from a book. Every counselor should try it.[14]

THE COMPREHENSIVE HIGH SCHOOL, THE DOUBLE-PURPOSE HIGH SCHOOL, AND THE AREA VOCATIONAL SCHOOL

In the first place, the basic assumptions, hypotheses, and guidelines, which were outlined in the first section of this chapter, will not become realities in vocational guidance unless the leadership of the superintendent and the policy of the board of education are directed toward those purposes.

In the second place—and this is what the present section is about—they cannot become realities unless the educational activities and the accompanying guidance program are embodied in such organizations as will enable the good will of soundly social educators to operate and such as will stifle the too-human individual jealousies, prestigious urges, and allurements to power that often bedevil the schools.

Such organizations are the double-purpose high school, the comprehensive high school, and the area vocational school, described in other parts of this yearbook. These descriptions must clearly set forth the circumstances that operate to attain these highly desirable

12. Daniel D. Feder, "The Emerging Role of the Professional Personnel Worker," *Personnel Services in Education*, pp. 208–9. Fifty-eighth Yearbook of the National Society for the Study of Education, Part II. Chicago: University of Chicago Press, 1959.

13. C. Gilbert Wrenn, "Philosophical and Psychological Bases of Personnel Services in Education," *Personnel Services in Education, ibid.*, pp. 68–69.

14. Gardner Murphy, *Personality: A Bio-social Approach to Origins and Structure*. New York: Harper & Bros., 1947.

results. The following brief summaries are offered here to establish
and emphasize the guidance phases.

The comprehensive high school.—The distinctive characteristics of
the comprehensive school is its inclusiveness, not only with respect
to clientele but also with respect to aims and purposes.

The comprehensive high school aims to serve the needs of *all* American
youth. That is to say, it accepts *without selection,* all the young people
in the area it commands—all races, creeds, nationalities, intelligences, talents, and all levels of wealth and social status. Such a school has as its
broadest objective the teaching of all varieties of skill, all kinds of knowledge to all kinds of youth bent upon living socially profitable lives. To
each one it seeks to give the course for which he seems best fitted. Its
design is to prepare one and all for potentially successful vocations. The
comprehensive high school prepares the college-oriented youth for college. It qualifies the non-college-bound youth and, as far as is possible, the
boy or girl who will drop out before graduation, for an occupation. It
is adapted to give everyone a general education for the common things
he will do in life and it may and should give some pupils of high capacity
preparation for both college and occupation. In this last area it functions
also as a double-purpose high school.[15]

The double-purpose high school.—The case for the double-purpose
high school rests upon the existence and identifiability of gifted students whose talents are not those of our potential scholars.

Just as there is a section of our school population gifted with high verbal
intelligence, our potential scholars and professionals, who seem well
served by straight preparation for college and high education, so there is
a significant proportion of young citizens who have dominant talents of
other kinds which they desire to develop to a skilled occupational level
during secondary school years. These are as truly our gifted children as
are those of marked academic interests. Many of these, perhaps a majority,
have also high IQ's. They have ability to carry on preparation for college,
side by side with as great a training as possible for a chosen occupation.
These are not students who need to have an interest 'teased' out of them.
They are those who know what they want. They frequently have great
capacity and eagerness for hard work. They can carry a double load of
work with zest and no great strain. These are the individuals the double-
purpose school serves *par excellence.* It accepts also those of marked occupational talent who know they have neither desire nor capacity for col-

15. Franklin J. Keller, *The Comprehensive High School.* New York: Harper
& Bros., 1955.

lege, but who know beyond a doubt what they desire to do from the moment of high school graduation. For all such pupils the double-purpose high school functions.[16]

The area vocational school.—An area school is organized in a fairly large area, often a county. From the surrounding academic high schools, on a half-day or week-in and week-out basis of instruction, it draws those pupils who are interested in the various offerings of the school, such as auto mechanics, machine-shop practice, agricultural-machinery mechanics, practical nursing, distributive education, electronics, beauty culture, auto-body repair, secretarial service, and so on. Of course, such a school requires close co-operation and co-ordination with the surrounding high schools. However, the actual operation in such schools as those in Bucks County, Pennsylvania, and Sussex County, Delaware, indicate that they can be highly successful.

A FLEXIBLE PROGRAM AND CURRICULUM

Flexibility of programing is fundamental in any school purporting to serve the needs of individual pupils. When a principal says, in answer to a proposed change in curriculum to meet the needs of individual pupils, "I can't program it," it is apparent that his school does not serve such pupils. Anything can be programed where there is the need, the desire, and the will. It is this flexibility that is essential, if vocational guidance is to be useful and practical.

RESEARCH

The feasible topics for research in vocational guidance are many and demanding. Outstanding among them are the following:[17]

Community-wide testing for vocational ability.—All the junior high school pupils in a community should be tested for vocational abilities. The results should be studied along with other pertinent data to determine how many pupils would benefit from vocational education. This is a most delicate task, but it ought to be carried out

16. *Ibid.*, p. 32. See also, Franklin J. Keller, *The Double-Purpose High School*, New York: Harper & Bros., 1953.

17. Quoted from Franklin J. Keller, *Vocationally Talented Pupils*. A co-operative research project of the United States Office of Education, sponsored by the Division of Field Studies and Research. New Brunswick, New Jersey: Rutgers, The State University, 1962.

intensively enough and often enough to produce worthwhile data that would give some indication of the desirable program in the community.

Sound guidance programs.—Parallel with such a study as the foregoing, there should be formulated a method of classifying and guiding these pupils so that they would gain the maximum benefit from instruction in vocational schools. As has already been indicated, enough excellent practice exists in various schools in the country to warrant the validity of such a study.

"Professionalizing" vocations.—There is a noticeable tendency to "professionalize" vocations, setting educational standards so high that actual age entrance into industry is postponed. Some of the more perceptive observers find that in some professions this works to the great disadvantage of the individual and society (in medicine, for instance). School courses are credited while job experience and personality assets are slighted, even ignored.

Status, status, status!—Closely related to professionalization is the whole matter of status. The problem of "white collars" and "blue collars" and its effect upon vocational-education practices requires most careful examination.

Analysis of physical condition.—Where rehabilitation cases are concerned, the closest attention must be given to physical condition, especially in relation to the requirements of any particular vocation. With presumably "normal" persons, this is not needed. Technicians' traits have been studied by British investigators. Similar studies should be made in this country of the physical requirements of all vocations and complete physical analyses should be made of all boys and girls contemplating entry into any of the newer occupations.

Personality in occupations.—One of the oldest clichés in vocational guidance and in personnel work is that more people lose their jobs through lack of appropriate personality than through lack of required skill. Good vocational schools keep this in mind, but, again, changing technologies require "good" personalities as well as appropriate physiques and skills. Study of personality is essential.

Motivation.—Frequent reference is made to that force (drive, persistence, "stickability," motivation) that makes workers work. This has been studied in many contexts, but little has been done with regard to vocations. Research in motivation as related to success in occupations is of the greatest importance, especially during times when the twenty-hour work week seems to be the most desirable goal to some people.

Intelligence and creativeness.—There should be no let-up in the attempts to improve the validity of existing tests of vocational ability nor of new attempts to formulate better ones. The United States Department of Labor is attempting to improve the GATB tests. There is always more to learn. Until fairly recently there seemed to be general acceptance of the standard I.Q. as a rating of intelligence, even to the extent of being used by high-school principals as measures of vocational intelligence. However, the researches of Getzels and Jackson[18] at Chicago and MacKinnon[19] at the University of California seem to show that the person who is highly creative may not be highly "intelligent," although he often *is*. So, the creative vocational person may not be, and often is *not*, intelligent in the I.Q. sense but may be a much more generous contributor to our culture than mere "intelligence" might make him. The area of testing needs some highly original attention.

A Hope, a Long-Range Perspective, and a Philosophy

No more fitting conclusion to this chapter could be written than is provided by the following quotations from previous NSSE yearbooks and from this author's *Principles of Vocational Education*.

A HOPE

[This hope] is that the personnel worker will study the differences that may exist between the philosophical and psychological concepts involved in the *establishment* of his educational function and those that are apparently utilized in the *practice* of his work . . . the philosophy and even psychology seem clear in what one is presumed to be responsible for doing, but personalities and the other exigencies of a given situation adulterate or even distort that purpose.

A student activity program is *designed* to provide opportunity for social learning, handling responsibility, and applying classroom learning to social situations. It may be so *organized and supervised* as to give the lie to all

18. Jacob W. Getzels and Philip W. Jackson, *Creativity and Intelligence: Explorations with Gifted Students.* New York: John Wiley & Sons, 1962.

19. D. M. MacKinnon, "The Nature and Nurture of Creative Talent," *American Psychologist*, VII (July, 1962), 484-95.

of these. The faculty adviser directs, sees that the outcome is good whether constructive learning takes place or not. The administration may hesitate to "take the rap" for learning that may result from failure or for mistakes that are made. . . . Counseling for student self-learning becomes counseling for counselor learning or for counselor-approved outcomes. Group guidance designed to contribute to self- and social-understanding becomes didactic classroom teaching far removed from student motivation and application.

Some of this is inevitable. No performance is perfect. Rather than denying the poor wisdom of the practice because of the excellence of the reasons for establishment, one should admit the gap between theory and practice, or see that the concepts concerning purpose are modified to meet reality. To promise much and deliver little is poor professional practice; it may be either the practice or the purpose that needs attention. Of most importance is to distinguish between the two.[20]

LONG-RANGE PERSPECTIVE

Long-range perspective on personnel functions seems to resolve them into the task of facilitating a creative process, not just an educing of what is already there in each personality, nor just a feeding in of information with the expectation that the human thinking machine will click out answers. Rather, it is a slow process of nurturing a life about which we know only too little. We present this personality with opportunities, deduced from research and experience, to learn about human life and the surrounding world; we help him probe within himself to discover what we cannot reach from our external vantage point; we guide him in the development of skill in organizing and interpreting the resulting knowledge—awareness of his emotions, attitudes, feelings, his value standards and his perceptions of his environment, as well as objective facts about manifestations of self. We cannot follow in all its ramifications the process by which specific choices are made, life plans are formulated, and adjustments are projected. We can find analogies in our own lives as we search for new lights on problems and find that solutions come often stealthily when we least expect them. Usually they do not seem to come without this intensive search. Perhaps this process within ourselves and those with whom we work is part of a universal creative process that goes on perpetually, and we are merely catalytic agents in keeping it moving ahead. If so, we need all the wisdom we can distill from research and experience and the humility that comes from awareness that we can neither determine nor know the ultimate direction of the process. Faith that there is meaning in every human life, hope that we can ever improve our services in foster-

20. Wrenn, *op. cit.*, p. 78.

ing this emergent creative process, and a quality of charity with respect to our own and others' limited efforts are beacon lights that beckon us forward in the pursuit of our goals.[21]

A PHILOSOPHY

The school as a benign habitat for good living.—Our secondary school . . . must have the kind of leadership that exemplifies the best kinds of personal relationship based upon the respect of person for person. This leadership must be evident in the way the school is managed and in the way that the whole staff goes about the task of studying ways of improving the school. It must be evident in the attitudes of teachers to students and in the types of student relationship the school cultivates. It must be evident in the emphasis the school puts upon learning situations and activities where the quality of human relations and effective ways of reaching group decisions are involved. This area of learning is so important that everything the school does or teaches must augment the ability and willingness of youth to participate more effectively in the activities of the different groups with which they are identified.[22]

The primacy of the person.—The inescapable fact about people is their diversity. The depressing truth about curricula is their uniformity. A curriculum is a course to be run—by the fleet-footed, the lame, the well, the sick, the bright, the dull, the intellectual, the athletic—and the well-educated are those who finish on time.

Schoolmen believe in the individual, they exalt him, but—he must run his course. If he takes too long or quits the race, he is a poor student or a "drop-out." Teachers, counselors, administrators give him good advice. They help him along. They may even change his course. But speaking generally—of general education—he must finish to win.

Now, recognition of the individual, respect for personality, carries with it the obligation of educating that human being in terms of his own nature as well as of the composite nature of two billion other human beings. Therefore, fundamental and precedent to the educational process itself is a determination of what education should be. This is not a single act, but a series of evaluations or re-evaluations. It is a guidance program. Such a program is not merely a diagnosis of the individual, it is, in the final analysis, an evaluation of education itself.[23]

21. Margaret E. Bennett, "Functions and Procedures in Personnel Services," *Personnel Services in Education, op. cit.,* pp. 132–33.

22. Will French, "Characteristics of a Secondary School Meeting the Needs of Youth," *Adapting the Secondary-School Program to the Needs of Youth,* p. 308. Fifty-second Yearbook of the National Society for the Study of Education, Part I. Chicago: University of Chicago Press, 1953.

23. Keller, *Principles of Vocational Education, op. cit.,* p. 68.

CHAPTER VII

Vocational Education beyond the High School

J. CHESTER SWANSON and ERNEST G. KRAMER

We must rid ourselves of the idea that anybody can ever finish his education. We cannot give our young people a good education. We can give them some education. We need extended education. We need to set up a program into which people can come at any time in their lives and get as much education as they can take.

—*Margaret Mead*

A Changing Society

Vocational education has traditionally been provided for youth during their high-school years or during early adolescence as apprentices or as beginners in the labor market. Immediately following World War II, the tempo of change in our society began to accelerate and with each passing year the acceleration has increased. The resultant social, economic, and political changes have had great impact upon vocational education, increasing the need for more knowledge, more extensive skills, and new skills.

The mechanization of agriculture, business, industrial, and service occupations has greatly expanded the scope of skills that vocational education should provide. While it is true that the second half of the twentieth century finds it possible to produce more goods and services with less human effort, it is likewise true that today's worker, whatever his occupation, needs more extensive skills and technical know-how in order to successfully compete in the labor market. Further, the rate of change means that today's worker must give continuing attention during his working lifetime to updating and changing his skills and knowledge in order to remain employed (see chap. iii).

One of the effects of the acceleration in the rate of change in our society has been to increase the importance of post-high-school preparatory vocational education as well as to dramatize the need for the availability of virtually lifelong upgrading and updating vocational education for those already employed. Indeed, no longer is it appropriate to say that vocational education and higher education have little in common—rather, it is becoming increasingly apparent that much of the needed preparation for entry into the world of work is sufficiently extensive and complex to make the four-year college-degree program one of the appropriate vehicles. During the last decade a significant number of college-degree programs have emerged for such sophisticated occupations as electronic technician, chemical technician, and accounting technician. There is every indication that not only will this trend continue but that it will accelerate in the immediate future.

Vocational Education in Higher Education

In the school year 1961–62, 420,485 persons received their bachelor's or first professional degree in the colleges and universities of the United States.[1] Of this number, 277,445 degrees were conferred in programs of studies which develop skills and provide knowledge with the objective of preparing the graduate for employment as a lawyer, a doctor, an engineer, a teacher, a scientist, or some other professional occupation.[2] This, too, is vocational education. Thus, about two-thirds of all persons in higher educational institutions are being trained for employment.

The issues and complexities of collegiate-level vocational-education programs of a baccalaureate-degree nature are beyond the scope of this yearbook and, indeed, are sufficient in themselves to warrant a separate treatise. This chapter deals only with junior-college and other types of post-high-school programs that do not normally lead to the baccalaureate degree.

Professional Training for the Vocational Teacher

The impact of society's changes and of the increased length and breadth of vocational education upon the preparation necessary to

1. Wayne E. Tolliner, *Earned Degrees Conferred 1961–62: Bachelor's and Higher Degrees*, Table 1, p. 2. United States Department of Health, Education, and Welfare, OE-54013-62, Circular No. 719. Washington: Government Printing Office, 1963.

2. *Ibid.*, Table 6, pp. 12–15.

successful vocational training are of considerable import. Just as there is a need for a more comprehensive program for the preparation of individuals to enter the labor force, so it follows that the program of preparation for the vocational teacher must be more rigorous and often quite different from those now provided. Collegiate preparation of vocational teachers—earlier thought by many to be somewhat inconsistent with the basic vocational-education philosophy—is becoming more and more accepted as logical and necessary. This is not to suggest that the vocational-education teacher's need for successful work experience in the occupation for which he will give training is considered any less important. It is imperative that he who would prepare students for successful vocational careers must first of all know, from experience, the skills and activities required for success in the occupation and must have been successful in it. However, it has become apparent over the years that each individual's educational development must include adequate general and liberal education. The preparation of the vocational-education teacher should, theerfore, include an appropriate liberal-arts education. This requirement presses most directly upon the preparation of trade and technical teachers, since training for agriculture, business, distribution, and home economics have been characterized by more general preparation. This is due to the fact that many aspects of the skills and knowledges necessary for the successful teaching of agricultural, business, distributive, and home-economics occupations are available in institutions of higher learning, whereas there is virtually no such opportunity for the trade and technical teacher. The trade and technical teacher must complete his "major" in the world of work.

Classification of Vocational Education

Vocational education beyond the high school is provided in various types of institutions, under many conditions, for many occupational skills, and for a number of objectives. It is thus difficult to classify vocational education adequately. An institution which provides vocational education beyond the high school may be classified as college, community college, junior college, vocational school, trade school, area vocational school, technical institute, high school with Grades XIII and XIV, industrial-education center, or adult-education center. There are other less frequently used names and many combinations of these names, but the program of instruction may be quite similar in each of these institutions.

Vocational education is often classified according to the nature of the program of instruction as pre-employment training, co-operative courses, apprenticeship training, or extension courses. Pre-employment training is vocational education provided for full-time students prior to employment. Co-operative courses are work-study programs in which a student works approximately half time and attends classes about half time. Often, some part of the instruction at school is related to his work task, but usually much of the school curriculum is general education and liberal in its objective. In the former case, a teacher from the school co-ordinates the classroom activity and the work assignment.

Apprenticeship training is also a work-study program. The student, however, is usually on the job 80 to 95 per cent of the total work week. His school activity is limited to no more than one day each week and is often no more than two hours each week. The school assignment is always directly related to the work task. The training program usually involves a formal agreement between the student, the employer, and the parent (if the student is a minor). Often the trade union is a party to the agreement. The agreement may also be subject to federal and state government regulations and may be negotiated through a federal or state government agency.

Vocational programs offered to employed persons in order to upgrade or update their job skills are often called extension courses or, sometimes, adult courses, part-time classes, or evening classes. These titles are used for the obvious reason that the students are usually adults. Classes are often held in the evening, and the student is not a full-time attendant.

Enrolments in extension classes have always been a major portion of the enrolments in vocational training subsidized by the federal government. In the school year 1961–62, 1,885,060 persons were enrolled in extension classes. This number is 52 per cent of the total enrolment in federally reimbursed classes. This number also represents an average of 20 students per 1,000 of the adult population, aged 20 to 64, of the United States.[3]

Extension classes subsidized by the federal government have been restricted by legislation to "confine instruction to that which is supplemental to the daily employment."[4] Current economic trends and job mobility make imperative the training of employed workers for other types of employment and the training of unemployed persons. The Congress recognized this urgent need and passed the "Manpower Development and Training Act" in March of 1962.[5] This legislation provides funds to be used specifically for the training of the unemployed and the displaced person in skills which do not have to be related to present or past employment.

This legislation has many features that are new in the history of federal subsidy of vocational education: It provides for the total cost of the program during its initial years; it designates no particular occupational categories; and it places a major part of the responsibility for the operation of the program in the Department of Labor. It is much more than just an act to implement a new phase of vocational education; it can, for example, provide more funds for vocational education in public schools generally than is now provided by other federal legislation. The Act stipulates only that the vocational education provided is for youth and adults who have completed or left high school. In any case, its potential impact has not been realized. It can change considerably the program and nature of vocational education beyond the high school. For instance, the law permits the Department of Labor to contract with private educational institutions to provide training if public schools cannot or do not provide it.

No person is approved for training under the Manpower Development and Training Act unless the Department of Labor certifies that there is a possibility of employment for persons with specific skills and that the person approved for the training has the ability to

3. *Education for a Changing World of Work*, Tables 22 and 23, pp. 75, 80. (Report of the Panel of Consultants on Vocational Education.) Department of Health, Education, and Welfare, OE-80021. Washington: Government Printing Office, 1963.

4. Public Law No. 347 (Smith-Hughes Act), 64th Congress, Section 11.

5. Public Law No. 87-415 (Manpower Development and Training Act of 1962), 87th Congress, Second Session.

achieve such skills. These requirements have a potential for providing quality factors often lacking in vocational education.

A portion of extension enrolments is provided for by college and university extension services. Many of the offerings of university extension are vocational. The trend is for the university extension to provide more postgraduate professional courses and fewer lower-division-college and post-high-school courses. These lower-division-college and post-high-school courses will more often be provided by the nonuniversity institutions previously listed. As an example, the enrolment in postgraduate professional courses in the University of California have increased from 30 per cent to almost 50 per cent of the enrolment in all courses in the past three years—while the lower-division classes have decreased from 17 per cent to about 12 per cent in the same period.[6]

There are three other terms which are widely used in vocational education for classification purposes. These are "adult education," "area vocational schools," and "technician training."

The term "adult education" is often applied to that portion of the public school program which offers classes to out-of-school youth and adults. This program is quite extensive but varies greatly from state to state and between different communities within a given state. The program may be offered in elementary-school, high-school or junior-college buildings. It may include related apprenticeship classes, vocational classes for upgrading and updating job skills or competency as a homemaker, classes for general or liberal education, and classes for leisure or recreational activities. Some high schools and junior colleges have as many adults in attendance on some evenings during the week as they have youth in attendance during a regular school day. In some states, fees, which are sufficient to support the program, are charged; in other states only a nominal registration fee is required. The adult-education activity of a school usually contributes directly to the vocational needs of the people of the community.

The "area vocational school" is a relatively new institution. It is a vocational school created to serve an area much larger than the usual school district. This administrative organization was developed to

6. University of California Extension, *A Decade of Transition*, Berkeley: University of California, 1963.

achieve two purposes: (*a*) to maintain a large enough enrolment to justify a diversified curriculum which would offer training for many employment opportunities, and (*b*) to provide a choice of vocational training to persons of a large area of residence.

This type of organization is growing in number. In the school year 1962–63, seventy-one new area vocational schools were put into operation. One hundred and six additional area schools are either under construction or in the planning stage. Twenty-four states now offer post-high-school vocational education in such institutions. Twenty additional states report new or pending legislation to increase the number of such schools or to expand existing facilities in such schools.[7]

The metropolitan vocational high school or technical school, which permits students to enrol from any of the residential areas of the city, serves the purpose of an area school for the district. Its large enrolment makes it possible to maintain a widely diversified curriculum. Since the normal residential restrictions are removed, students are not restricted in their occupational choice to only those vocational programs provided in their local school.

The area vocational school, therefore, becomes much more significant than just another institution or administrative device. It is the most effective means yet devised to make it possible to expand vocational programs for many additional occupations. The desirability of such an administrative unit was recognized by federal legislation when the National Defense Education Act of 1958 included Title VIII, "Area Vocational Programs," which provided states with funds to establish and operate schools to serve more than one school district.[8]

Title VIII of the National Defense Education Act, which provided for assistance to area vocational schools, restricted these funds "to train highly skilled technicians in occupations necessary for national defense."[9] The need for this type of training is indicated by the rapid growth in enrolment of technicians in training. Approximately

7. "Area Vocational Schools—a Summary of State Developments." United States Department of Health, Education, and Welfare, Office of Education, Division of Vocational and Technical Education, July, 1963 (mimeographed).

8. Public Law No. 85-864, 85th Congress, Second Session, Title VIII.

9. *Ibid.*

50,000 persons were enrolled in this program during the first year of its operation. This number had increased to almost 150,000 by the end of its fourth year[10] at which time more than 600 different schools were involved in the program.

The services offered by the area vocational school should not be confined to the training of technicians, although federal legislation emphasized this type of training because the need for technicians was so great. A major justification for the area vocational school, however, is that it makes possible provision of a diversified curriculum, offering training for many occupations.

Technical Education[11]

"Technical education" is used synonymously with "vocational education" in many countries of the world. It is not a standardized term in our own country. As communications systems, industrial controls, cyrogenics, laser development engineering, medical advances, and other technological developments demand more engineers and scientists, there is, in consequence, a greater need for highly skilled and knowledgeable persons to assist and to work with the professional engineer and scientist. In a study of the present employment and future demands for technicians, the National Science Foundation, with the assistance of the Bureau of Labor Statistics, found that almost 600,000 technicians were employed in industry in 1960 and that about seven technicians were employed for every ten engineers or scientists.[12] It also indicated that the ratio of technicians was increasing and suggested that the ratio could be considerably higher if more qualified technicians were available. The estimate developed from this study indicated that more than 1,000,000 technicians would be needed by 1970. This figure would have to be increased appreciably if government employment and employment in

10. *Education for a Changing World of Work, op. cit.,* p. 45.

11. See a detailed discussion of this subject by Lynn A. Emerson, "Technical Training in the United States," *Education for a Changing World of Work,* Appendix I. Department of Health, Education, and Welfare, OE-80022. Washington: Government Printing Office, 1963.

12. *Scientific and Technical Personnel in Industry,* 1960. National Science Foundation, NSF 61-75. Washington: Government Printing Office, 1961. (See also, *The Long-Range Demand for Scientific and Technical Personnel.* NSF 61-65).

nonindustrial activities were included. The National Science Foundation estimated that more than 65,000 additional technicians would be needed each year until 1970.

The training of technicians demands extensive knowledge of certain areas of science and mathematics, the accurate and skilful handling of specific instruments, and the analysis of electrical circuits, control devices, or measuring devices. The persons in training for such vocations must possess certain aptitudes and must be motivated to study rather abstract science and mathematics, and the teachers of such classes must have had extensive experience and training, similar to that of an engineer or scientist.

The term "technician," however, is often applied to occupations other than those which are designed to assist the scientist or engineer. The terms "food technician," "medical technician," "dental technician," "nursing technician," "agricultural technician" are just a few of the many job titles which designate the worker as a technician. Efforts to restrict the title to a more narrow segment of workers have not been successful; in fact, there is evidence that the term will be used even more widely. It thus becomes even more difficult to define. The term "technician," however, should be restricted to persons who are engaged in occupational activities and who perform in the manner indicated in the following list of criteria:

1. The activities as technician require a person:
   a) to possess and use extensive specialized knowledge, and/or
   b) to make very accurate measurements, and/or
   c) to use delicate and complex instruments, and/or
   d) to accept unusual responsibilities for the safety and welfare of persons and equipment.
2. A technician works:
   a) directly as an assistant to a very highly skilled person, or
   b) in a process or with equipment developed by very highly skilled persons.

As production and service processes and equipment become more complex, more occupations will justify and use the title of technician.

On-the-Job Training

Education for employment is provided by a variety of agencies other than the public schools. Clark and Sloan studied vocational education in industry, merchandising, and the armed services, and studies indicate that large numbers of persons are being trained by these groups, many at levels above the high school.[13] They estimate that the armed services have more persons in training than all the colleges and universities in the United States, private and public combined.

If the training requires very expensive equipment, it will usually not be available at a public school. Or, if the skill requirement is peculiar to a single industry, a public institution often cannot justify a training program. An institution which accepts the responsibility of training for employment should be aware of occupational training by business, industry, and the armed services and should assist its students to take advantage of such opportunities. It should also consider supplementing such training to increase the student's prospective economic security.

The work-study programs of "Distributive Education" and "Diversified Occupations" have been very successful in the employment experiences of their students. These programs are "on-the-job-training," in that the student learns the job skills as he works in the business office or industrial plant. These programs were originally developed for high schools. They should be expanded in post-high-school programs to take advantage of the laboratory and shop experiences and the necessary equipment, supplies, and much of the supervision and instruction which business and industry will supply.

A large segment of in-service training has always been provided by the employing agent. This type of training is very important at this time when the unemployment rate is higher than normal and when automation is making many jobs obsolete; it, too, should be expanded.

The Junior College or Community College

Many of the programs of occupational education are provided in junior colleges or community colleges. They can provide a widely

13. (a) Harold F. Clark and Harold S. Sloan, *Classrooms in the Factories.* Rutherford, New Jersey: Fairleigh Dickinson University, Institute of Research, 1958.
(b) Harold F. Clark and Harold S. Sloan, *Classrooms in the Stores.* Sweet Springs, Missouri: Roxbury Press, 1962.
(c) Harold F. Clark and Harold S. Sloan, *Classrooms in the Military: An Account of Education in the Armed Forces.* Published for the Institute for Instructional Improvement. New York: Bureau of Publications, Teachers College, Columbia University, 1964.

diversified curriculum to serve the educational needs of the high-school graduate and of adults who desire an educational program of two years beyond high school. The first two years of a liberal-arts college program are usually provided in junior colleges, and a variety of vocational courses is offered. The number and type of vocational courses will vary greatly among various institutions. Some may offer no vocational courses; others may have a diversified offering. But generally they are characterized by flexibility: they often serve as area vocational schools; they may provide pre-employment training for older youth or adults; they may provide training to update and upgrade skills of those at work; and they provide retraining under the Manpower Development and Training Act.

TABLE 1

JUNIOR COLLEGE ENROLMENTS IN
CALIFORNIA FOR 1962–63*

Type of Curriculum	Total Enrolments
Liberal Arts	252,694
Vocational	184,732
Other	542,918

* "Student Majors by Curriculum Fields and Other Related Data in California Public Junior Colleges, October, 1962." California State Department of Education, Bureau of Junior College Education, Release No. 4, April 1, 1963 (mimeographed).

California has the most extensive system of junior or community colleges in the country. Tuition is free, and there are no residence restrictions within the state. Table 1 shows the enrolments in liberal-arts and vocational courses in the junior colleges of the state of California for the school year 1962–63. Such an enrolment breakdown is not available for the United States as a whole.

Table 2 lists vocational curricula and the number of junior colleges offering each curiculum. This tabulation indicates the great variety of courses which can be made available by a state system of community colleges.

Some states provide vocational education beyond the high school in separate institutions rather than in combination with liberal or general college courses. These institutions are usually called technical institutes.

The technical institutes of Connecticut are examples of a type of post-high-school vocational-education center which is developing in a number of states (see Table 3). They do not have a strictly limited place-of-residence requirement; they maintain a relatively large enrolment; and they provide a large variety of occupational training opportunities. They accept all students above high-school age who can benefit by the instruction provided. These technical institutes are simliar to the junior colleges of California in these respects.

TABLE 2

VOCATIONAL CURRICULUM IN CALIFORNIA JUNIOR COLLEGES*

Vocational Curriculum	Number of Junior Colleges Offering Curriculum
Agriculture, horticulture, and forestry	
Agriculture—business...................	11
Animal husbandry......................	10
Floriculture and ornamental.............	10
General agriculture....................	10
Others...............................	32
Applied and graphic arts	
Advertising and commercial art...........	25
Journalism...........................	10
Photography..........................	14
Publishing and printing (graphic arts)......	12
Others...............................	28
Business and commerce	
Accounting and bookkeeping.............	51
General business management............	31
General clerical.......................	50
Real estate...........................	20
Retail merchandising...................	36
Secretarial and stenographic.............	60
Others...............................	86
Trade and technical	
Automotive and diesel...................	38
Building construction...................	24
Civil and construction..................	28
Drafting.............................	40
Electronics technology..................	51
Welding and oxygen cutting.............	19
Others...............................	143
Health services	
Dental assisting.......................	20
Licensed vocational nursing..............	30
Medical assisting......................	15
Registered professional nursing...........	18
Others...............................	14
Miscellaneous occupations	
Cosmetology..........................	15
Law enforcement......................	36
Others...............................	25

* *A Directory of Occupation-centered Curriculums in California Junior Colleges and Schools for Adults.* Compiled by J. M. Jacobsen. Sacramento: California State Department of Education, 1962.

North Carolina initiated a state system of industrial-training centers a few years ago, which had grown into twenty centers by 1963. Each center serves as an area vocational school, offering a number of curricula. The General Assembly of North Carolina, in 1963, provided for a state system of community colleges, which will probably be developed around the existing industrial-training centers as well as existing and future junior colleges.[14]

Other states are planning similar vocational-training centers. In some states these institutions will be a state-operated and state-financed system of schools; in others they will be part of a local school system but will enjoy major financial support from the state.

TABLE 3

TECHNOLOGY ENROLMENTS IN THE TECHNI-
CAL INSTITUTES OF THE STATE OF
CONNECTICUT, 1962–63*

Curriculum	Number Enrolled
Mechanical technology	225
Electrical technology	275
Tool technology	120
Chemical technology	85
Civil technology	79
Computer technology	135
Total	919

* Letter of October, 1963, from Joseph T. Nerden, Director, Division of Vocational Education, State of Connecticut.

In some states these schools will be exclusively vocational-training centers; in others they will be combined with a two-year college curriculum. They may even include vocational students in the upper high-school years. In some states these schools will be considered a part of the state system of higher education; in other states they will be a part of the secondary-education system.

There is sufficient evidence to indicate that vocational education beyond the high school can be provided effectively by many patterns of curriculum organization and administration. But whatever

14. a) *An Act To Promote and Encourage Education beyond the High School in North Carolina.* Raleigh, North Carolina: State Department of Public Instruction, 1963.

b) *A Guide for the Establishment of Comprehensive Community Colleges in North Carolina.* Raleigh, North Carolina: State Board of Education, Department of Community Colleges, 1963.

curriculum organization or administration is followed, efficient and effective operation requires:

1. A diversified curriculum related to the employment possibilities available to those completing training.
2. A student body large enough to justify a diversified curriculum related to employment possibilities available to those completing training.
3. Policies and regulations which free the student from local residence requirements.
4. A program of studies which provides necessary and sufficient related knowledge as well as manipulative-skills development.
5. A continuing contact with business, industry, and agriculture which prevents obsolescence of the instruction.
6. An adequate program of guidance, student selection, and placement.

Any program which follows similar guidelines and evaluates the placement and success of its graduates should be effective in its service to its students and to the economy of the region it serves.

The privately financed trade school has provided large numbers of vocationally trained persons. The most common pattern among private vocational schools is the highly specialized curriculum. Typically, these schools train the auto mechanic, electronic technician, beautician, barber, office worker, and so on. If these are well endowed (few are), they may offer a more diversified curriculum, but the private school must, in general, support itself from its fees and usually must show a profit on its capital investment. This restricts the private trade school to programs for which there is considerable demand for the training and which do not require too extensive capital investment. In metropolitan centers, private schools may serve large numbers of persons and provide very satisfactory training. The profit motive, however, makes much vocational training impossible as a private venture and at times may severely limit its quality.

The Scope of Vocational Education beyond the High School

The changing nature of our industrial society is such as to place increasing emphasis on the importance of continuous educational opportunity. The fluid nature of our workaday world and the very real possibility that a significant number of the individuals in tomorrow's labor force will have more than one occupation during their working life places a new importance on adult education and on the need for retraining workers and upgrading and updating skills of those employed. This characteristic has caused many analysts of the vocational-education program to ponder a possible change in the balance of effort between the amount and type of vocational education that should precede entrance into the labor market and the amount and type of vocational education better done after one has become a worker. It would appear that pre-employment programs should tend to be broader based and that highly specialized, narrower-based curricula of short duration and high intensity should be more often provided to those who have already entered the labor market.

If we are to use the concept of adult education as connoting such programs, then, in the future, the largest vocational effort will be in the area of adult education. Since the tempo of change is increasing so rapidly, it is imperative that our society be able to meet these needs for upgrading and retraining swiftly and efficiently. The advent of the Manpower Development and Training Act of 1962, which provides generous federal subsidy for highly specialized training programs designed to re-establish unemployed workers in gainful employment is but a dramatic indication of the national recognition of such a need.

Attention to the general-education development of the adult is no less important. Indeed, limited experience with programs designed to retrain unemployed workers has indicated that one of the principal deterrents to individual success in such programs is the significant lack of an appropriate general-education background. This very fact suggests that many adult-education programs of tomorrow will need to concern themselves with the development of such basic competencies as reading comprehension, arithmetical reasoning, and scientific understanding. This, likewise, connotes a broader competence spectrum that will need to be typical of so-called knowledges related to occupational competence.

Perhaps nowhere in the total program of education is the opportunity to meet needs less bound up with pedagogical tradition than is the case in adult education. Therefore, it seems that dramatic successes in the immediate future may be possible.

Many organizational patterns are encountered when one reviews the manner in which our educational programs go about meeting the needs of the adult worker for supplementary instruction. Typical of such organizational patterns are evening high schools, classes for adults attached to day high schools, evening junior colleges, classes for adults attached to day junior colleges, classes for adults in summer sessions at either high schools or junior colleges, and specialized schools for adults offering classes day or night, or both. Since many of those individuals needing to enhance their long-term job security will need general-education development as well as opportunity to upgrade their vocational competence, the desirability of providing such opportunities as part of a comprehensive high-school or junior-college program is self-evident. To meet the needs of workers for retraining or upgrading, it is of primary importance to develop and to establish short, intensive programs at once. These programs will need to be sensitive to the current needs of both industry and workers. The consideration of organizational placement of such a program in the school structure is of secondary importance.

Emerging Imperatives

It becomes increasingly apparent not only that youth will stay in school longer before they enter the labor market but also that it will be essential for them to return to school from time to time after entrance upon employment in order to stay employed. This trend will increase the need for consideration of vocational-education programs of a post-high-school nature. As the pressure of students increases in post-high-school institutions, it would seem that some problem areas may well be further aggravated to the point that they might be identified as emerging imperatives.

TENDENCY OF JUNIOR COLLEGES TO BECOME PREOCCUPIED WITH CLASSICAL CURRICULA

It has been generally accepted that the junior college serves several functions, which are best described by the concept of a community college. One of these functions is to provide the first two years of a baccalaureate-degree program. Another of these functions, of equal importance, is to provide vocational-education opportunities. In recent years, the number of students seeking the first two years of a baccalaureate degree in the junior college has increased to the point that some junior colleges tend to consider the transfer program their only purpose. In other instances, junior colleges select only the so-called prestige occupations for which to provide appropriate pre-employment instruction.

Much has been said and much more written about the fact that too many individuals are preparing for the area of our occupational life that employs approximately 10 per cent of the total work force. One of the difficulties in getting students to make realistic occupational choices is a result of our accepted status patterns. Florence Nightingale is reported to have said, in respect to hospitals, that whatever a hospital does, it should not spread disease. The same could be said of the junior college—that whatever else the junior college does, it should not aggravate the problems of our society by downgrading vocational education, either directly or by implication.

NEED FOR BETTER ARTICULATION BETWEEN HIGH-SCHOOL AND POST-HIGH-SCHOOL PROGRAMS

As our youth stay in school longer, it follows that considerably more of the student population can be expected to go beyond the twelfth grade. This would call for a re-evaluation of the need to closely articulate high-school programs with post-high-school institutions—particularly the junior colleges. Many technician occupations, for example, lend themselves to a basic program that would be appropriate in the high school and upon which the post-high-school institution could build in greater depth to the ultimate advantage of the student entering industry.

NEED FOR SEVERAL DIFFERENT TYPES OF POST-HIGH-SCHOOL INSTITUTIONS

There appears to be a tendency in some quarters to argue that the institution which offers post-high-school instruction should be either a junior college or a technical school. It does not seem wise to assume that the determination of the type of an institution appropriate for post-high-school vocational-education opportunities is an "either-or" matter. Rather, it appears more likely that there is possibly a need for several different types of institutions. Some types of vocational education which are closely allied with the general-education development of the individual probably are best taken care of in the traditional junior college. Other instances of highly specialized, complex pre-employment training might best be taken care of in an area vocational school or technical institute.

Some types of institutions lend themselves to serving geographic needs better than others. In some areas of the country, tradition and practice tend to emphasize the technical-institute type of institution, while other areas appear to be able to accomplish essentially the same results through a regular junior-college program. What must be done, in whatever form, is to provide the necessary vocational education to meet the needs wherever they are and whatever they are.

CHAPTER VIII

Impact of Federal Legislation and Policies upon Vocational Education*

MAYOR D. MOBLEY and MELVIN L. BARLOW

Introduction

Federal aid for vocational education had its beginning in the early years of the twentieth century. The first federal vocational-education act was signed into law on February 23, 1917, by President Woodrow Wilson. Fifty-five years earlier the Congress had sought to provide for vocational-education needs of agriculture and industry at the college level through the Morrill Act. This Act led to the establishment of agricultural and mechanical colleges in all the states. The Morrill Act was extended by Congress in 1890. The Hatch Act of 1887 and the Smith Lever Act of 1914 rounded out the government's participation—prior to the passage of the Smith-Hughes Act—in vocational education at the college level and provided added stimulation for the development of agriculture and agricultural education. The effect of this early legislation relating to agricultural education at the college level was to focus attention more clearly upon the need for similar education at the secondary level. Prior to the enactment of the Smith-Hughes Act a number of states had developed programs of vocational education in the secondary schools; the Act brought these programs into public view and facilitated similar development in other states.

For years there had been much agitation for such legislation on the part of leaders in agriculture, industry, and organized labor. Until about 1900, most of the skilled workers in the United States had come

* The authors are indebted to Walter Arnold, Assistant United States Commissioner of Education, and to Edwin Rumpf, Lane C. Aash, Earl M. Bowler, and Mary P. Allen, Division of Vocational and Technical Education, United States Office of Education for their helpful suggestions.

to this country from Europe. As immigration laws were tightened, leaders in government, agriculture, industry, and labor realized that vocational-education programs would need to be developed if the United States was to move forward in economic growth.

An Overview of Legislation Prior to 1963

THE SMITH-HUGHES ACT

The Smith-Hughes Act followed and, to a great extent, was in the spirit of the report of the Commission on National Aid to Vocational Education, which was created by an Act of Congress in 1914. The Commission was headed by Senator Hoke Smith of Georgia. Congressman Dudley M. Hughes of Georgia was also a member of the Commission. Both had been active in the establishment of agricultural and mechanical schools in each of the congressional districts of Georgia.

The Smith-Hughes Act provided approximately $7 million annually, as a permanent appropriation, for vocational education in agriculture, trades, home economics, and industry and for teacher training.

THE GEORGE-REED ACT

Twelve years after the enactment of the Smith-Hughes Act, on February 5, 1929, President Coolidge approved the George-Reed Act, which was a temporary measure. It authorized an appropriation of $1 million annually (expiring in 1934) to expand vocational education in agriculture and in home economics.

THE GEORGE-ELLZEY ACT

On May 21, 1934, President Roosevelt signed the George-Ellzey Act. This Act replaced the George-Reed Act and authorized an appropriation of $3 million annually for three years to be apportioned equally for training in agriculture, home economics, and trades and industries.

THE GEORGE-DEEN ACT

The George-Deen Act was signed into law by President Roosevelt on June 8, 1936. It authorized, on a continuing basis, an annual appropriation of approximately $14 million for vocational education in agriculture, home economics, trades and industry, and, for the first time, in distributive occupations.

WAR-PRODUCTION TRAINING

In 1940 Congress began making appropriations to states to train defense-production workers (later called war-production workers). The appropriation for the first year was $15 million. After the United States entered World War II, annual appropriations were increased rapidly until the amount exceeded $100 million per year. This program was discontinued at the war's end in 1945.

THE GEORGE-BARDEN ACT

The George-Barden Act amended the George-Deen Act and superseded it. It increased the authorization for appropriations for vocational education from $14 million to $29 million annually. The measure was signed into law by President Truman on August 1, 1946. Funds for vocational education were authorized for agriculture, home economics, trades and industry, and distributive occupations. The Act also authorized the use of funds for guidance and teacher training in all of the several fields and for research in vocational education.

BILL OF RIGHTS FOR WORLD WAR II VETERANS

The so-called "GI Bill of Rights" for World War II veterans was signed into law on June 22, 1944, by President Roosevelt. It provided almost unlimited funds for the education of World War II veterans. Vocational educators throughout the nation played a major role in developing and operating vocational-training programs under the provisions of this Act.

EFFORTS TO ELIMINATE FEDERAL FUNDS

During the early fifties, efforts were made to eliminate federal funds for vocational education.[1] For several years the Bureau of the Budget either recommended cuts in federal funds or the elimination of all vocational-education laws. Instead of following these recommendations Congress greatly increased federal funds for vocational education.

1. The economy drive during the 1930's included recommendations that funds for vocational education be reduced; funds were actually increased by the George-Ellzey and George-Deen Acts.

PRACTICAL-NURSE TRAINING

On August 2, 1956, President Eisenhower approved the Health Amendments Act of 1956, which authorized $5 million annually for five years for the expansion and improvement of practical-nurse training. In 1961, this law was extended for three additional years, to terminate on June 30, 1965.

TRAINING IN THE FISHING INDUSTRY

To provide for training in the fishing industry, an amendment to the George-Barden Act was approved by President Eisenhower on August 8, 1956. It authorized, on a continuing basis, $375,000 annually as aid to states for vocational training "in the fishing trades and industry and distributive occupations therein."

AREA VOCATIONAL-EDUCATION PROGRAMS

On September 2, 1958, President Eisenhower signed into law the National Defense Education Act of 1958. Title VIII of this Act (Title III of the George-Barden Act) authorized $15 million annually for the training of highly skilled technicians. This Act was scheduled to terminate on June 30, 1962, but subsequently was extended to terminate on June 30, 1965.

AREA REDEVELOPMENT ACT

Section 16 of the Area Redevelopment Act authorized an appropriation of $4.5 million annually for vocational training and retraining of unemployed workers living in areas of redevelopment. Under the provisions of this measure, the training of unemployed workers is by law a responsibility of the Department of Health, Education, and Welfare. The actual training is done in states under the control and supervision of state vocational-education boards. This was a temporary act, scheduled to expire on June 30, 1965.

MANPOWER DEVELOPMENT AND TRAINING ACT OF 1962

The Manpower Development and Training Act of 1962 authorized $161 million annually for three years, terminating on June 30, 1965. About one-third of the funds authorized under this Act may be used for training purposes under the control and supervision of state vocational-education boards. Appropriations under provisions of this Act are made to the Department of Labor and the funds for training are transferred to the Department of Health, Education, and Welfare for distribution to state vocational-education boards.

TRADE EXTENSION ACT OF 1962

The Trade Extension Act of 1962 contains provisions authorizing the training of displaced workers. The training program under provisions of the Act is the responsibility of the Secretary of Labor. There is no mention in the Act of any responsibility of the Department of Health, Education, and Welfare or of state vocational-education boards.

PUBLIC WELFARE AMENDMENTS ACT OF 1962

The Public Welfare Amendments Act of 1962 authorized training for certain welfare cases to be carried on under co-operative arrangements of welfare agencies and state authorities responsible for the administration of vocational and adult education. It is assumed that any vocational programs developed under this Act will be carried out on a contractual basis with state vocational-education boards.

SUMMARY

The brief review of federal laws for vocational education shows to some extent the trend as it relates to federal aid for vocational education. Earlier acts earmarked funds for special programs and established standards to be maintained. Recent acts were more general in nature and did not earmark funds for specific programs.

However, provisions of the Manpower Act, approved in 1962, specifically limit the training to unemployed individuals who, after receiving training, have a reasonable opportunity for employment. By regulations and by law, considerable control of the program is placed in the hands of federal authorities.

Significant Results of the Legislation

GENERAL RATIONALE

Financial support for vocational education from the federal government was first regarded as temporary, "stimulating" legislation. Charles A. Prosser predicted in 1925 that there would be no additional federal legislation but, rather, a gradual tendency to accept federal partnership in maintaining education. The Smith-Hughes Act had, however, provided a continuing appropriation.

It is clear that the vocational-education program of the nation has advanced more rapidly with federal funds than would have been the case without them. States that had lagged in developing vocational-education programs were induced to take action.

There are several schools of thought regarding the impact of federal legislation on vocational education. Some persons contend that the legislation has narrowed the offerings in vocational schools and that school authorities have not developed programs in keeping with actual needs but have followed rather blindly the development of programs that are aided with federal funds. Although this may be true in some communities and in some states, there is nothing in the federal laws that encourages the limitation of vocational education to those occupations for which federal funds are provided.

Federal funds for business education (office-occupation training) were not made available in the federal acts prior to 1963, even though several attempts were made to include this area in the federal-aid program. These efforts were defeated largely as a result of private interests.

Although federal funds were not available for office-occupation training, this program was developed on a large scale by the public schools. Many persons contend that, had federal funds been made available over the years for office occupations, it would have been easier to establish nation-wide standards which would have made the program more effective and more valuable to those enrolled.

It is the opinion of most students of federal support for vocational education that the current trend is toward legislation of a broad nature, without earmarked funds for specific occupational categories. They contend that state and local education authorities, after almost fifty years of experience in developing and promoting vocational education, should be given greater autonomy in the development of the kinds of programs needed.

The recommendations of the Panel of Consultants on Vocational Education indicated the desirability of greater autonomy on the part of the states to plan and develop programs tailored to fit their needs. The report does not recommend earmarked funds for the several occupational categories of vocational education. On the other hand, the Panel did not recommend the repeal of existing laws that now earmark funds for the several phases of vocational education.

Until recent years, it was generally accepted as policy that vocational programs should be tailored to meet the specific needs of a community—that training should be offered only in those occupations in which people could find employment near their homes. For some time, however, leaders in vocational education have advocated the development of programs in keeping with the interest and needs of individuals regardless of their place of residence. This new trend in vocational education may be attributed, in part, to the mobility of workers. In recent years, workers have moved from state to state and from city to city in greater numbers than has been the case in the past. Mobility of labor has an influence upon vocational-education programs in all parts of the nation. The fact of mobility should encourage the preparation of individuals for occupations in which they are interested and for which they have talent rather than limiting training to occupations which are available locally. This seems to be a desirable trend.

SPECIFIC IMPACTS

A student of the history of vocational education becomes aware of trends and changes in vocational education; he is led to believe that many of these have been and are directly influenced by federal legislation for vocational education and that changes would have occurred less rapidly and trends would have been less pronounced had there been no federal legislation. It is acknowledged that the general impact of the legislation upon vocational education has not produced a finite number of specific effects, well identified and ordered but, rather, a very large number of effects of varying import. It is probable also that geographical location, administrative position in vocational education, age, and experience help to identify and order the effects observed by a particular investigator and that others would see these influences in a different manner and would weigh them differently. Nevertheless, there seems to be no question but that legislation has had an impact upon the general development of vocational education. The following specific impacts represent, primarily, the views of the chapter authors and those of many other persons as well.

Promotion of the national welfare.—The war record of vocational education in two world wars is, in itself, conclusive evidence that legislation had produced in the states a line of defense that could act immediately when called upon in a national emergency. During World War II, more than eleven million people were given specialized training for jobs and occupations needed to arm, equip, and feed our armies and allies. These millions of vocationally trained Americans contributed greatly to America's "arsenal of democracy." Many believe that these skilled and semiskilled workers spelled the difference between victory and defeat. They turned out the guns, ships, and other ingredients of victory.

Similarly vocational education has responded to the call by Congress for efforts in the direction of meeting the critical national needs for skilled manpower. Also, the millions of people who have attended the classes and either entered upon work or made additional progress in their work have improved their earning power and have consequently achieved a higher standard of living for themselves and for the nation.

Development of standards.—The federal acts have set the stage for the development of standards in vocational education. The Division of Vocational and Technical Education of the United States Office of Education (from 1917 to 1933, Federal Board for Vocational Education) promotes the development of vocational education in many ways, not the least of which has been through the variety of publications, including compilations of statistical data. This "central" office stimulates the exchange of information so that changes and trends in program development are known throughout the nation. This has had a stimulating effect on states that have poor programs and has also made it possible for the programs of good states to become better.

Improvement of administration and supervision.—An adequate and effective framework for the administration and supervision of vocational education has developed in response to the federal legislation. The requirement that states develop plans forced them to give attention to quality controls at both the state and local levels. Acceptable levels of quality and criteria for the development of supervisory and administrative practice have evolved from the influence of the legislative acts.

Development of teacher education.—Federal legislation made it mandatory that vocational-education programs in the states have adequate programs of teacher education. Accordingly, all states have developed a means of providing teacher education either on a pre-service or in-service basis for teachers of vocational education. These programs differ widely because each state developed teacher-education programs which were appropriate to its particular needs; the states were not required to conform to a standardized national pattern. National and regional conferences called by the United States Office of Education, Division of Vocational and Technical Education, have made it possible for educators who train teachers to exchange ideas about the purpose, method, and content of teacher education. Such conferences have led to an increasingly improved program of teacher education throughout the United States.

Leadership development.—The importance and necessity of continuous leadership development in the various states is inherent in the federal legislation. Accordingly, over the years national and regional conferences have been devoted to leadership development. These conferences have encouraged state and local review of the quality and potential availability of leadership, have caused higher standards for leadership positions in vocational education to be established, and have assisted the state and local community to improve their practices in the selection of administrators, supervisors, and teachers. This general upgrading of leadership development, an influence of the federal acts, has been stimulated by the publication by the Office of Education of studies, summaries of practice, and suggested optimum goals for leadership development.

Evaluation.—The states were required to live within the minimum requirements of the federal acts, to conduct a program of vocational education according to their own plan, and to report regularly upon certain aspects of their program to the United States Office of Education. Although these activities do not of themselves insure quality in vocational education, they do provide the environment in which quality and ideas can develop. Professional associations in vocational education have been inspired to develop useful and excellent criteria for vocational education. Many states and local programs have used such evaluative instruments in studying their programs of vocational education. Evaluation of vocational education was not specifically a requirement of the federal acts until 1963, but, prior to 1963, the inspiration and desire to make evaluations stemmed, in part, from the influence of federal legislation.

Development of a national consciousness of vocational education.— A consciousness of vocational education as a national concern has come about through the participation of the federal government in vocational education. The national, state, and local structures of vocational education make possible the general communication of ideas, collaboration in experimentation, and realistic determination of vocational-training needs on a nation-wide scale. The national consciousness of vocational education has been stimulated also by professional associations which have worked on important issues and problems with state and local groups. The net result of this total consciousness has been the development of an approach and design for vocational education which make it possible to match needs for labor, training, and employment on a much more effective basis.

Development of the "area" concept.—One of the most significant trends in recent years has been the development and spread of area vocational-education programs. Some states have had such programs for many years. For example, Connecticut started area vocational programs in 1915. These were state-owned and -operated schools and were available to pupils from any part of the state. In recent years, Connecticut, as well as many other states, has greatly expanded vocational-technical schools of this character. If this trend continues, and in all likelihood it will, there will in due time be a system of area vocational programs throughout the nation. Some of these programs are operated as a part of a junior college and some as separate vocational-technical institutes or institutions. They have come into being in recognition of the fact that it is not possible to develop broad multiple offerings in vocational education in small high schools. Many of these area schools are serving youths who have completed high school or have dropped out of school and are beyond high-school age. They are serving a real need in the field of vocational education.

State boards for vocational education.—Long before the passage of the Smith-Hughes Act, the National Society for the Promotion of Industrial Education had recognized with approval the tendency in American education to broaden the responsibility of the state for the education of its youth. Bulletins of the Society emphasized the need for a board functioning at the top administrative level of education in a state. In order for a state to secure the benefits of the Smith-Hughes Act, it was required that the state accept the provisions of the Act through legislative authority "and designate or create a State board" to co-operate with the federal board to implement the programs contemplated by the Act.

Establishment of a state board for vocational education brought vocational education clearly within the purview of the top educational authorities of the state. Designation of a person as a "state director" gave further emphasis to programs of vocational education. State directors meet in professional association to consider problems of the state function of vocational education. Such meetings have produced standards of performance in the practice of vocational education and have, in addition, provided feedback to the state boards; thus, vocational education has been more than a casual concern of the board. The existence of the state board for vocational education has had far-reaching effect upon the place of vocational education in the state educational structure.

State plans.—The Smith-Hughes Act required that the "State board shall prepare plans showing the kinds of vocational education for which it is proposed that the appropriations shall be used. . . ." This requirement of the federal legislation has had a significant impact upon the development of vocational education in the states.

The states have given specific attention to teacher qualifications, kinds of schools and equipment, courses of study, methods of instruction, and a variety of other items. With the exception of adhering to the minimum provisions of the Act, the states have been free to develop vocational education to fit their own needs and desires. Inspection and enforcement at the federal level for a state was in terms of the state's own plan. The state plan for vocational education is notable in federal legislation; every federal law since the Smith-Hughes Act has upheld the policy adopted in that Act. The total impact of the state plan upon the development of vocational education in the states has been most significant. In the best situations, the state plans represent a consensus of those responsible in any way for the development of vocational education.

Matching of federal funds.—Underlying all federal legislation for vocational education is the principle of matching federal funds with state and local funds. This financial partnership has produced in each of the states an effective vocational-education fund which has increased in size over the years since 1917.

Increase in expenditures, for vocational education has been most pronounced at the local level. Thoroughly reliable data have not been collected on the actual expenditures for vocational education at the local level. However, it is known that availability of federal money for vocational education has led to the provision of larger amounts at the state level and significantly larger amounts at the local level. As an example, "for every $1 of Federal funds [spent for trade and industrial education in 1961], State expenditure was $2.26 and local expenditure $3.33."[2] The matching principle has had a considerable impact in making funds available to provide for the vocational needs of the youth and adults of the nation.

IMPLICATIONS AND TRENDS

The trend throughout the United States is to expand vocational-education programs. One of the major reasons for this expansion is the fact that more and more occupations require specialized training, and there are fewer and fewer opportunities for employment on the part of unskilled or semiskilled persons.

In recent years, thousands of young people have been unable to find employment largely because they possess no marketable skills. There was a time when almost any young man or young woman who had finished high school could obtain employment. No longer does a high-school diploma guarantee employment; the individual must also possess marketable skills. This fact has caused school authorities throughout the nation to consider seriously the need for expanding and modernizing vocational-education offerings.

Federal legislation has tended not only to "raise the sights" of vocational education but to extend its scope as well. For example, emphasis placed upon practical-nurse education by federal legislation produced an immediate response in the states. Enrolment in these programs increased rapidly. Development of practical-nurse education led to the expansion of offerings in education for other health occupations.

2. *Education for a Changing World of Work*, p. 35, United States Department of Health, Educaton, and Welfare. Washington: Government Printing Office, 1963.

Similarly, attention of federal legislation to the need for highly skilled manpower brought immediate response throughout the nation in the form of classes for a variety of technical workers. Classes to prepare workers to enter employment as technical workers and classes for persons who were employed as such grew rapidly.

America's unemployment problem is causing many persons to look to vocational education for at least a part of the solution. Every month, year after year, the skills of thousands of workers become obsolete. The hope of these workers to find gainful employment is dependent in a large measure on retraining programs. The relation of training to employment was recognized by the Congress in 1962, when it passed by an overwhelming vote the Manpower Development and Training Act, which provided funds for the training of unemployed and underemployed youths and adults. Manpower authorities tell us that we are likely to be confronted for many years with unemployment problems having their origins in scientific and technological developments. Many workers of the future, because of these developments, may reasonably expect to change occupations or jobs at least five times during a lifetime. Many of these changes of occupation will call for highly specialized training programs.

Then, there are millions of workers who, in order to retain their present jobs, must obtain specialized training to update or upgrade their skills and their knowledge. Much of the effort of vocational educators in the years ahead will be devoted to training unemployed people and offering specialized training for updating employed persons to prevent them from becoming unemployed.

The Vocational Education Act of 1963
(Public Law 88-210)
INTRODUCTION

The report of the Panel of Consultants on Vocational Education bears the same relationship to the Vocational Education Act of 1963 that the report of the Commission on National Aid to Vocational Education does to the Vocational Education Act of 1917. Each of these legislative milestones in vocational education (the Acts of 1917 and 1963) was preceded by intensive study of certain needs of the society. In 1917, the task was to construct a program for vocational education which would provide an educated labor force. In 1963, the task was to review the past achievements and to modernize and redirect the program in terms of the extraordinary developments in technology and in terms of a variety of social and economic needs.

During the forty-seven-year history of federal aid to vocational education, millions of people have been prepared to enter the labor force, but the total enrolment in 1964 is entirely too small in comparison with the millions entering the labor force. The scope of the program has increased since 1917 to the point that it includes a wide variety of occupational instruction, but the scope of occupational coverage is small in comparison with the need. The investment of federal funds in 1917 was large and adequate for the needs of the period, but in 1964 the amount of the federal investment in vocational education is entirely too small. The total federal appropriation for vocational education during the entire period, 1917–61, was less than the federal appropriation for one year, 1961, for the school lunch and school milk programs. The "hue and cry" of federal control which has persisted over the years was not based on facts; such control was difficult to find. It is true that the acts and the federal policy set requirements to be met by the states and local communities, but these requirements were minimal and exceedingly small. It was alleged that control follows money, but the largest portion of the vocational dollar came from the local community; thus, control was located where it belonged—in the local community.

Vocational education suffered many ills in 1963. The Panel sought to diagnose these ills and, assisted by the informed opinion and considered judgment of many persons and groups, selected the ingredients of a prescription most likely to provide an immediate cure and to prevent a relapse. The Congress wrote the prescription for a new era in vocational education—one to strengthen and improve the quality of vocational education and to expand the vocational-education opportunities of the nation.

PRESCRIPTION FOR CHANGE

Legislation dating back to 1917 influenced the development of vocational education, and the national program grew up around certain well-defined occupational areas. With few exceptions the program of vocational education served the American people well. The only trouble was that it served too few people, was found in too few schools, and was organized in too few occupational areas. The legislation of 1963 recognized the achievements made under the previous acts and no attempt was made to change significantly the existing structure of the vocational-education program. The emphasis in 1963 was upon providing vocational education where it had not been developed previously.

The controlling fact in the definitions of vocational education has always been the definitions found in the federal acts. Since the first years of federal legislation for vocational education, two intentions are clearly visible: (*a*) the intent to meet the growing needs of the individual as he attempts to adjust to a changing technology and a variable job market, and (*b*) the intent to meet the needs of business and industry—the economy of the nation. The Vocational Education Act of 1963 was no exception; its purposes remained the same.

Central purpose of the Act.—Authorizations for federal grants to the states were intended for the following purposes:

1. To assist states to maintain, extend, and improve existing programs of vocational education.
2. To develop new programs of vocational education.
3. To provide part-time employment for youths who need such employment in order to continue their vocational training on a full-time basis.
4. To provide instruction so that persons of *all* ages in *all* communities will have *ready access* to vocational training or retraining which is of high quality, realistic in relation to employment, and suited to the needs, interests, and ability of the persons concerned. Such persons were identified: (*a*) those in high school, (*b*) those who have completed or discontinued formal education and are preparing to enter the labor market, (*c*) those who have already entered the labor market and who need to upgrade their skills or learn new ones, and (*d*) those with educational handicaps.

The intent of the Congress was to provide vocational education for all persons and all occupations, except those which the Commissioner of Education identified as professional occupations or as requiring a baccalaureate or higher degree. Never before had vocational education been charged with such broad responsibility.

Other purposes.—In order to secure quality in all vocational-education programs, Congress provided in the Vocational Education Act of 1963 for a variety of *ancillary services*, such as: (*a*) teacher training and supervision, (*b*) evaluation, (*c*) special demonstration and experimental programs, (d) development of instructional materials, (e) state administration and leadership, and (f) program review in relation to manpower needs and job opportunities. In addition, special attention was focused upon research in vocational education, and funds were authorized to support such research.

The Act also provides that funds may be used for the construction of facilities for area vocational-education schools and for the construction, equipment, and operation of residential schools to provide vocational education for youth 15 to 21 years of age. The latter is to be conducted on an experimental basis to determine the feasibility and desirability of residential vocational schools.

Flexibility and advisory services.—It is apparent that the Vocational Education Act of 1963 places more responsibility than heretofore placed upon the state and local community for the development of programs of vocational education which meet the fundamental purposes of the Act. If only one characteristic is used to describe differences between the vocational-education acts of the past and the Act of 1963, that characteristic should be *flexibility*.

New also in the Act of 1963 is the provision for an advisory committee on vocational education, of twelve members, who "shall advise the Commissioner in the preparation of general regulations and with respect to policy matters arising in the administration of this part, the Vocational Education Act of 1946, and supplementary vocational education acts, including policies and procedures governing the approval of State plans under section 5 and the approval of projects under section 4(c) and section 14."

In addition, an advisory council on vocational education is provided for the purpose, at intervals, of "reviewing the administration of the vocational education programs for which funds are appropriated pursuant to this Act and other vocational education Acts and making recommendations for improvement of such administration, and reviewing the status and of making recommendations with respect to such vocational education programs and the Acts under which funds are so appropriated."

These significant innovations in vocational education will direct attention continuously to the purposes, processes, and content of vocational education.

THE PAST IS PROLOGUE

The Vocational Education Act of 1963 makes possible a brighter future for all phases of vocational education and provides a greater opportunity for meeting one of the essential needs of society. The tendency to look back, from this vantage point, over the program of the past is irresistible. Here and there we find the purposes, principles, and symbols of vocational education which still influence the direction of vocational education. Insight into earlier points of view is indicated in remarks attributed to Dudley M. Hughes. His rationale of 1916 leading to the conclusion that vocational education is a concern and a responsibility of the federal government was stated as follows:

National efficiency is the sum total of efficiency of all individual citizens, and the national wealth is the sum of their wealth producing capacity. While, therefore, our national prosperity in the past has been largely based on the exploitation of our natural resources, in the future it must be based more and more upon the development, through vocational education, of our national resource of human labor. In the markets of the world we compete, not as individuals but as a unit, against other nations as units. This makes the protection of our raw material and of our productive skill and human labor a national problem, and unquestionably introduces a national element into vocational education, making the right preparation of the farmer and the mechanic of vital concern to the nation as a whole.

One may find in these thoughts the foundation blocks of vocational education—relevant and modern a half-century later. Now, as then, our human resources are critical to our continued economic development. Federal legislation and policies relating to vocational education have been directed toward fundamental issues in American life. Federal legislation has provided a national motivation for states and local communities and has caused programs to develop in areas where such development would have otherwise been slow and halting.

CHAPTER IX

Local, Regional, and State Policies and Policy-making

HERBERT M. HAMLIN

The Nature of Policy

The term "educational policy," as it is used in this chapter, refers to a body of guiding principles for the development and operation of an educational program which has been adopted by the public or its authorized representatives. Educational policy is made by boards of many kinds, legislatures, and the Congress of the United States. Not all of the actions of these bodies are at the level of policy, but they should be.

A statement of policy is organized and internally consistent. It is intended to endure for a long time. Perhaps our prime example of a statement of public policy is the Constitution of the United States. The statement originally adopted includes only 2,200 words. It has been amended only 23 times in 175 years. The Smith-Hughes Act is a good example of an expression of policy relating to vocational education. It provided the framework within which a national program of vocational education could be developed.

Policy is not to be confused with philosophy (although a philosophy must underlie policy) or with rules and procedures for conducting an educational program or curriculum (also necessary). Programs and procedures can only be developed properly by public educational agencies with public policy as a guide.

One way of arriving at the nature of policy is to determine the questions which can only be answered ultimately under our system by the citizens or their representatives. The basic questions in formulating policy for vocational education seem to be the following:

1. How is policy to be made? Who will share in its development? Who will enact it?

A policy-making body can enact in five minutes all of the policy it should enact. It may take years to formulate the policy to be enacted. Policy-makers may use any help they can get, lay or professional. They need a vast amount of help.

2. Who are to be served by vocational education? How? How much? When? Where?

There are never enough resources to serve well all who might be served. Choices must be made.

3. What public purposes will be served?

Public education is conducted for the benefit of the public; benefits to groups and individuals are coincidental. The public owes to those who conduct vocational education a clear definition of feasible purposes it expects them to achieve.

4. How will the public determine whether its purposes are being accomplished?

Evaluations of vocational education by the public, or on behalf of the public, will be made and should be made. They are essential for its improvement. Arrangements for regular, systematic, and fair evaluations must be provided in policy.

5. How is vocational education to be organized and administered?

Decisions relating to the organization and administration of vocational education may involve a reconsideration of the organization of public education as a whole, since the development of vocational education has been restricted by the structure of public education, which is inadequate for almost all forms of education and which sometimes makes vocational education impossible.

6. How are programs and procedures to be planned?

It is the responsibility of professional educators to develop programs and procedures in line with public policy, but the public must insure that there are planned programs and procedures.

7. How will adequate personnel be secured and maintained?

There are special problems in providing adequate personnel for vocational education since occupational as well as educational competence is required and the schools must compete with business and industry for personnel.

8. What provisions will be made for research, development, and innovation?

Research, development, and provision for innovation must be built into any sound program.

9. What funds and facilities will be provided? How will they be provided?

The funds for conducting public vocational education come from the public. Questions relating to funds will be answered by the public or its representatives. To answer them well, all the previously stated questions must be answered.

These policy questions apply at every level: in the school districts; in regional units with junior or community colleges, vocational schools, or technical institutes; in the states; and at the national level. Only firm and good answers to these questions at every level, plus co-ordination of the policies developed at all levels, can provide the vocational, technical, and practical-arts education that is needed.

The public is responsible for public policy. All of the ultimate controls over public education are in its hands. Professional educators are responsible for the execution of citizen-made policies; they should have the right to advise about policy, but no more. Vocational educators are constantly tempted to take over functions that belong to citizens, instead of insisting that citizens perform them adequately and aiding them in that performance. Although citizens may neglect their responsibilities or delegate them to educators, the means are always at hand whereby they can be reclaimed.

The Development of Present Policy-making Arrangements

Arrangements for making local, regional, and state policies for public education have developed haphazardly in the United States and are much in need of review and revision.

ARRANGEMENTS FOR LOCAL POLICY-MAKING

The first local policies for public education were enacted in town meetings in New England during the seventeenth century. In 1789 the first "school committee" was established in Massachusetts. The sole responsibility of the early school committees was to evaluate the schools and report their evaluations to the town meetings for appropriate action. As public education developed and became more complex, the town meetings gradually relinquished their control over the schools; boards of education, the successors of the school committee, assumed their functions.

Concepts of the nature and functions of local boards of education evolved as the states provided a variety of structures and functions for them and the courts interpreted state legislation regarding them.

Over a long period, there was little communication among boards or among members of different boards. The first state school board association was organized in Pennsylvania in 1896. In 1940, the National School Boards Association was formed. Now all states have associations affiliated with the national association. Primarily as a result of the activities of these organizations, there has developed a better understanding of the functions and responsibilities of local boards of education.

Many boards now accept the modern concept that a board of education has two functions: (*a*) to enact the local policies it is empowered to enact and to see that these policies are executed, and (*b*) to see that the state policies which apply to the district are executed. Boards still have many powers that go far beyond this concept. Within broad limits set by their states, they may deal with anything that comes to their attention. Some boards are still dictating details of the curriculum and the choice of textbooks, employing and discharging teachers, disciplining pupils, selecting equipment, and performing other functions outside the area of policy. The boards that confine their efforts to making policy and seeing that policy is executed do so because they realize that they serve best when they do—not because state laws require them to function in this manner. They find that they have all they can do well in dealing with policy matters.

Professional educators, and administrators especially, have an important influence upon the functioning of boards of education. They may insist effectually that boards leave to them responsibilities they are better able than the boards to discharge. They may bring to the boards matters with which they themselves could deal if there were adequate board policies to guide their decisions.

Until recently nearly all boards of education have enacted individual policies sporadically as the need for them has arisen and have recorded their actions in board minutes. Recently, and particularly in the complicated schools situations of our larger cities, organized "policy statements" have been developed as alternatives to chaos. Many of these deal primarily with rules, regulations, and procedures; many others are mixtures of philosophy, policy, program, and procedures. There is probably no school system in the United States that has a comprehensive statement of policy that could be called adequate. Few policy statements have been developed democratically with adequate representation of those affected by them. Few of the smaller schools have policy statements.

The state legislatures are the primary policy-making bodies in the states. They share their responsibilities in various ways with state boards and commissions. All but two states have state boards of education for the elementary and secondary schools, some with limited and some with broad functions. Typically, each state has several boards of higher education; most states now have a board for co-ordinating higher education; a few have a single board for higher education. Special functions, one of them educational television, have sometimes been given to special state agencies.

The Smith-Hughes Act of 1917 required that each state receiving federal aid for vocational education have a state board of vocational education.

The federal government has also required that states receiving federal funds for vocational education shall submit to the United States Office of Education state plans for conducting vocational education. These state plans have usually been the only policy documents for vocational education that the states have had. Like most other "policy statements," they have usually been mixtures of policy, program, and procedure. They do not answer the basic policy questions because the outline for a state plan which the Office of Education asks the states to follow does not ask these questions.

A few states have recognized that the state plans they submit to the Office of Education are inadequate statements of policy. In some states the state funds for vocational education not required to match federal funds are being spent under state policies which do not have to be approved by the Office of Education.

Antecedents of Present Policies for Vocational Education

Policy for vocational and practical-arts education has been evolving for a long time. It did not originate with the Smith-Hughes Act, although the Act has had a profound effect upon local, regional, and state policies as well as upon national policy. The origins of policy for vocational education were in the school districts and the states;

the development of policy for vocational education has been a "grassroots" movement.

LOCAL AND STATE POLICIES PRIOR TO THE SMITH-HUGHES ACT

There were notable examples of local initiative in establishing vocational and practical-arts education prior to 1917. Manual training was introduced into many schools during the last quarter of the nineteenth century. Milwaukee established its vocational school in 1902. Agriculture and domestic science were taught in scattered school systems before there were state policies to encourage their development.

A majority of the states had enacted policies for vocational and practical-arts education before the Smith-Hughes Act was passed. Some states provided earmarked funds; some required that agriculture be taught in all schools or in certain classes of schools; some established requirements for the certification of teachers of vocational subjects; and some set up special vocational or agricultural schools.

STATE AND LOCAL ADJUSTMENTS TO FEDERAL LEGISLATION

State and local funds for vocational and practical-arts education were very limited in 1917. To gain the added funds the federal government had made available, the states met the federal requirements, —sometimes abandoning programs they had been developing for a decade or more or changing them materially.

Agriculture had been taught to a great variety of persons prior to 1917: elementary and high-school pupils, boys and girls, men and women, town and country residents. After 1917, it was largely converted into a "vocational" subject or at least one which could meet the requirements for receiving federal funds for vocational education, and the clientele served in most schools was restricted to male farmers and male prospective farmers. Little more was done until recently toward including agricultural education in general education.

Home economics has been taught with and without federal funds. Industrial arts and business education have developed generally over the country with no use of federal funds.

The patterns of local, regional, and state policy for vocational education have been too largely shaped by national legislation because the states and the local and intermediate school districts have lacked initiative, sense of responsibility, and capacity for organization needed to develop appropriate policies to supplement those of the national government. This situation has not arisen from the nature of national legislation, which was designed to limit federal control and to encourage state initiative. The framers of the federal legislation recognized that effective vocational education would be possible only if the states and the school districts were to formulate the policies required to implement the broad provisions of the federal acts.

Current Policy-making

LOCAL POLICY-MAKING

Although the local board of education is the official policy-making body of a school district, some policy questions must be referred to the electorate of the district. Commonly, for example, funds for major school building construction and major increases in operating costs must be voted upon by the people of a district.

The official and legal process of policy-making is, however, only a small part of the total process. The people of a community provide the climate in which the schools are conducted and they set most of the real expectations. It is impossible to impose a good school system, or a good program of vocational education, upon a community that does not want it.

The policy of a school district is usually the result of many forces: pressure groups of lay citizens, school employees, state requirements and recommendations, requirements of accrediting associations, the influence of school board associations, national trends, competition with Russia, and other forces. Too often, policy is made with only immediate needs in mind, and those who determine policy do not represent adequately those who are affected by the policies enacted.

A few school districts have gone far toward developing fair and democratic procedures in policy-making. Boards of education are aided by able and representative citizens' committees and by school staffs. Consultants are used. Time and thought go into the making of policy decisions. Policies are evolved which can endure.

REGIONAL POLICY-MAKING

The need for policies for vocational education for regions or areas within the states has arisen recently as area schools—junior and community colleges, vocational schools, and technical institutes—providing vocational education have developed. There is no uniformity in the process of developing policies for them. Some of these institutions which serve regions are attached to local boards of education; some are largely controlled by the states. Often, the governing boards are not doing their jobs, so that policy-making is largely left to the administrators. The potential tasks of these area schools are so large and important that special machinery for policy-making for them is needed in the regions and in the states, manned by policy-makers who understand the machinery and will do what is required.

STATE POLICY-MAKING

At the state level, political, lay, and professional organizations apply pressures on the legislatures to move them in directions approved by the organizations. Legislatures, however, commonly follow tradition except when they must deal with school emergencies. The policies they formulate ordinarily serve only to enable the schools to continue as they are or to survive from one emergency to another. State boards of education more commonly do long-range planning and develop the policies necessary to carry out their plans. However, their powers are often limited, and sometimes they are ineffective because they are in conflict with the executive or the legislative branch of state government.

INCLUDING POLICY FOR VOCATIONAL EDUCATION IN
PUBLIC EDUCATION POLICY

Public policy for vocational education in some states and localities has been developed separately from policy for other forms of education. Vocational education has sometimes been organized completely outside "the public school system." There is growing realization that public education must be seen whole and that all of its parts (elementary education, secondary education, and the various forms of education beyond the high school) must be related to each other.

If general policy for public education is well conceived, very little special policy for vocational education is required. Special policies and special arrangements for vocational education have developed because those responsible for the public schools have not always been willing to accept some of the basic tenets of vocational education:

education should prepare for useful work; schools should not discriminate on the basis of age; it should be expected that what is taught in the schools will be useful outside the schools and taught so that it will be used. No one should object to applying these principles generally in the public schools.

INFLUENCE OF NEW NATIONAL LEGISLATION ON STATE,
REGIONAL, AND LOCAL POLICY-MAKING

The National Vocational Education Act of 1963 could have a profound effect upon state policy-making and perhaps upon regional and local policy-making. The states are being given a large amount of new money. Decisions regarding its use will have to be made. New possibilities have been opened. The federal government has asked the states to assume a larger share of responsibility for policy decisions about vocational education than formerly exercised by them. The new funds are appropriated for services to designated groups of peoples, not for use in the traditional areas of agricultural education, industrial education, and the like. The range of choice allowed the states may be narrowed considerably by regulations which the Office of Education will adopt, as previous regulations have narrowed choices, but the states have always been free to make more decisions than they have made. Now they are likely to be forced to make decisions they have been reluctant to make.

The new legislation may or may not affect regional and local policy-making within the states. The states which have a tradition of centralized control will probably make most of the new decisions at the state level. Those accustomed to sharing control with the school districts will probably pass on to the districts responsibility for making the new set of decisions.

VARIATIONS IN STATE POLICIES FOR THE FEDERALLY AIDED PROGRAM

Harrington has shown that there are more variations in the school programs supported in part by federal funds for vocational education than there are in school programs supported wholly by state and local funds.[1] National controls are very light, permitting wide variations in practices. The controls that exist are not always in effect

1. Gordon M. Harrington, "Vocational Education Moving in Diverse Directions," *Nation's Schools*, IX (July, 1957), 45-48.

because the states may ignore them and the federal government lacks adequate means for determining whether or not they are enforced.

If control is in ratio to financial contributions made, as some hold, the states and the school districts have acquired increasing control over the federally aided program. In 1940 the states and the school districts together contributed $1.75 for each federal dollar; in 1950, $3.85; and in 1960, $4.27. In addition, the states and the school districts provided the buildings, equipment, and teaching aids used.

DECISIONS THE STATES MAY MAKE

Only a part of the total program of vocational and practical-arts education in the public schools is nationally aided. The states are free to conduct all of their vocational and practical-arts education without federal aid, but they use nearly all of the national funds made available to them. Apparently, the national controls are not very objectionable. However, since all states contribute to the federal funds, it would be expected that all would attempt to benefit from them.

There are many decisions left to the states even when federal funds are used:

1. They must decide how state policy for vocational education is to be made, who are to share in making it, and how they will share.
2. They may use the federal funds for some or all of the purposes for which they are provided.
3. They may assume complete control over the programs conducted in the local and area schools or delegate a large part of these controls.
4. They may match the federal funds, dollar for dollar, or may require local and area schools to match them, if they want the program, or may join with the local and area schools in matching them.
5. They may or may not provide adequate state services for the development of vocational education in the local and area schools including supervision, teacher education, research, and development. In short, the states, and not the national government, hold the decisive controls over vocational education, even in the federally aided program. There is much more danger of undue and unwise state control over vocational education than there is of "federal dictation."

DECISIONS THE LOCAL AND AREA SCHOOLS MAY MAKE

In nearly all of the states the school districts are free to decide whether they will participate in the federally aided program or in any part of it. The school districts in most states are able to make the following decisions when they are sharing in the federally aided program:

1. They may decide whether there is to be organized, written, local policy for vocational education and how it is to be made.
2. They may decide the specific purposes of the program provided, select the clientele to be served, evaluate and improve the program, determine curricula and courses, choose teachers from among those approved by their states, and provide buildings and equipment better than the states require.
3. They may decide how vocational education is to be organized and administered in their schools.

In the states where local decisions of this order can be made, they are far more important than those made by the states or the nation. Only the local people have thus far been effective in providing program evaluation. However, federal and state funds continue to flow into many communities with programs that are ineffective because the local people do not exercise their responsibilities for evaluation. On the basis of local evaluation, programs are continued as they are, discontinued, or improved.

PROGRAMS CONDUCTED WITHOUT FEDERAL AID

Reference has been made to two of the largest programs of vocational and practical-arts education which are financed without federal assistance: business education and industrial arts. In certain large cities, the programs financed without federal aid are much larger than those that are financed with it. The public often misconceives vocational and practical-arts education because there are accurate, nation-wide statistics for only the federally aided program. The new and more comprehensive federal legislation of 1963 authorizes funds for education in office occupations and in other occupations for which federal funds have not been available. A more comprehensive picture of vocational education in the public schools will be presented as statistics on the newly aided programs begin to appear.

State, regional, and local policies for vocational and practical-arts education are usually developed separately for the federally aided and the unaided portions. The two may be administered separately.

Much state supervision may be provided for the aided program while little or no supervision is provided for the unaided program. The workers in the aided program are much better organized than the workers in the unaided programs.

CHANGING RELATIONSHIPS OF THE STATES TO THE SCHOOL DISTRICTS

The relationships of the states to the local and intermediate-school districts are undergoing change. In North Carolina, the school districts are required to submit to the state a plan for vocational education in agriculture which parallels the plan the state submits to the United States Office of Education. In several states, supervisors have been renamed "consultants." Consultant services from the state have been extended to school administrators and sometimes to local boards of education. Much more should be done by the states toward aiding the boards of local and intermediate districts to evolve policies for vocational and practical-arts education. Consultant services should be separated as completely as possible from administrative and regulatory functions. Those responsible for enforcing state policies and regulations cannot often serve as consultants. Consultant services should come in part from state agencies independent of state departments of education, particularly from the state universities.

The state departments of education are being called upon to perform more and more services in support of local and area programs of vocational education. Demands are increasing for state-level research and development, in-service education of vocational-education personnel, the preparation of curriculum guides and teaching materials, and many kinds of consultation services. While retaining some administrative and regulatory functions, these departments seem destined to become, to a far greater extent than they now are, service agencies for the schools.

The federal legislation of 1963 encourages co-operation among districts in providing broad programs of vocational education rather than provision of separate and perhaps narrower programs by each district. It is important that state departments of education be reorganized so that they will be able to advise more effectively with respect to local and area schools. Policy-makers will take more interest in a broad program of vocational and practical-arts education than they will take in a program for one of its subdivisions. Hope for getting adequate local and regional policies is increased by the 1963 legislation.

In many parts of the United States, the county has been the intermediate district; about a third of the counties of the United States are local school districts. But as the smaller elementary and secondary schools have been combined, the traditional intermediate districts have lost their significance. New types of intermediate districts are rapidly emerging, often to provide the vocational education the local schools cannot by themselves provide.

Deciding the nature and functions of these new intermediate or regional districts is one of the most important policy decisions the states now face.

New districts are being set up to provide junior or community colleges, vocational schools, and technical institutes. The concepts guiding the formation of these districts are usually limiting; the districts could be used for many purposes that have not been recognized in their formation. Districts have been created to provide training in a few industrial occupations for boys and young men or college-parallel courses for transfer students. Some of these districts never go beyond the precedents they have established; others organize additional programs as demands for them arise, so that they are forever adding patches instead of developing a program in keeping with a grand design.

Adequately conceived, these districts could provide continuing education for two-thirds or more of those who have left the local schools. They could also provide education for older high-school students, supplementing that available in the local schools. They should not only provide a central school for an area but extension centers for adult education and education for youth that the smaller high schools cannot offer. The feasibility of a comprehensive approach in developing education for a relatively large area of a state has been demonstrated.

Organizing for Policy-making

State-wide planning for the organization of the districts sponsoring area schools is urgently needed. Without such planning, the larger metropolitan areas will, no doubt, develop rather satisfactory schools; weak institutions will develop sporadically over some other sections of a state; and the rural areas will remain unserved.

State and area policies for area schools should be developed without delay. Some of the critical policy issues to be faced are:

1. How large must the area and the population be to support an adequate area school? Few states need or can support more than ten of these comprehensive institutions.

2. How can these institutions be designed so that they will serve all who need, want, and will profit from further education and will, at the same time, maintain appropriate standards in all that they do? New institutions strive for prestige. Some of them are seeking it by providing only college-level courses or programs in technical education with admission requirements as high or higher than the requirements for college entrance. In either case, they are excluding most of the population from services they need.

3. How can vocational and general education be balanced in these institutions? There is justified fear on the part of vocational educators of domination of these institutions by academic administrators and faculty members. If vocational-technical education is to receive its proper emphasis, provision for it must be built into the basic body of policy which the public or its representatives accept and to which continuing allegiance and support will be given. Competent administrators of vocational education must be employed and given all of the freedom they can appropriately be given. Special campuses for vocational-technical education may be justified in some cases. Advisory committees of citizens should be provided for the vocational-technical programs.

4. What assurances can be provided that adult education will receive proper attention? The number of adults eligible for services from these institutions is much greater than the number of youth of high-school age or just past high-school age. The education many adults require is both more extensive and intensive than adults have been getting in the programs of adult education that the public schools have been providing. Vocational education for adults may involve preparation for entering an occupation, upgrading in an occupation, or retraining for a new occupation. Any one of these may be time-consuming and expensive.

5. How are these new institutions to be related to the local public schools and the public colleges and universities? If area schools develop as they might and should, they will have a tremendous impact upon all public education from the kindergarten through the graduate school. Now is the time to measure their potential impact and to make the adjustments in thinking about the whole of public education that will be needed.

The local schools, relieved of a part of their responsibility for vocational education, will be able to perform better the functions that are left them. They can improve their programs of basic education, essential as a foundation for vocational education and employability. They can provide the vocational counseling that their charges need. They can step up their programs of practical-arts education, provided as a part of general education but helpful also as a background for vocational education. They can offer some specific vocational education for potential dropouts and those who will enter work after graduation from high school, providing them with salable skills. They can provide the beginnings of vocational education for clusters of occupations, with the expectation that specialized education for particular occupations will follow in the area schools. They can provide, with the help of the area schools, types of adult education that can best be offered in the local school districts.

The colleges and universities will be able to settle down to their traditional tasks of professional education, scholarship, and research instead of attempting to be all things to all men. The present trend toward college attendance by an ever rising percentage of high-school graduates can only result in frustration on the part of those who do not fit into the colleges and cannot get in college the education they need, and in ruination of the colleges for the purposes they have long served well.

ORGANIZING FOR LOCAL POLICY-MAKING

Much needs to be done toward developing policies for vocational education in the school districts; vocational educators have done little to promote their development.

Participants.—The board of education formulates official policies. It should be aided in developing these policies by administrators, the professional and nonprofessional staffs, citizen consulting committees, organizations interested in public education, agencies other than the public schools engaged in education, and consultants.

Public information and public hearings.—Existing policies and proposed changes in policy should be publicized widely in a school district. Public hearings should be held before a comprehensive policy statement is adopted. The support of the public is required. The public is entitled to know and to speak.

Time required to develop policy.—It is sometimes held that time will not permit consultation by a board of education with other agencies or with individuals. If decisions are being made so hurriedly that nonmembers cannot be consulted, one can be sure that the board is not developing long-term policies. Real policy is so important and its effects are so enduring that time must be taken. It may take two years to develop a statement of school policy in a district which has not had such a statement. Changes in policy will be necessary thereafter. If, however, sufficient time and thought are given in shaping an initial statement of policy, few changes during a generation are needed.

ORGANIZING FOR STATE POLICY-MAKING

There is need at the state level for the same broad participation in policy development and for the allotment of adequate time for policy development.

Legislatures and state boards which are responsible for vocational education occasionally set up commissions to make special studies. When this is done, it is usually because long-standing problems have become acute. These problems might not have developed if the state had provided the needed machinery for policy development.

The counterparts of the persons and agencies involved in policy development in the school districts are needed in developing state policy.

USE OF CITIZENS' COMMITTEES

Ours is a representative democracy, not a pure democracy. It is necessary to decide how much and what kind of representation of citizens is required in making public policy for education. Generally, the representation provided by the members of boards of education and legislators is inadequate. It needs to be supplemented by the use of citizens' advisory committees.

No other group of educators has been as enthusiastic as vocational educators regarding the use of citizens' committees. Sometimes advisory committees for vocational education have assumed functions that belong to boards; sometimes they have encroached upon the prerogatives of professional educators. It should be recognized that policy is the proper realm of the lay citizen and the one in which he can make the greatest contribution. Since there are authorized agencies for official policy-making, anything that an advisory committee does about policy must be related to the work of some official body.

Advisory committees that are parts of school systems should be appointed by and responsible to the policy-making body of the system. They can serve their sponsoring body by suggesting policy to be enacted and by reacting to current and proposed policies. In all of their work on policy development they must remain in regular communication with the official policy-making body.

Advisory groups of citizens serve also in advising the professional staff. This is a minor function in comparison with their contribution to the development of official policies for vocational education.

A discussion of the organization and use of citizens' committees in policy development is too involved and would be too long to be included in this chapter. The procedures suggested by the author for use in a school district can be adapted for use in dealing with state citizens' committees.[2]

The Policy-making Process

Codifying existing policies.—It is, first of all, necessary to organize existing policies that may be scattered in various places and to reduce unwritten policies to writing. When this has been done, it is possible to know what current policy really is, to detect gaps and inconsistencies, and to criticize particular policies.

Answering the basic policy questions.—The basic policy questions

2. Herbert M. Hamlin, *Citizen Participation in Local Policy-making for Public Education.* Urbana, Illinois: College of Education, University of Illinois, 1960.

have already been listed. Members of a policy-developing group should be allowed to think freely about these questions without being influenced unduly by present policies or the policies of other school systems.

Comparing policies with those of other systems.—Statements of policy adopted by other school systems cannot be copied in toto. Good examples of policy are few. However, much can be gained from a study of the policies adopted by other school systems.

Trial and revision.—No set of policies is likely to be completely satisfactory as first initiated. It must be tried and revised. Those who administer policy should be allowed to make exceptions when they are warranted, reporting the exceptions to the policy-makers so that policy changes can be made, if they are justified.

Summary

The federal government has provided, through successive acts, good examples of policy for vocational education. Unfortunately, there has not been continuous attention to national policy for vocational education. Major policy actions, preceded by reasonably adequate study and discussion, were taken in 1917 and 1963, forty-six years apart. In neither case was policy for vocational education integrated into national educational policy.

Nevertheless, the nation has done better than the states or the school districts in developing policy for vocational education. National policy has influenced state and local practices and, too often, has been substituted for state and local policies. The national government has demonstrated what can be accomplished when policy issues are carefully examined and action is taken regarding them. The states and the school districts could profit from the national example.

BIBLIOGRAPHY

HAMLIN, HERBERT M. *Citizen Participation in Local Policy-making for Public Education.* Urbana, Illinois: College of Education, University of Illinois, 1960.
———. *Public School Education in Agriculture: A Guide to Policy and Policy-making.* Danville, Illinois: Interstate Printers and Publishers, 1962.
HARRINGTON, GORDON M. "Vocational Education Moving in Diverse Directions," *Nation's Schools,* IX (July, 1957), 45–48.
NATIONAL SCHOOL BOARDS ASSOCIATION and AMERICAN ASSOCIATION OF SCHOOL

ADMINISTRATORS. *Reference Manual on Written School Board Policies and How To Develop Written Policies*. Evanston, Illinois: National School Boards Association, 1960.

O'NEAL, JOHN F. "The Status, Structure, and Functions of Citizens' Advisory Committees," *Journal of Educational Research*, LV (September, 1961), 29–32.

TUTTLE, EDWARD M. *School Board Leadership in America*. Danville, Illinois: Interstate Printers and Publishers, 1958.

WARMBROD, JAMES R. "State Policies for Distributing State and Federal Funds for Vocational Education in Agriculture to Local School Districts." Unpublished Doctoral dissertation, University of Illinois, 1962.

CHAPTER X

Rationale for Organizing, Administering, and Financing Vocational Education

WILLIAM P. MCLURE

Introduction

The issues concerning the general purpose of vocational education in our society are well drawn. The important questions concern the individual and society in general. As the child grows up, he must be educated for effective performance in all aspects of living. In a world of work there is no escape from the necessity for formal preparation of the individual for vocational pursuit. A strong society depends upon educated citizens. These are axioms which have less need for defense than for appraisal in the light of changing conditions.

The moot questions are specific. They are: What does the individual need to learn at various stages in his development? How long should he pursue formal education before entering full-time employment? Under what conditions, if any, should he resume formal education?

There are some differences of opinion expressed by authors of preceding chapters. These differences suggest the need for establishing educational policies at the various levels of government. They help to explain why practices vary throughout the country. Likewise, they help to explain the delay in adopting public policy to meet emerging needs.

This country must not provide less than a broad, comprehensive program of formal education for its citizens. No individual should suffer the lack of opportunity for his fullest development. Yet, about a third of the nation's youth leave high school before graduation. Less than half of those who graduate from high school enter college; and, of those who enter college, about half graduate.

In one way or another vocational education, or the lack of it, has an important bearing on this total pattern of dropouts and graduates. We cannot afford anything less than a system of education from kindergarten through the university which moves the terminal points of dropouts to successively higher educational levels. An increasing number of high-school graduates must continue formal education through junior college as well as beyond. This expansion and extension of opportunity will call for revisions in organization, administrative arrangements, and financial support of education.

Education through High School

What is the most probable future pattern of vocational education? More attention must be given to vocational work in the elementary and secondary schools, and more guidance relating to vocational work must be given to all youth. Specialized training is needed for some youth in high school. It is especially important for those who will enter employment after graduation. It is likewise important for some students who will pursue vocational programs in junior colleges and other institutions of higher education. In the upper elementary grades, starting in Grade VI, some retarded youth who are potential dropouts should be introduced to vocational work.

Leaders in government have as a common purpose the keeping of educational policies up to date. The principal difficulty lies in maintaining an effective structure of education in relation to the dynamic factors of social demand and individual choice. All too frequently the arguments about vocational education deal with little pieces of a large, complex problem, which involves every individual in one way or another at all stages of his development.

THE CONCEPTUAL PROBLEM

It might be helpful in resolving some issues to examine the general structure of education in terms of learning experiences of individuals. An outline which seems defensible is shown in Chart 1. The scheme presented in this diagram recognizes an expansion of knowledge and skill as the individual progresses (year by year) from kindergarten upward. The idea of expansion represents far more than mere accumulation of facts: it suggests everything that is known about the development of intellectual processes.

CHART I

THE STRUCTURE OF EDUCATION

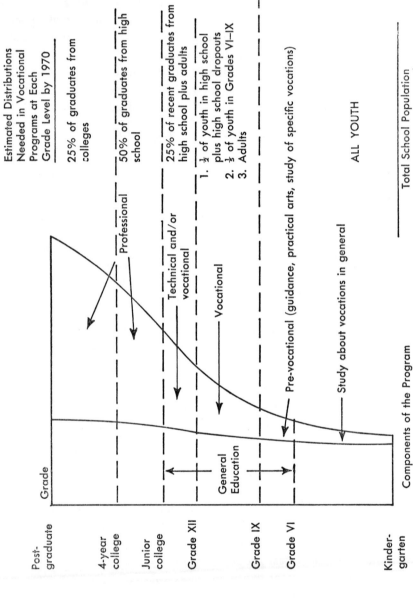

Grade		Estimated Distributions Needed in Vocational Programs at Each Grade Level by 1970
Post-graduate		
4-year college	Professional	25% of graduates from colleges
Junior college		50% of graduates from high school
Grade XII	Technical and/or vocational	25% of recent graduates from high school plus adults
Grade IX	Vocational — General Education	1. ½ of youth in high school plus high school dropouts
	Pre-vocational (guidance, practical arts, study of specific vocations)	2. ⅓ of youth in Grades VI–IX
Grade VI		3. Adults
Kinder-garten	Study about vocations in general	ALL YOUTH
	Components of the Program	Total School Population

No matter how we define them in detail, there are two basic components of education, the general and the vocational. The two are often indistinguishable except by operational definition. Whatever exists in practice relative to these components should meet the test of contributing to a well-rounded education of the individual.

THE LOCAL SCHOOL DISTRICT

The provision of adequate programs of vocational education in high schools raises some serious problems of organization. Local school systems have not been planned or organized in a way to make possible the provision of programs to meet the needs of youth and adults. In most states distribution of the population accounts for the existence of relatively few school systems of sufficient size to organize the variety of instructional programs and services needed.

In the great cities, the size of school population is not a primary factor in organization. Rather, the overriding problems are high population density, high rate of migration, excessive retardation, and social and economic deprivation as it affects a large part of the school population.

The rural areas and villages of America are, for the most part, areas of declining population. These are the areas that contain most of the school districts of inadequate size. There is a great deal of evidence to indicate that school districts need at least two thousand high-school pupils (not necessarily in one school) to organize effective and economical programs of instruction in all fields, including vocational education. This means that a twelve-grade district would have about eight thousand pupils in all grades.

The problem of reorganizing local districts into administrative units of adequate size in rural areas and small cities is an old and tiresome story. Consolidation of small districts has been slow and has fallen short of creating units with school populations of adequate size. There were 37,025 districts in the United States in 1961, 30,287 of which operated schools.[1] Of the 17,376 districts which provided elementary schools, only 533 enrolled over 1,200 pupils. Of the

1. United States Department of Commerce, Bureau of the Census, *Public School Systems in the United States, 1961–62*. 1962 Census of Population, Preliminary Report Number 3, GC-P3. July 6, 1962, p. 3.

1,240 high-school districts, only 261 had more than 1,200 pupils. Only 12,378 districts operated elementary and high schools. Of this number only 5,047 had more than 1,200 pupils in all grades. The estimated number of districts that enrolled 2,000 high-school pupils was about 2,000. In short, as late as 1961, about a third of the youth of the nation were in districts that were too small to offer programs of more than a general character.

One plan for securing a minimum population base—the consolidation of school districts—has been advocated for many years. But this plan runs head on against the desire to retain existing local control rather than to yield control to a community of larger size. Consolidation is the most logical solution if it does not result in transporting students excessive distances and in the loss of effective communication between the central office staff and the schools and neighborhoods.

THE REGIONAL UNIT

If the school population of a local district is too small to offer effective and economical programs in all fields, there is an alternative to consolidation. Two or more local districts could be organized into a regional (sometimes called area) unit which can provide special programs like vocational education. This plan is highly developed in New York State where a number of programs and services are offered through regional units called "boards of cooperative educational services." The office of county superintendent of schools in California similarly provides a number of services to underlying districts. A few other examples are found scattered throughout the nation. There are some examples of regional vocational schools, a few of which date back to the origin of the county vocational high school. In some of the large cities, there are special vocational high schools serving regions which include several regular high-school attendance areas. This latter arrangement seems feasible for the large city but not for the thinly populated areas.

The most promising arrangement in the sparsely populated areas is centralized special vocational programs for part-time attendance of students who choose them. Thus, students would be permitted to remain in the neighborhood high school for the general (basic) subjects. The vocational center could provide programs for three groups: (a) students in school, (b) youth who drop out of regular school, and (c) adults.

The crucial issue with respect to regional units of education is not whether they will or will not develop. The important question is whether they will develop as an *ad hoc* collection born of adversity and destined for an uncertain life of struggle or whether they will be planned and developed on a state-wide basis as powerful auxiliary units to all local school districts of the state.

There are many medium-size cities which have very limited programs of vocational education for their youth and adults. Expansion of the geographical base (attendance areas), without exceeding a reasonable commuting distance, would provide a school population of a number sufficiently large to allow a greater variety of offerings than could be offered in a neighborhood school such as is maintained in attendance districts as now defined. One of the greatest obstacles and points of difficulty in organizing large regional units is the division of social and political structures between rural and urban areas.

The growth of urbanization in America, accompanied by improvement in the means of transportation, has made it possible to organize educational programs of wide and easy accessibility to all. In Illinois, for example, a recent study[2] found that although 52 of the 102 counties in the state did not have a school district offering a single course in vocational-industrial education, it is possible to organize some 40 to 44 regions which could provide programs in all vocational fields. Too much of our school population is found in operational units (school districts) that are too small to provide adequate programs of vocational education.

At the other extreme, perhaps a third of the school population is in large cities. The circumstances in this situation are also unique. High population density, high rate of mobility, and a large measure of social and educational maladjustment present problems of organization. These communities have a much larger demand for vocational education than is found in most smaller communities.

2. William P. McLure, and Others, *Vocational and Technical Education in Illinois*, p. 163. Urbana, Illinois: Bureau of Educational Research, College of Education, University of Illinois, 1960.

THE STATE CENTRAL UNIT

There is considerable variation among states in the structure of central units of educational government. Forty-eight states now have state boards of education with general regulatory powers over public elementary and secondary schools and, in some cases over post–high-school institutions of junior college level as well. Eight states have special boards for vocational education, the type of agency created to administer federal vocational funds under the Smith-Hughes Act of 1917.

A separate agency at the state level for vocational education has proved to be an unsatisfactory arrangement. In forty-two states, the state board of education with general authority over the public schools is now designated as the agency to administer vocational education. However, there may yet be a question as to whether this unification of function at the policy-making level has achieved sufficient unification in the professional staff organization of state departments of education.

Many states need to adopt more functional arrangements in state central units in order to facilitate efficient organization in regional and local units of operation. Some states will have to decide whether it is better to leave education at the junior college level under the jurisdiction of the agency with responsibility for the public schools or to establish arrangements designed to make this institution a part of the system of higher education. Other states must decide whether to have two systems or one; that is, one for vocational and technical curricula and another for preprofessional (college-transfer) programs or an administratively unified system offering a comprehensive program. This is a basic policy decision which will determine the nature of organization for vocational education in the state central agency.

FINANCE

The problem of finance is ubiquitous. In many respects it is more basic than organization. This is especially true in situations in which the size of the school population or of the segment in need of particular programs in vocational education is not limiting. The large systems are operating at such a marginal level of support that necessary improvements cannot be effected in the scope and quality of the education they offer without raising this level.

Significant adjustments in the large cities come in large packages. The extensive changes that they require often involve from three to five thousand students. For example, the writer recently observed two high schools in a large city, one in a depressed neighborhood and another in a reasonably affluent section. Each school had about three thousand students, but the composition in terms of achievement, ability, motivation, and other characteristics differed sharply. The pupils of the former had a median I.Q. of 87, and the rate of retardation was high. Only 25 per cent of the Freshmen stay in school to graduate. The pupils of the latter school had a median I.Q. of about 115, and the rate of retardation was low. Ninety per cent of the Freshmen in this school graduate. Less than a third of the graduates of the former school attend college. Eighty per cent of the graduates of the latter attend college.

The programs of these two schools are similar. There are no vocational subjects—only industrial arts for a relatively few students. Both schools are located on sites that are too small for building expansion. The buildings are about fifty years old, structurally sound, in the eyes of the public too good to abandon but, in reality, too poor for economical renovation.

Each school needs to have its program reorganized to include some vocational education. The problem is too complicated to be solved by merely substituting a few shops for some academic classrooms. This would only accentuate the crowded conditions and leave the basic program of general education unchanged. These examples illustrate the problem and one cause of rigidity, which so commonly besets the public schools. They do not have ample fiscal resources to cope with this difficulty.

The financing of vocational education cannot be taken out of the context of support for the total program. A half-century of experience with specially earmarked funds leaves the basic problem of financing this phase of education unsolved. What has happened is that special administrative and financial structures have tended to unbalance the entire system. This tendency has resulted from a distribution of intergovernmental revenues on the principles of stimulation of a narrowly defined program. Grants have been limited to defined programs meeting specified characteristics, and for this reason work of a prevocational nature has not been introduced. In 1960 the United States Office of Education[3] reported a total current expenditure of $238,811,800.00 in the public schools for vocational education, as it is defined, for federal reimbursement. Of this total, $45,313,200.00 (about 19 per cent) were obtained through grants from the federal government. The total figure does not represent the true expenditures for vocational education in the public elementary and secondary schools, however. Expenditures are not reported for instruction in any field which does not receive federal reimbursement.

During the past decade the trends in state fiscal policy (with respect to education) have been toward the development of a comprehensive and unified policy. The federal government has gone counter to these trends with renewal of the long-standing practice of special federal aids through the National Defense Education Act of 1958, the Manpower Development and Training Act of 1962, and the Vocational Education Act of 1963. It remains to be seen whether a more unifying principle will be invoked by the federal government at some future date after evaluating developments under the present policy.

Two common methods have been used in the distribution of state grants for special programs. One is matching local funds, either on a fixed or a variable percentage basis; the other is a distribution based on budget approval, with certain criteria defined as the basis for determining the amount of the grant. These methods are used in conjunction with the federally reimbursed programs.

Various means for the improvement of financing vocational education have been considered. A first promising step would be the establishment of a broad definition of vocational education of an integral character. A coherent program of guidance and counseling, prevocational instruction, and vocational work should extend from elementary school through high school. Earmarked funds should not be attached to fragments or narrowly defined categories as has been the practice too often in the past. Instead, funds should be allocated in such a manner as to foster a program of adequate scope and proper

3. *Digest of Annual Reports of State Boards for Vocational Education.* United States Department of Health, Education, and Welfare, Office of Education. Washington: Government Printing Office, 1960.

sequence in both the general and vocational components of education from the early orientation stage to the level of specialized training.

Education beyond the High School

The turmoil in education beyond the high school is no less than it is at the lower levels. To some observers, the emotional attachments and biases that develop from widely different experiences suggest a lack of central purpose. To others, the experiences of the past half-century represent a period of experimentation, the consequences of which result in erratic development on a broad front.

Education at this level has experienced the throes of change similar to those experienced by the high school as it attempted to expand its offerings from a narrow academic program for the few to a comprehensive program for all youth and for adults. Post-high-school institutions are now faced with mass education for an increasingly heterogeneous population. The demands for effective social and occupational performance (of individuals) require that increasing numbers of persons continue formal education to higher levels than seemingly were necessary in previous years.

FORCES OF CHANGE

It is important to note the implications of the current social and economic forces which call for changes in vocational education at the junior college[4] level. This level is defined as education which is suitable to the intellectual and social development of individuals who have completed high school or its equivalent. Programs normally require two years for completion, but a few may require only one year, and others as many as three. There are two general purposes to be served: One is that of preparing some individuals for vocational

4. The term "junior college" is not an ideal one. Some persons in the vocational and technical fields dislike it for good reasons. Traditionally, most junior colleges offered mainly the Freshman and Sophomore work of the four-year academic institutions. Until recent years only a few of them ventured to expand their programs to include specialized curricula in the so-called vocational and technical fields. Other terms are likewise inadequate. "Community college" is too provincial. "Two-year college" is inadequate because a few curricula are one year in length and others require three years. The writer prefers "junior college" because it suggests programs of less than four years. He would hope that time will erase the early stigma which some attach to this name as these institutions enlarge their mission and develop comprehensive programs. In the meantime, a more generic term than this one will be welcomed if someone invents it.

and technical work which requires higher skills and knowledge (cognitive) than high school can provide. The other is that of providing general education for some students whose choice of vocation requires four or more years of college work and who expect to transfer to senior institutions.

These two types of curricula, the vocational or technical and the preprofessional (college-transfer), have a common core of general or academic education. The student who is studying to become an electronics technician should pursue some study beyond the high school in such basic fields as English, history, economics, and mathematics. The prelegal student would devote all his time during these years to a selected group of general subjects. These characteristics of programs are important considerations in developing criteria for organizing and financing education at the junior-college level.

There are then certain realities which each state must face sooner or later in deciding what patterns of organization and finance will be adopted to meet the challenge of vocational and technical education at the junior-college level. The major ones are as follows:

1. The need to educate a larger segment of the population
2. The need for a broadening educational purpose.
3. The need for a common core of general education for specialized vocational-technical curricula and preprofessional curricula.
4. An increasing demand for institutions to provide educational opportunity within commuting distance of the student's home
5. The growth of urbanization with concentrations of population in a relatively few centers
6. The increasing numbers of youth seeking post-high-school education who are financially unable to attend the traditional residential type of institution
7. The increasing numbers of employed adults seeking post-high-school education
8. The need for counseling service on a broader scale and better related to the public schools than at present

ASSESSMENT OF THE STATUS QUO

Given these circumstances, the next questions logically relate to the organization and financing of needed programs. How can such programs as outlined in previous chapters be organized and operated to accomplish the currently perceived purposes of vocational education at the post-high-school level? How can financial resources be

utilized efficiently to accomplish these ends? These are the types of
questions which call for reassessment of educational policy by state
governments. The few states that have considered these questions
have concluded that the problems involved are of such magnitude as
to require a new interpretation of the responsibility of the state.

Traditionally, state responsibility has been interpreted generally
as responsibility which could be delegated to the administrative units
which operate locally as part of the fabric of individual communities
of varying sizes and occupational composition. The local operating
unit has had to bear the awesome responsibility of interpreting the
purpose of education. At the same time it has had to make its choices
in terms of the circumstances which it could control.

What we have in most states, therefore, is a loosely co-ordinated
aggregation of local operating units, consisting in most cases of single
institutions. Limited financial resources and size and character of the
population force most of these institutions to establish highly eclectic
purposes and, thus, to offer programs of very narrow scope. A high
degree of provincialism has been inescapable. Under such conditions,
the concept of meeting the needs of the community has come to
mean a local educational program designed to match the manpower
requirements of local occupations as far as local resources permit.

The problem ultimately gets reduced to simple economic terms
of balancing input with output. The total educational program tends
to be built around this economic law as it applies locally. Since financial support is predominantly local, it is expected that the investment
in trained manpower will remain in the community. High priority
tends to be placed on programs that promise to be of local benefit.

The educational needs of youth and adults who must find employment elsewhere are given a low priority. Resources put into programs
for these individuals are exported, and the indirect benefits accruing
locally through membership in a more prosperous state or nation,
though real, are difficult for citizens to perceive. Certainly some
communities would receive more indirect benefits than others,
though such benefits have not been measurable.

The establishment of programs in the specialized areas of vocational and technical education has suffered more public resistance
than the establishment of general programs for students planning to
transfer to senior institutions. Programs which train for the profes-

sions are older and better established. Citizens have become accustomed to paying taxes to support a state institution which opens doors to a wide variety of opportunities for its youth. They have grown accustomed to the type of higher education which provides for all communities the specialized training of workers in the professions. It is understandable, therefore, why the junior college, though a local institution, has gained comparatively wide support. It has served primarily the function of the state institution for Freshmen and Sophomores. But this type of junior college has problems related to the aforementioned interpretation of the input-output economic equation. Many citizens who pay local taxes to support local junior colleges argue that they pay double, since they also pay taxes to support the state institutions. The benefits of local investment in the junior college are thought of primarily in terms of benefit to the community rather than to the individual.

The possible range of specialization in vocational and technical education is so great that a state system of junior-college education is imperative. It is difficult to see how anything less can cope with the problem. The educational needs of individuals are not circumscribed by social, political, and geographical boundaries of communities. They extend to the state and even to the entire nation. There is no problem of either state or national concern which does not in some way reach down into every community.

This does not mean that educational institutions must be located in every community or that every institution must offer everything needed by all individuals in the state or the nation. The most compelling need today is an organization with state-wide coverage which omits nothing of importance. A rational state system, in other words, is a necessity. In addition, supplementary participation of the federal government seems necessary to make good the shortcomings of states, to remedy the lack of interstate articulation, and to deal with problems of superstate responsibility.

STATE SYSTEM OF COMPREHENSIVE JUNIOR COLLEGES

The most imaginative structure for vocational and technical education of less than four-year-college level is a state system of comprehensive junior colleges. This system would consist of regional administrative units located strategically with reference to distribution of population and co-ordinated by a state agency for higher education. Most states can be divided into a few regions centered around the larger cities in such a way that programs can be offered within reach of most potential students who are willing to commute. Only very sparsely settled areas would find such a pattern impractical. Where possible, a region should have a minimum of about 500,000 inhabitants, which would provide an enrolment demand of full-time and part-time students sufficient to justify 20 to 25 curricula or specialized programs. This is about half the number of two-year programs needed in each of the large industrial states. These figures are optimal. Establishing regional units with a smaller population would be justified in sparsely settled areas in order to maintain reasonable commuting distances for their youth. Regional units with larger and more concentrated population could provide more than 25 programs.

Regional systems could operate more than one operating unit or instructional center. Extension branches could be combined with a central unit to offer a great diversity of educational opportunity within commuting distances of most students. Some students will prefer the traditional, residential pattern of living on or near the campus. Others will find this a necessity when lack of a preferred program requires transfer to a school some distance from their homes. The least mobile students are the part-time ones—those who are employed and want further education for retraining or for upgrading themselves. Hence, it is important for them to have a wide choice of specialized programs.

The American experience in the governance of public higher education suggests that a regional board of junior-college education would be an appropriate agency of control. The regional board, which would be responsible to a state board of higher education, would have powers to discharge responsibilities delegated to it by the state board and as prescribed by state legislation.

Each region would consist of a single administrative unit in charge of the operating units. Existing public junior colleges would be integrated into the regional system and reorganized appropriately in accordance with local and regional needs. The professional staff would be organized with a chief executive officer responsible to the regional board. A central staff would provide fiscal, personnel, guidance, and other services for the whole system.

This brief description is illustrative of a basic principle of organization: namely, a state structure of large-scale operation with flexibility to meet the problem of diversity. Such an organization can respond with vigor to the choices of individual students and the needs of society. This design would not call for eliminating existing public institutions but for strengthening them. Some might continue their traditional role. Others would prefer to enlarge their offerings.

Such a system organized on a state-wide basis would take into account the existence and work of private institutions. In some communities the private institution may be meeting the local needs satisfactorily. In other cases, this institution is concentrating on a few highly specialized fields which draw relatively few students from the community. Thus, the public system would augment rather than duplicate or compete with the private institution.

A state system of comprehensive junior colleges would be adaptable to atypical structures such as technical institutes and lower-division departments in some univeristies. These institutions make unique contributions, but they do not show evidence of representing a pattern of organization for general coverage of a state.

The regional system is conceived as a single administrative unit which is prepared to handle large numbers of students. Enrolments would range from around 3,000 upward. The system would be unique in terms of its programs, purposes, and clientele. The central operating unit would have a campus with buildings designed for various purposes. Extension or auxiliary centers, too, would need adequate facilities, but ordinarily they would not be complete colleges. They would include the academic courses for which elaborate outlay of laboratories and shops are not required. Some of these branches might well offer the total program for college-transfer students of the locality. Specialized staff might be utilized in more than one center. The students in the vocational and technical curricula might take their general subjects in these branches and commute to the central unit for their specialized work. These are examples of the kinds of flexibility which could exist under a large regional system.

ARTICULATION

The junior colleges face a problem of articulation with the high schools and the senior institutions of higher education. In addition they need a functional relationship with agriculture, business, industry, and government. These relations can be maintained only by planned programs with competent staff for special assignments.

Articulation with the high school depends heavily on working with the school in guidance, counseling, and other ways. Some mutual planning of instructional programs is essential. In this planning, two purposes are uppermost for the junior college: One is to assist the student in making the most intelligent choice of occupation. The other is to assist the high school in planning the best possible background for the student who is to enter the junior college.

Articulation of junior with senior institutions of higher education is equally important to college-transfer students. Advisement of students requires projecting plans of individuals beyond the junior college. To this end effective communication with all departments in the senior institutions is necessary. Planning of courses in terms of content and sequence is an important consideration in all areas.

Articulation between the junior college and the world of work requires a large amount of time from the staff in the areas of specialization. Guidance, instruction, and placement must be kept in close relation to the various occupations.

DUAL SYSTEMS

There is an alternative to the state system of comprehensive junior colleges. This is a dual system consisting of institutions, two basic types of which would predominate. One would offer a general academic program for students planning to transfer to senior institutions. The other would concentrate on the terminal vocational and technical programs, with supporting work in general education. The technical institute and the area vocational school are examples of the latter. The technical institute has limited its program primarily to subengineering work of a highly technical nature, necessitating a a heavy reliance on science and mathematics. The basic or general education component varies from one-third to half of the total program. There has been a tendency in recent years to increase the amount of general education to provide a better balanced program.

Vocational schools have tended to train for jobs requiring less knowledge of an academic nature and more manipulative skill. Many of these schools do not clearly distinguish between the level of work of high school and post high school. However, there is a distinction which can be made for most of the work. Many of these institutions accept students who either have not graduated from high school or who have had no vocational work in it. The initial work offered to these individuals is essentially deferred work and is elementary in character. Much of the vocational preparation in some junior colleges and vocational schools of presumed post-high-school level could be done equally well in high school or in regional programs, described earlier in this chapter. The lack of clear distinction between these two levels of educational performance undoubtedly has contributed to the lower prestige of some of these institutions as compared with other institutions whose programs are all of post-high-school grade.

There is ample evidence to support this conclusion in the experience of the newer type of comprehensive junior colleges in California, New York, and Florida. Among these institutions there are programs covering a wide range of occupations in agricultural, business, distributive, and industrial fields. The specialized training is usually not so highly technical as that of the engineering fields, but the depth of knowledge and skill goes beyond the capacity of the high-school student. Students enrolling in those programs meet general academic standards comparable to those entering the professional and highly technical fields. Moreover, these students continue study, along with other students, of such general-education subjects as English, history, and economics. Thus, the broad range of vocational preparation at the junior-college level is achieving a status of quality that is comparable to education for the technical fields.

Some states may become embroiled in the issue of whether to establish a system of comprehensive junior colleges or a dual system consisting of academic junior colleges and vocational-technical institutes. If they decide upon the latter, they may drastically reduce the degree of freedom of opportunity available to students.

The roots of dual systems already exist. In most states, junior colleges are of the academic type. They are staffed by academicians to offer academic programs. Only in recent years have some of them begun to introduce a few vocational courses in response to the general demand for expansion of the purpose of this kind of institution. On the other hand, there is another professional group with specialization in industrial-arts and vocational fields. This group has been con-

cerned primarily with operating prevocational and vocational programs in high schools, special vocational schools, and technical institutes.

Naturally, each professional group tends to favor its own field.
These biases can be managed in a competitive yet constructive manner in a single, comprehensive system. The organization can establish
policies and procedures to insure fair and impartial emphasis on each
of these two fields.

If, however, there is not a working consensus between these two
groups, the result can lead to dual structures of organization and
control. Each one develops its own arguments and justification for its
type of institution. Loyalties are developed in the populace for each
type. In the end, some intrinsic values may be lost. Duplication, excessive cost, eliminated or foregone educational offerings, and limited
choices for many individuals may be some of the hidden outcomes of
dual systems.

The justification for dual institutions should rest on the same basic
educational criteria as the comprehensive type. These consist of such
things as breadth of opportunity, accessibility to the maximum number of potential students, capacity to insure high quality of instruction, economy of operation, and administrative feasibility in terms of
basic interpersonal relations.

STATE FISCAL POLICY

An administrative structure under which essential programs of
junior-college education can be organized and operated is one of two
fundamental necessities. The other need is the establishment of
appropriate fiscal policies.

It is difficult to see how any state-wide system of junior colleges
can function with great flexibility and capacity without state support.
The principle of state and local partnership borrowed from the public schools is hardly adequate for junior colleges. Since most junior
colleges have evolved as an extension of high schools, it is understandable how this principle became established as a basis for their
support. If states find it difficult to break entirely with this tradition,
the major emphasis, at least, should be placed on state support and
only minor emphasis on local or regional support. The source of rev-
enue for local administration is the property tax. But this source is

already hard pressed to support of public schools and local government.

The tradition of state support for senior institutions of higher education is well established in every state. The method of legislative appropriation is a sound means of meeting the budget requests of higher educational institutions. This procedure would be equally feasible for a state-wide system of comprehensive junior colleges and vocational technical institutes.

States like California, Florida, and New York which have divided the support between the state and the regional unit have only transitional policies. As their institutions increase in size and complexity to cope with the needs of the times, these states will inevitably move farther toward complete state support.

Other states which have not established long-range policies are confronted with these fundamental problems of organizational and financial structures. College enrolments will increase very sharply by 1970 if facilities are available. Any state which does not make significant strides toward meeting this need by that time will then begin to experience the economic effects of its failure.

What will be the cost of this type of education? One study[5] recently presented some estimates for an extensive program for Illinois. Estimated costs were based on a selected group of newly maturing comprehensive-type junior colleges with campuses designed to offer comprehensive programs. Operating costs in 1959–60 were averaging over $800.00 per full-time pupil and over $500.00 per full-time equivalent pupil in part-time evening classes in the vocational and technical programs. The costs per full-time college transfer student were about $700.00 per year. Estimates for 1965–66 were about 18 per cent higher, or about $1,000.00, $625.00, and $850.00, respectively. The costs of capital outlay at 1960 prices were estimated at an average of $3,000.00 per full-time student. These figures are close to predictions of national averages for the period 1965 to 1970.

FEDERAL POLICY

The organization of the United States Office of Education reflects the pattern in the various states. The Division of Vocational and Technical Education has been organized to work with state boards of

5. McLure et al., op. cit., p. 159.

education which have supervision over the public elementary- and secondary-school programs and over other agencies which have jurisdiction over vocational programs in junior colleges and special vocational schools.

The Division of Higher Education in the Office of Education is not functionally related to the vocational and technical programs in the junior colleges and other post-high-school institutions. It would appear that there is a need at the federal level somewhat analogous to that of the states, namely, that functional structures for post–high-school education should be separated from those for the public elementary and secondary schools.

Post-high-school education of college grade, regardless of the nature of the program, is higher education. Grade level is more important as a principle of organizing units of operation and control than the existing division along vocational and academic lines. It is true, as pointed out earlier, that some courses and even programs in the junior colleges, particularly for dropouts and adults, are of high-school grade in difficulty. But these courses represent a minor rather than a major function of these institutions and, thus, should not be a determining factor in the location of control.

Some important changes in federal fiscal policy appear to be essential. The first change should be to make a distinction between public school (elementary and secondary) and post-high-school vocational programs. Policies for all higher education are in need of reassessment. The complexity of the problem, however, suggests that education at the junior-college level has a uniqueness of purpose and operation for which federal policies should be clarified.

The second needed change in federal policy is a shift from the existing narrowly defined categories to broader bases for financial aid. At the high-school level the total vocational component, including prevocational work, should constitute the basis of grants.

At the junior-college level the total curriculum of a given occupational field should be the basis for grants rather than the specialized vocational component. This principle recognizes programs as integral units. The general-education component is essential to the well-rounded development of the specialist and should not be omitted from consideration. Specialization in occupational fields is sufficiently advanced at this level to define the total curriculum or program for each field of work. This is not true of programs in the high school, hence this principle appears to be less valid for that level.

The principle of determination of fiscal policy by the program or curriculum is not new. It is established, to a limited extent, in the present Rehabilitation Act, which takes into account the costs of all factors essential to the accomplishment of the individual's educational goals.

Such a policy applied at the post-high-school level would result in relating programs to manpower needs better than do present policies. Also, the policy would be neutral with respect to patterns of organization. In technical institutes, the total enrolment might be the basis for consideration. In comprehensive junior colleges, only the enrolments in vocational and technical curricula would be included. Part-time programs could be included easily by converting part-time course loads of students to full-time equivalents.

A third needed change in federal policy is the substitution of a more comprehensive sharing of support with the states for the present procedures of reimbursement. It is time for the federal government to adopt a broad base of sharing by matching state expenditures for these programs at high-school and post-high-school levels. The share of the expenditures derived from the federal government should be determined by a formula based on the taxpaying ability and effort of the states to support the respective phases of education.

Such a policy would move the federal government away from its present position as a stimulator. Instead, it would serve as a means of enabling every state to provide adequate financial support for a defensible program. Adoption of this principle might foreshadow an eventual policy of federal assistance for support of the total public educational system, which many advocates have long urged. In the meantime, if policies are revised to raise the position of vocational education, the total system will gain sorely needed strength.

BIBLIOGRAPHY

1. AMERICAN EDUCATIONAL RESEARCH ASSOCIATION. "Vocational, Technical, and Practical Arts Education," *Review of Educational Research*, XXXII, No. 4 (October, 1962).
2. ARNOLD, WALTER M. "Area Vocational Education Programs." (Reprint from *School Life*, January, 1960). Washington: United States Office of Education, 1960.

3. CLARK, BURTON R. *The Open Door College: A Case Study*. New York: McGraw-Hill Book Co., Inc., 1960.
4. *Economics of Higher Education*. Edited by Selma J. Mushkin. United States Department of Health, Education, and Welfare, Office of Education, OE-50027, No. 5. Washington: Government Printing Office, 1962.
5. *Education for a Changing World of Work*. Report of the Panel of Consultants on Vocational Education. United States Department of Health, Education, and Welfare, Office of Education, OE-80021. Washington: Government Printing Office, 1963.
6. EMERSON, LYNN A. *Vocational-Technical Education for American Industry*. United States Department of Health, Education, and Welfare, Office of Education Circular No. 530. Washington: Government Printing Office, 1958.
7. FIELDS, RALPH R. *The Community College Movement*. New York: McGraw-Hill Book Co., Inc., 1962.
8. FLESHER, W. A.; FLESHER, MARIE A.; REESE, ROBERT M.; and OTHERS. *Public Vocational-Technical Education in Oregon*. Columbus, Ohio: School Survey Service, 1958.
9. HAMLIN, HERBERT M. "Adult Occupational Education," *Handbook of Adult Education in the United States*, chap. xlvi, pp. 542–50. Chicago: Adult Education of the U.S.A., 1960.
10. HENNINGER, G. ROSS. *The Technical Institute in America*. New York: McGraw-Hill Book Co., Inc., 1959.
11. JARVIE, L. L. "Plans and Programs for Post-High-School Education Outside the Usual Patterns of Higher Education," *Review of Educational Research*, XXIV, No. 4 (October, 1954), 277–84.
12. MEDSKER, LELAND L. *The Junior College: Progress and Prospect*. New York: McGraw-Hill Book Co., Inc., 1960.
13. McLURE, WILLIAM P., and OTHERS. *Vocational and Technical Education in Illinois*. Urbana, Illinois: Bureau of Educational Research, College of Education, University of Illinois, 1960.
14. McLURE, WILLIAM P. *Federal Financing of Vocational Education*. Report to Panel of Consultants on Vocational Education. United States Department of Health, Education, and Welfare, Office of Education, August 10, 1962. Washington: Government Printing Office, 1962.
15. NATIONAL MANPOWER COUNCIL. *Improving the Work Skills of the Nation*. New York: Columbia University Press, 1955.
16. SMITH, L. F., and LIPSETT, L. *The Technical Institute*. New York: McGraw-Hill Book Co., Inc., 1956.
17. THORNTON, JAMES W., JR. *The Community Junior College*. New York: John Wiley & Sons, Inc., 1960.
18. *Vocational Education for Rural America*. Edited by Gordon I. Swanson. Washington: Department of Rural Education, National Education Association, 1958.
19. WOOD, HERBERT S. *A Study of Techincal Education in California*. Sacramento, California: California State Department of Education, September, 1959.

CHAPTER XI

Responsibilities of Nonpublic Agencies for Conducting Vocational Education

CLAUDE W. FAWCETT

Rapid technological advancement in the past two decades, with the consequent shortage of highly skilled manpower, has forced employers and nonpublic organizations supported by them to assume more and more responsibility for vocational education. The extraordinary expansion of human knowledge, and its subsequent inclusion in the public school curriculum, has caused many curriculum specialists to strive to eliminate some vocational education from the crowded program of instruction of the public school. Competition for the scarce tax dollar in fast-growing metropolitan centers has forced educators to seek elimination of educational services that might possibly be cared for in any other way. Despite the fact that this country is moving toward a maximal industrialism faster than any other in the world, the temptation to shift responsibility for vocational education to nonpublic agencies has been almost irresistible.

The arguments to support the shift of such responsibility are manifold and often seem reasonable. Vocational education is expensive. Space to house a program is the most expensive of any part of the public school plant. Machinery and equipment are special; in a period of rapid technological development, they become obsolete almost before their special features are learned by the instructors. New processes, machinery, procedures, and unusual solutions to problems constitute the average corporation's major resources for competing with others in the market place; they are often closely guarded secrets and deliberately made unavailable to others. It seems to some that the vocational-education program of public agencies tends to lag behind current vocational practice. This line of reasoning inevitably leads to the suggestion that it is the nonpublic agency that should bear the prime responsibility for vocational education.

It is simple to declare that someone else must bear the responsibility for what amounts to a public service essential to the common good of the society, but it is quite another thing to make sure that he is willing or, by the very nature of his unique role in that society, is able to bear such responsibility. Whether employers, trade associations, employee associations, proprietary and nonprofit institutions, or voluntary organizations, singly or co-operatively, can provide sufficient vocational education to meet the needs of our society is largely determined by their purposes and resources. It is well to inquire concerning their potential in this matter.

Employers

The success of any enterprise depends upon its ability to select, develop, and retain individuals whose skills, attitudes, and knowledge are essential to the accomplishment of its goals. Since work assignments made to individuals within the work plan of the organization are usually unique in terms of the goals of the organization, it is normal to expect that no person at the time of first employment will possess completely the highest skills, the most desirable attitudes, or the most complete knowledge essential to the best possible execution of his assignment. Goals of the organization change and this necessitates reassignment of individuals. When such change occurs, the organization can either employ new people and train them or it can retrain old employees. All employees, if they have truly identified their own hopes and desires with the goals of the organization, are motivated to develop their potential service. Some show promise of developing rarer skills which may be useful to the organization, but identification is soon lost unless opportunities for development are provided for them. These facts suggest that vocational education is an essential part of the normal personnel process of a healthy organization.

Phelps and Gallagher describe the personnel-planning process to determine training needs in a business organization as follows:

1. The office of corporate planning must be able to anticipate and identify the shifting requirements for technical capabilities within the com-

pany. The number of personnel needed, their level of competence, and the date by which they should be ready must be forecast.

2. Each job requirement must be run through the matching process in order to:

—establish the relation of the present mix of capabilities to the capabilities forecast for one, two, three, and five years hence (showing those capabilities for which there will be a continuing demand, those which will be in short supply, and those which will be in excess).

—locate any qualified employees.

—identify the capabilities of the most likely groups of trainees for each requirement.

3. Training activities must be planned which will bring employees to the level of competence needed at the time requisitions for the additional capabilities are anticipated. Other training programs must be established for the employees who have potentially unneeded capabilities in order to develop new qualifications which would enable them to be moved into areas of need.

4. The number of trainees to be brought into the company each year from all sources . . . must be estimated.[1]

It is clear from the foregoing that each organization, if it is to succeed in accomplishing its purposes, must enter into the vocational-education field. Phelps and Gallagher have established some dimensions of the program. It is significant that their statement of the fourth need includes the expression "the number of trainees." This suggests that an organization will normally need to commit itself to a vocational-training program for most entering employees. The extent and nature of such threshold training will inevitably be determined not only by the demands of the jobs into which recruits are to be placed but also by the supply available. One Southern California aircraft company needed machinists for a very difficult mechanical process. Research determined that an extraordinarily high intelligence level was required to learn the skills involved. Its own employees, when canvassed, could not provide the number needed; nor could exterior sources provide the additional required number of skilled machinists. Therefore, the company established a recruiting policy of employing unskilled individuals who displayed the essential intelligence level and mechanical aptitude for learning. The vocational-education program established was complete; trainees were taught the skills during a lengthy training period. This is an example

1. Ernest D. Phelps and William Gallagher, "Integrated Approach to Technical Staffing," *Harvard Business Review*, XLI, No. 4 (July-August, 1963), 122-29.

of the length to which an organization may have to go in threshold training to satisfy its staffing needs.

Another type of threshold vocational-education need arises when the organization has adopted a process, or installed a machine, which is unique. No person recruited could normally have had any experience with it. If the current work force fails to provide sufficient numbers of potential trainees for the machine, it will be necessary to recruit and to train new employees for the positions required. Often it is possible to rely on the makers of the machine for this service. For example, the International Business Machines Corporation, because of the relatively small number of some of its large computing and recording machines, is estimated to have trained during the past year in excess of 100,000 employees for companies using its machines. This training activity of the company developing the machine, of course, increases the market demand for the product, since availability of skilled operators is almost always a condition of purchase.

The training program for employees of a company has several facets other than threshold training. Practically no one on original employment has all the skills, attitudes, or knowledge that represent the most complete capabilities for the assignment. It is imperative that an in-service-training program be directed toward developing the next most difficult skill, the next most desirable attitude, and the next most needed body of knowledge. Any organization that fails to take this essential upgrading problem into account will suffer losses in its attempts to meet its goals. Another facet is the need to prepare individuals for more difficult assignments. Retirements, deaths, and separations inevitably cause skill losses within an organization. If the organization fails to anticipate these skill losses and fails to have individuals within the organization in training to provide the needed skills, it must struggle manfully to select persons with the lost skills from other organizations. Often the new employee comes in with a long retraining program facing him, and the organization suffers until it is completed.

Yet another facet of training within the organization is the essential process of change. New processes, products, and new solutions to operational problems effect changes in requirements for skills, attitudes, and knowledge. In adjusting to changes, however, familiarity with the organization represents a major reservoir of knowledge that is not lost. Employees who can be retrained for new organizational needs present a lesser job of training. Nevertheless changes are essential to an organization which wishes to keep current its capabilities for meeting organizational goals. Consequently, retraining is also essential.

Employers meet these needs for vocational education in many ways. The most common, of course, is the placement of the responsibility upon the employee's supervisor. This procedure is reminiscent of the guild system of master and apprentice and is the chief source of instruction in vocational education in any organization. But this personal tutoring is seldom sufficient to meet the demands of the organization. Supervisors have other specific organizational responsibilities; training of employees is often done casually, after other work is done. Another solution is the formal educational programs which have grown up in some organizations.

Clark and Sloan report that factories in our industrial complex have carried vocational education farther than almost any other organization. They say:

> Factories today have classrooms, organized programs of studies, faculties, textbooks and examinations, and even graduation exercises with diplomas. Educational budgets often rival those of good-sized colleges, and expenditures per student are not infrequently two and a half or three times the national average for conventional institutions.[2]

They report that one corporation, for example, offers 111 separate courses. There are two semesters of instruction per year of either 10 or 16 weks. Classes meet twice per week, usually from 1:00 to 3:00 P.M. or 7:00 to 9:00 P.M. Most classes are held on the employee's time. Some are restricted to employees, and others are open to employees' families and the public. Tuition is charged but kept low. Of the 111 courses, 60 are technical and are specifically designed to meet company needs. Twenty-three courses are managerial and supervisory; thirteen are clerical; and fifteen cover academic subjects.[3] Other companies report that they hold classes on the company's time and restrict courses to those that can be shown to be specifically directed toward advancing the company's goals.

2. Harold F. Clark and Harold S. Sloan, *Classrooms in the Factories*. Rutherford, New Jersey: Institute of Research, Fairleigh Dickinson University, 1960.

3. *Ibid.*, pp. 97–98.

In summing up the significance of these industrial schools, Clark and Sloan evaluate this movement as follows:

It is possible that we are now witnessing, in the educational activities of American industry, the birth of a third great educational force of far-reaching consequences. For, just as the first [growth of medieval universities] has perpetuated learning, the second [development of the free public school system] has provided bulwarks for democracy and for a free economy, so this third innovation is adapting civilization to a new technological era, the ultimate consequences of which stagger the imagination. Nor is this merely an adjustment to mechanical wonders. It is an integration of the new technical skills and revitalized human relationships, envisaging a world augmented not only in material comforts but, far more important, in spiritual values.[4]

Strong as the vocational-education program may be in the industrial sector of our economy, it is not clear that other sectors are following this practice with as much vigor or insight. Clark and Sloan repeated their study of industrial education in retail establishments. They summarize their findings as follows:

There are classrooms in the stores, but not many. Even among the 36 largest retailers to which the present study is primarily directed, three reported no educational activities falling within the definition adopted for the study. And, as the stores decline in size, the percentage of establishments maintaining no formal training programs grows rapidly. Although there is a definite trend toward larger retail organizations in the United States, the shift is not sufficiently strong as yet to make retailing anything but a predominantly small-store operation. The total amounts of formal education conducted by retail establishments, therefore, is extremely limited.[5]

Despite the fact that we are indebted to a retail company, Lord and Taylor of New York, for the first business program of personnel evaluation (1914), it is apparent that retail establishments have failed to follow up with personnel-training programs to develop skills found to be wanting. This is not intended to suggest that no training is done in retail stores. Whatever is done is usually left to the employee's immediate supervisor.

Another plan used by many business firms to provide vocational education for their employees is to send them to either public or

4. *Ibid.*, pp. 134-35.

5. Harold F. Clark and Harold S. Sloan, *Classrooms in the Stores*. Sweet Springs, Missouri: Roxbury Press, 1962.

private schools. This program has several facets also. Sometimes the company is willing to pay tuition, fees, and costs of instructional materials for the employee in those courses of instruction which are clearly identifiable as tending to assist the employees to more nearly achieve company goals. Sometimes the subsidy is dependent upon the employee having earned a passing grade in the course. One of the most unique programs is sponsored by a manufacturer in Los Angeles. The company furnishes, as a loan, the funds for all costs of instruction. While completing the course, the employee pays a proportionate part of the loan back to the company at each pay period. At the conclusion of the course, if the employee has satisfactorily completed it, the entire cost, now paid back to the company, is refunded to him. This procedure is designed to secure regular attendance and a satisfactory level of participation.

Vocational-education programs in public institutions are used extensively and supported by business firms. International Business Machines, for example, not only conducts its own training programs but co-operates with schools and colleges in the development of skills of its own employees. The Chrysler Corporation spends about a quarter of a million dollars per year in supporting vocational education in public schools through trouble-shooting contests and similar programs. The Sears Roebuck Foundation contributes time of its employees and money to the support of vocational education in public institutions. The Distributive Education Clubs of America are supported by funds from a number of companies. These are but a few examples of the types of support given to public institutions by business firms to assure the continuation of quality vocational-education programs in public institutions.

Some public support for vocational programs comes indirectly from government funds through business firms. Many governmental contracts, designating specified amounts for the training of personnel, are awarded to private contractors. Businesses may spend these funds for the creation of vocational-educational programs of their own, but most such funds are utilized in the development of co-operative programs of instruction in either public or private institutions. This method of distributing public funds was chosen so that the contractor could assure himself of training programs tailored to his corporate needs.

There are problems in co-operative vocational-education programs: Courses offered by an institution normally conform to institutional customs and traditions. Often they cannot be designed to be
of more than casual assistance to a single company. Frequently, the
relationship between the course of instruction and the employee's
service to the company is not really defined or clearly understood
either by the employee, the company, or the training institution.
Often there is little continuity from one course to another. The
temptation of the employee is to complete a degree or achieve some
other noncompany goal. As a result of these "squeaks" in the co-
operative training process, sometimes these activities, unless specifically designed to meet company needs, are of doubtful value either
to the employee or the organization for which he works.

During recent years the demand has grown for companies to educate managerial personnel by providing them a year of instruction at
company expense in liberal-arts colleges. For the year of college
attendance, the company pays all costs of instruction and the full
salary of the individual. Companies have paid full costs of instruction
to provide opportunities for individuals to train themselves for the
more unusual occupations within their organizations. The controlling
factor in these activities of companies is the scarcity of the supply of
individuals for given activities and the scarcity of the individuals with
capabilities for learning them.

Thus, we see that the employer is forced to treat the component
skills, attitudes, and knowledge of the employees as an economic
resource which provides, as do tools, buildings, and land, an important and valuable means by which organizational goals can be attained. The method of husbanding them and treating them has been
described by Phelps and Gallagher as follows:

1. Classify and index the knowledge, skills, and experience of all . . .
employees in the company.

2. Classify and index the qualifications of all prospective candidates for
employment.

3. Match the qualifications which are required in job openings (as they
are made known) with the qualifications of present and prospective employees. (Then the candidates meeting these requirements should be referred in an order which gives precedence to present employees.)

4. Conduct joint planning by (what are now) the recruitment and

training groups to fill the openings estimated by the corporate long-range planning committee. (A policy of promoting and/or transferring employees whenever possible should be followed.) Hiring from the outside should be done only at customary entering levels—except for those key positions where no candidates exist in the company.[6]

Several problems are readily identifiable when one contemplates abandoning the responsibility for vocational education in our culture to employers only. Even though some segments of industry are working extremely hard at the task of providing vocational education, only the larger companies are deeply involved, have comprehensive programs, and are succeeding in carrying on reasonably successful programs of instruction. Smaller companies (90 per cent of all businesses in this country employ fewer than 100) can afford few programs; their interests are narrow, and their needs cover only a small spectrum of the vocational-education needs of the society. Some businesses are almost unaware of their organizational stake in vocational education for employees. The interests of the employer in vocational education are necessarily restricted to the vocational education that will serve to develop the skills, attitudes, and knowledge of the employees that are pertinent to the goals of the organization. In the light of these quite-restrictive factors, it seems unwise for our culture to rely too much on the employer for vocational education, even though he must rely on a self-supported program to develop the resources vital to his organization.

If vocational education came to be provided entirely by employers, some additional dangers to society would necessarily be encountered. Public programs are essential for the employee who wishes to move from one employer to another. They are vital to secure for the workman an opportunity to move from one occupation to another, particularly if he is occupying what is considered to be his proper niche in the organization for which he works. Vocational education includes many things besides skills, attitudes, and knowledge essential to one employer. It involves general concepts of ethics, human relationships, and public responsibility that are broader than the needs of a single employer. The public, consequently, must maintain programs designed for the interests of the society as a whole.

6. Phelps and Gallagher, *op. cit.*, p. 127.

Trade Associations

The vocational-education programs of trade associations are not designed to assist society in meeting many of its needs. These groups are made up of representatives from similar businesses. They are formed for many reasons. Most are concerned with the ethical practices of members. Almost all foster some kind of defensive procedure against government regulations. Almost all provide some central service in connection with collective-bargaining procedures with unions. Many are gravely concerned with tax allocations. Some have directed their activities toward common research, particularly in developing new uses for products and new products from waste materials. Vocational education is a peripheral function growing out of other organizational activities.

Nevertheless, trade associations do provide some vocational-education programs. The Merchants and Manufacturers Association of Los Angeles conducts an annual training conference for business executives generally oriented to personnel and general management problems. The National Association of Manufacturers conducts training programs for personnel executives. The Forest Products Laboratory of Ann Arbor, Michigan, trains representatives of lumber-producing and processing companies in manufacturing new products. The Iron and Coal Institute has provided materials for instruction in public schools, as has the American Petroleum Institute. These activities can be classified as vocational education only if it is given the most general definition possible. They represent more an extension of other purposes of the trade association than an organized interest in providing functional vocational education for the public as a whole.

Employee Associations

Nor is direct responsibility for vocational education central to the purposes of the employee association at the present time. This is a strange conclusion to reach in the light of the history of apprenticeship in this country. There was a time when the apprenticeship program, modeled after the medieval guild system, was about the only path to successful completion of a vocational-education program. The employee association has acquired other goals and purposes which have been described as follows:

The reasons [why people join labor unions] are exclusion of competitors for jobs now held by union members; control of salaries and wages; regularizing standards of performance in jobs held by members; setting standards of education for admission to jobs; controlling conditions that keep the organizations supplying jobs healthy; maintaining union membership; and participating in political activity. . . .[7]

There was a time before the advent of the industrial union that the craft union was directly concerned with the vocational education of its members. The craft union controlled apprenticeship by the exercise of its power over work permits. The educational program for an apprentice was specified by the union itself. Responsible members of the employee association were gravely concerned about the capability of a member of the union to produce. After the passage of the Smith-Hughes Act of 1917, which the American Federation of Labor strongly supported, the grave concern of the union for the apprenticeship declined. There were several contributing factors.

The mild boom of the late twenties gave way to more than a decade of economic depression. Reduced working staffs in most organizations caused unions to emphasize the restriction of membership to its older members. The depression was broken by the advent of World War II. The expansion of the economy combined with the withdrawal of large numbers of technically trained personnel for military service created such a shortage of skilled workers that the normal processes of vocational education were inadequate to provide the individuals needed. Two lines of activity were instituted to meet the shortage. First, complicated technical jobs were broken down into components that could be filled with individuals trained through short, intensive courses of instruction. The thirty-hour training program was more the rule than the exception. Second, more and more skills were built into new machinery so that the age of automation was accelerated in our industrial complex. In addition, by 1941, the movement of population in this country from locality to locality, county to county, and from state to state began to accelerate rapidly. And another development that materially changed the union's direct interest in vocational education was the growth of the industrial union under the Wagner Act of 1934 and the Labor-Management

7. Claude W. Fawcett, "Education and the National Economy," in *Foundations of Education*, p. 312. Edited by George F. Kneller. New York: John Wiley & Sons, 1963.

Relations Act of 1946. The competition between craft and industrial unions for membership has changed the character of the craft union's interest in vocational education. Principally, the craft union has had to be less restrictive in its membership.

During the depression years the restrictive, protective impulse of the unions caused them to severely limit the number of persons admitted to apprenticeships. When the great demand for vocationally educated persons came along during the war years, it was obviously impossible to utilize the apprenticeship to fill the burgeoning needs of the economy. Government-sponsored programs of vocational education emphasized the utilization of women and other casual workers for less skilled occupations. Movements of population, however, have had the greatest depressing effect on the maintenance of training standards in the crafts. Fast-growing centers of population created needs for skilled craftsmen faster than any local employee association could provide them. We entered the era of the verbal apprentice. Individuals who used to be called "boomers" in a more stable economy simply reported to employers their capabilities for performing certain skilled jobs. They were put to work; they were needed so badly that the union had to accept them regardless of formal apprenticeships or prior skills. The movement was encouraged by the competition of the industrial union, which was willing to accept all the individuals in a particular industry into its membership. In order to adjust to these changing conditions, the employer was forced during the fourth decade of this century to institute and develop company training programs to assure the development of competence among employees.

As a result of these developments, the usual employee associations have lost direct interest in vocational-education programs. They normally co-operate fully with the state agencies interested in developing the apprenticeship. Their members serve on labor-management-state committees on the apprenticeship. They admit to work large numbers of apprentices. The San Diego area alone has more than a thousand apprentices involved in forty-two classes of skilled jobs and more than seventy different occupations. The program of instruction, however, is carried on jointly by the employer and co-operating public education agencies. The chief contribution of the union to this process is the issuance of work permits, participation in the setting of standards, and acceptance of the apprentice as a journeyman on completion of his training period.

Thus, it is possible to note that the shifting purposes of employee associations have caused them to assume a different role in vocational education. Conscious of their political strength in the society, employee associations have become strong advocates for increased federal, state, and local expenditures for vocational education. During recent national planning for vocational education, some of the strongest advocates for extended federal expenditures in this field were representatives of employee associations. Full support for expanded state expenditures can be expected from these groups. Thus, the traditional role of direct participation in vocational education has gradually been displaced by group support for public programs.

Direct participation has not been entirely lost, however, because many union contracts call for both union and employer contributions to educational funds. The electrical workers in California, for example, have established such a contribution on the basis of each hour of work done. These funds are used for upgrading employees in the association, for retraining individuals whose skills are obsolescent because of technological change, and for general programs of improving the education of members. Much of the actual teaching is done by public agencies.

This role in vocational education is quite a contrast to that of the American Medical Association, for example, which not only sets standards for admission to the profession by developing training programs and qualifying examinations but also accredits medical schools, admits to specialties within medicine, and disciplines inept practitioners of the medical arts. An exception occurs occasionally among labor unions. In an earnest attempt to improve the capabilities of master plumbers to cope with building codes, health regulations, and modern construction, the plumbers' union has developed, with many junior colleges, two-year programs to provide collegiate training for their members. This trend is consistent with the growing necessity for collegiate training to provide technicians for our more difficult occupations in society. We may anticipate further growth of this trend as automation creates the necessity for a technician to know as much as an engineer knew in 1930 and to have learned all of it in no more than two years of post-secondary-school instruction.

Proprietary and Nonprofit Institutions

It is difficult to differentiate between proprietary and nonprofit institutions. Tax laws in our society today have given so many advantages to the latter that many proprietary institutions have been turned into nonprofit organizations with the founder and originator receiving a salary rather than a profit from the organization's operation.

The role of the proprietary and nonprofit institution in vocational education is vital to the success of vocational education as a whole. As has been noted, public agencies, through no fault of their own, do tend to be behind the times. In addition to the aforementioned secrecy of employing organizations, there is the normal reluctance of any organization supported by public funds to venture into any new and untried program of instruction. By virtue of its uniqueness, a program may encounter so much opposition that funds for its support are withheld. If funds are provided, the program may be so unusual that it is misunderstood and criticized severely enough to affect other activities. As a result, it is often difficult to maintain a growing edge of experimentation among educational programs conducted by public agencies.

The history of education is replete with instances demonstrating that the slowness of public agencies to take on responsibilities essential to the culture has led to the creation of proprietary or nonprofit institutions to carry on the work. Usually, in our society, the experimentation done by private agencies has finally, when proved successful, forced public agencies to assume the responsibility formerly borne by the private agency alone. Some notable instances can be cited. Augustus Storrs started the Storrs Agricultural School in Mansfield, Connecticut, in 1881—seven years before the University of Minnesota established a secondary school of agriculture in connection with its Department of Agriculture, and long before agriculture was an acceptable program of instruction in public schools. The Workingman's School, established by Felix Adler in New York, emphasized the idea of work as a cultural rather than a vocational aspect of the regular curriculum. This school later became the Ethical Culture Society, and the need to teach industrial arts as a general-education function in an industrial society has been accepted. The

Drexel Institute in Philadelphia, the Mechanics Institute in Boston, the Case Institute in Cleveland, all are instances in which proprietary or nonprofit organizations have experimented with new programs or new curricula for the eventual benefit of the society as a whole.

This pattern continues, and it is to be hoped that it always will. There are specialized proprietary and nonprofit schools devoted to the preparation of individuals in highly specialized occupations. The Gibbs School for secretaries, for example, prepares medical, legal, and executive secretaries for highly specialized work. It is difficult for the public agency to operate a program for a few people. Certain vocational schools are supported largely by corporations within a particular industry to prepare individuals rather specifically for those industries. Schools, such as the New Haven Junior College, pioneered in the preparation of sales engineers for firms manufacturing specialty products. The proprietary or nonprofit vocational-education school has advantages in that it can experiment with new programs of instruction. It can feel free to co-operate directly with a group of employers, tailoring its program largely to suit their interests. As a matter of fact, a private school in this sector of the vocational-education field is forced to experiment with the new, the unusual, and the experimental in order to maintain a clientele which will support its activities. In being forced to do the new and the unusual in order to survive, the production of practices and programs of benefit to the society is speeded up. This activity is essential to continued growth and development of vocational education.

It should be noted, however, that the opportunity to experiment, to develop new ideas and programs, to carry on a program of real benefit to vocational education is dependent upon support and fiscal health. There are private proprietary and nonprofit schools that are literally one jump ahead of bankruptcy. They have neither experimental programs nor unusual students. These organizations succeed only in preying on unsuspecting students who are, all too often, unaware that they are being exploited.

A few trends in the development of successful private organizations can be anticipated. The rapid growth of automation, and its consequent requirement for technicians, will almost certainly push proprietary and nonprofit institutions devoted to vocational education to some semblance of collegiate instruction. It is to be expected that they will identify themselves largely with the junior college. Growth of corporate training programs will encourage small businesses to seek a joint program that will serve the common needs of several organizations which are too small individually to justify a complete educational program. New occupations, such as that of computer technician, for example, are likely to become the focus of these new organizations. It should be noted that the schools may not be new in the sense that they are newly created entities; they may be new only in the sense that prior organizations have shifted emphasis and programs to adapt to a new market in the culture. In any event, these experimenters are essential to continued growth and development of vocational education in this country.

Voluntary Organizations

The history of vocational education is filled with the names of voluntary organizations designed to promote the interests of vocational education. Some, like the National Society for the Promotion of Industrial Education organized in New York in 1906, were designed specifically to promote the establishment of vocational-education programs. Its successor, the American Vocational Association, was designed not only to provide professionals in the field with opportunities to exchange information but also to exert influence in securing governmental action to carry on vocational-education work. This influence is exerted by providing consultants to legislative committees, to administrative officers of the government, and to various governmental bodies. It assists members of Congress to obtain data essential to the preparation of legislation concerning vocational education. It summons up essential field support to urge senators and representatives to act in the vocational field.

Other organizations have been devoted to gathering information and distributing it to employees in particular occupations or industries. Some of the early societies established for this purpose were as follows:

1744—American Philosophical Society
1781—New Jersey Society for Promoting Agriculture, Commerce, and the Arts
1785—South Carolina Society for Promoting and Improving Agriculture and Other Rural Concerns

1792—Massachusetts Society for Promoting Agriculture
1794—Society for Promoting Agriculture in the State of Connecticut
1809—Columbian Agricultural Society
1811—Society of Virginia for Promoting Agriculture.[8]

The American Home Economics Association was organized in 1909 with the avowed intent of improving living conditions in the home, in institutions, and in the community. Other voluntary associations could be named, but the purposes of these groups are clear; interested citizens voluntarily are contributing their time either to gather and disseminate vocational information deemed by them to be essential for public welfare or to seek better ways through existing institutions to fill an observed public need.

Federal and state governments have assumed so much responsibility for vocational education and have provided so much monetary support that the role of the voluntary association has, at times, been assumed to be largely political in character. Organizations enrolling teachers and administrators of vocational education have often been labeled institutions of the "Establishment," the implication being that they were primarily concerned with conserving the program as it was in order to maintain positions for their members, continuing support from the government, and occupational respectability. Laymen belonging to voluntary organizations have been branded as tools of employers, dupes of the profession, and amateur politicians dedicated to the satisfaction of selfish ends, either political or economic. Such charges are undoubtedly true in the case of a minority of individuals within a minority of the organizations, but the nature of the political process demands that some group or groups of individuals in the society take responsibility for studying the problem, actively supporting their recommendations, and informing government representatives of their thinking and research. If this is not done, it is quite likely that no one will take direct responsibility for a process quite essential to the survival of an industrial culture. The long-range expectation of the public must be that the voluntary organization dedicated to selfish ends must inevitably fail, because its operations must reveal its selfish ends so clearly that it will lose, as many self-

8. Melvin L. Barlow, "Vocational and Practical Arts Education," in *Foundations of Education*, op. cit., p. 543.

seeking groups in the past have lost, the public support it must have to exist.

It is particularly important in this period of rapid change that the voluntary organization be encouraged to grow in influence and in numbers. A relatively free market for ideas about education now exists. Groups, overwhelmed with the mass of new knowledge being produced, have been pushing harder than ever for the elimination of almost all but academic instruction in public schools and universities. The idea of compelling the study of mathematics and science has spread to other academic subjects. At the same time, the fact that scientific discoveries have been translated into major changes in products, processes, and machinery in industry has gone almost unnoticed. These changes have revolutionized the job assignments in our modern business activity. If we fail to maintain a labor force capable of utilizing and intelligently understanding the new work required, the new knowledge is quite likely to become ineffective in our culture. Competitive organizations devoted to the dissemination of knowledge concerning the vocational needs of our industrial culture are essential to insure intelligent public judgment concerning the balance of instruction essential to our modern life.

Summary

The foregoing discussion suggests that the hope of some educators that vocational education can be largely abandoned in the public schools and universities is vain. Employers are performing, and shall probably expand, the vocational-education activities that are relevant to their organizations. They, however, should not be expected to work outside the framework of their organizational goals. Education provided by employers does not constitute a program sufficiently broad and comprehensive to meet the needs of our society. Trade associations and employee associations can be counted on to assist in the vocational-education process, but again, only when it is related and supportive to the goals of their organizations. Proprietary and nonprofit vocational-education organizations may shift their forms, but they are essential to the conduct of the experimentation in vocational education. From such experimentation, adaptations can be and historically have been accepted in instructional programs of public institutions. Voluntary associations are essential to the maintenance of the dialogue concerning the educational process in the public forum which resolves the educational issues of the society. It would be disastrous for either the public or nonpublic agencies dealing with vocational education to abandon their time-honored functions which have developed through the thought and practice of the past two centuries. The problem is to allocate resources so that both public and private organizations can make their full contribution to vocational education in a time of great change.

CHAPTER XII

Research in Vocational Education

GEORGE L. BRANDON and RUPERT N. EVANS

Structure of Research

Research is a quest for new knowledge or for a more useful interpretation of facts which are already known. Research of any type can be classified under one or more of the categories appearing in Table 1, which also presents examples of types belonging to each category and drawn from two fields of specialization.[1]

This chapter, since it is concerned with research in vocational education, will discuss only types 3, 4, 5, and 6, as presented in Table 1. We must recognize, however, that unless the results of research types 1 and 2 are known to our researchers, their work will be seriously handicapped and may be completely worthless.

Purposes of Research in Vocational Education

PROGRAM-PLANNING

More than most other types of education, vocational education must change its structure and content to adapt to rapidly changing occupational requirements. New groups of trainees may need to be served. Programs in unusual occupations may need a new area-school structure if they are to be implemented. Expansions and contractions of existing programs may be needed.

The basic research tools for program-planning in vocational edu-

1. Based on a paradigm developed by David Clark in conjunction with Ernest Hilgard and Lloyd G. Humphreys at a meeting sponsored by the Social Science Research Council on "The Behavioral Sciences in Education" at Cornell University on June 23–25, 1961. As recorded in *Dissemination and Implementation: Third Annual Phi Delta Kappa Symposium on Educational Research*, p. 107. Edited by Keith Goldhammer and Stanley Elam, 1962. The last two columns have been added by the authors of this chapter.

cation include (*a*) community occupational surveys; (*b*) recommendations of local advisory committees, representing management and labor; and (*c*) occupational analyses. Vocational education has pioneered in the use of these three techniques of research. Until quite recently, no other phase of education planned its program on as sound a research basis as did vocational education.

However, changed social and economic conditions have tended to outmode the research tools we have used so successfully in the past.

TABLE 1

CATEGORIES FOR THE CLASSIFICATION OF RESEARCH

CATEGORY	EXAMPLES FROM TWO AREAS OF SPECIALIZATION	
	Testing	Guidance
1. Basic scientific investigation (content indifferent)	Learning theory	Decision-making
2. Basic scientific investigation (content relevant)	Transferability of skills	Theory of occupational choice
3. Investigation of educationally oriented problems	Development of a test of skills	Effect of vocational-education classes on occupational choice
4. Classroom experimentation	Norming, validating, standardizing	Trial of units on occupational choice in selected classes, with revision as necessary
5. Field testing	Packaging, feasibility testing	Test of new program in a broad sample of schools
6. Demonstration and dissemination	Advertising and marketing	Installation of new program in schools which agree to explain it to visitors, plus other dissemination activities

Increasing worker mobility demands that we replace community surveys with state, regional, or national occupational surveys. Increased worker mobility and a desire for vocational education in less common occupations demand that recommendations be obtained from advisory groups representing larger areas than a single school district. The rise of occupations which require a high level of knowledge and a low level of manipulative skill demands new forms of occupational analysis based on factors other than "operations" or "jobs."[2]

2. R. M. Gagné, "Military Training and Principles of Learning," *American Psychologist*, XVII (1962), 82–91.

OPERATIONS RESEARCH

Every vocational teacher, head of a vocational department, or principal of a vocational school is concerned with the operating effectiveness of his program; but research techniques for determining such effectiveness have been almost entirely unused. Studies of cost per student clearly showed that costs of vocational education were much higher than those of most other educational programs; consequently, these studies have been little used, even for comparative purposes. Except in a few states, it has been assumed (not tested) that teachers with ample occupational experience know the subject matter that they are expected to teach; that students who study three or four hours per day learn more than those who study two hours per day; that skills learned in school are transferred to jobs; that students who observe demonstrations and read books learn more than students who observe demonstrations; and that students at the close of a vocational program know more than they did at its beginning.

EVALUATION

One of the best techniques of evaluation has been the follow-up of graduates to determine the extent to which they were placed and succeeded in the occupations for which they were trained. The results of follow-up studies have obvious implications for both program-planning and operations. Unfortunately, this type of study has been of little use to the homemaking-oriented home-economics program or to the farm-oriented agriculture program. In the former case, almost every student became a homemaker; and in the latter case, relatively few were able to become farmers. In other areas of vocational education, including the more modern types of agricultural and home-economics education, it is valuable to know that placement rates of 60 per cent for high-school programs and 80 per cent for classes completing part-time co-operative (work-study) programs are typical.[3] Unfortunately, data on success in the occupation are much less frequently available.

3. T. J. Cote *et al.*, *Follow-up Study of 1961 Graduates of Trade and Industrial Programs in Public Vocational and Technical High Schools, North Atlantic Region* (Washington: United States Office of Education, Trade and Industrial Education Branch); "Placement Record of Vocational Graduates by Trade, 1960–61" (Columbus, Ohio: State Department of Education, Division of Vocational Education, Trade and Industrial Service, 1961, mimeographed).

Since vocational education is usually justified on economic grounds, it is surprising that we have almost no studies of the economics of vocational education.[4] The few studies of the economics of education as a whole invariably assume that each school curriculum has the same economic utility. This assumption is absurd.

EVALUATION OF PAST AND PRESENT RESEARCH ACTIVITIES

Too often in vocational education only one type of research—program planning—has been stressed. Even here, there has been a regrettable tendency to conduct such studies only once—when the program is begun—and not to repeat them periodically. Operations research and evaluation have been too often nonexistent except in theses for college degrees. Unfortunately, thesis research in vocational education, as in most social sciences, is too unrelated and covers too little ground to add much to new knowledge.

It is perhaps true of most new fields that a missionary spirit, rather than a questioning spirit, prevails. Vocational education is surely old enough and sufficiently well established and accepted to allow it to adopt a questioning and discriminating attitude about each of its practices and programs.

Data for Research

SOCIAL BOOKKEEPING

Data are needed for program-planning at local, state, and national levels. Some persons must be the bookkeepers for society if we are to make intelligent plans. Two sets of books are needed for our planning: we need to know the supply of trained workers, and we need to know the demand for them.

We know how many new automobiles are produced each year, but we do not know how many automobile repairmen complete training in vocational schools, on the job, or in schools of the armed forces. Moreover, we have almost no information on the *quality* of the supply.

Program-planning for School "A" must take into account the number and quality of students prepared in all other schools and

4. One exception is D. J. Pucel and R. N. Evans, "Manpower Economics and Vocational Education," *American Vocational Journal*, XXXIX (April, 1964), 18–22.

agencies. As Ginzberg points out, opportunity for vocational education is a function of its distribution. We know less than we should about the geographic distribution of vocational education, and we know practically nothing about other factors which limit certain individuals in the choice of occupational training.

Perhaps equally important for program-planning is information about the *demand* for workers. We know about how many loaves of bread will be needed next year and five years hence, but we do not know the number of new wheat farmers, new bakers, and new bakery salesmen that will be needed in the future. The task of predicting demand for trained workers is particularly difficult in new and in rapidly changing occupations.

As Arnstein points out in chapter iii, we have no accurate data on job vacancies. It seems obvious, however, that we know more about the demand for trained workers than we do about the supply. Moreover, we have better quantitative than qualitative data.

Because worker mobility makes bookkeeping on the labor force almost impossible at the state level, it would appear reasonable for the federal government to assume responsibility and to utilize in the task its relationships with the growing chain of regional and state offices. A logical division of the task among government agencies would be for the Department of Labor to collect data on demand and the Department of Health, Education, and Welfare to collect data on supply.

OPERATING PROGRAMS

Each local and state vocational program needs to collect data and conduct research aimed at improving the quality and efficiency of its operations. Studies of student and teacher selection; comparative studies of methods of organization, instruction, and placement; and cost accounting would provide a basis for more efficient local operation and could be used as bench marks for other programs.

EXPERIMENTAL PROGRAMS

Each state should encourage the development of experimental and pilot programs, which would gather data to help answer such questions as the following: Which of several types of prevocational programs is best? How much supervision is desirable in part-time co-operative programs? What time allotments work best for each instructional area? What are the relative merits of different methods of training teachers? Findings from such studies would allow much more valid generalizations than those from the operational research noted in the preceding paragraph.

RESULTS FROM RELATED FIELDS

Research effort in vocational education is seriously weakened by the failure to utilize results from studies in industry and the armed forces and the failure to utilize research techniques developed by economists, psychologists, and sociologists. It will be one of our major tasks to acquire an intimate knowledge of these and other techniques and to apply that knowledge to vocational education. When one considers the volume of technical, personnel, and basic research production from other disciplines and fields with which vocational education is directly related, he becomes aware that it is staggering. Specific personnel and provisions of the nature of a center or clearinghouse are required for its proper dissemination and use.

The following selection of research results and techniques in various disciplines and fields of application indicate just a few of the interesting and profitable avenues for our exploration and study:

1. New methods of teaching and learning through many new media, numerous "synthetics," programed-learning, computer-based instruction, and so forth. Many aspects of so-called "related instruction" in vocational education are uniquely adaptable to these media.

2. The sociology and economics of occupations, mobility, basic literacy, status and prediction of population age groups, women in multicareers, obsolescent and promising careers, gross national product and the economic value of manpower, implications of automation and technology, international production and competition, and so forth. Vocational education cannot plan or evaluate its program without insights which research in these and other areas will provide.

3. The broad fields of personnel research, training, and utilization: skill levels of employment, occupational analysis, personnel classifications, classification and description of occupations, worker traits and qualifications, occupational testing and selection, transferability of skills, industrial training and evaluation, training curriculum re-

search, civilian counterparts of military occupations, new categories of workers and needs in government, industry, agriculture, business, welfare, public service, and so on. Vocational education has profited from research in these areas in the past, but we have not systematically kept abreast of new knowledge and techniques.

Inasmuch as a great many of the results and techniques in these broad, related fields are rigidly tested in pilot programs and field trials, it is critically important that vocational educators, particularly researchers, keep abreast of developments and results. Resources in many of the fields are too many to be appraised and consolidated, in fact the careful selection and appraisal of resources and results constitute a major research problem in itself. For the proper solution of the problem, specific personnel and a center or clearinghouse are required.

The Recruitment and Development of Research Personnel

VAST SCOPE AND NATURE OF RESEARCH

Research demands have far outstripped research manpower and resources. The decision to meet our multitude of research needs may be the most critical decision in this age, requiring our utmost determination. The needs and nature of modern vocational education as they are presented in this volume, and the goal of our research effort, are made evident by Arnold:

> The very nature of work is changing . . . occupations which were once well defined are now blurred into functions that combine a cluster of skills. Within each and every one of the categories of vocational education, as we define them today, there is a wealth of opportunity to blend the specialized knowledges of teachers and administrators for the purpose of creating new categories and defining new occupational fields in which there is new demand for manpower. . . .[5]

Essentially, the existence of the situation described by Arnold means that our research needs will not be fulfilled by any realization of unrealistic expectations of research production on the part of our already overburdened teachers, supervisors, and teacher-education personnel. Not only must full-time personnel be allocated to the

5. "News," *Industrial Arts and Vocational Education*, LII (November, 1963), 4.

research function but personnel from the various disciplines and professions must also be enlisted for the task. Vocational education as a powerful social, economic, and technological force can only be the product of knowledge originating from a research-team effort. Research—data and methodology—must become interdisciplinary in nature, attack, and application.

RECRUITMENT OF RESEARCH PERSONNEL

If our research needs are interdisciplinary, we cannot recruit research personnel solely from the ranks of professional or higher education. Interested, competent personnel must also be recruited from research scholars in government, industry, business, agriculture, and the social sciences. Unless there is a new covenant which accepts and deliberately provides for interdisciplinary recruiting in our research organization, the strait jackets of our traditional requirements, administrative regulations, and state plans will nullify our effort toward interdisciplinary research. We must locate, recruit, and educate research personnel; they must be attracted by compensation and opportunities in line with their interests. If the role and nature of occupational education are to be clarified by the various professions, only federal and state administrative policies that alone can make possible such clarification must be adopted. Our research program should utilize research administrators, project directors, designers, technicians, statisticians, and others, and, in addition, those persons who are needed to perform the essential reporting, dissemination, implementation, and education functions. However, if it were presently possible to recruit and finance the operations of such a staff of researchers, current regulations which primarily require experience in both occupations and vocational teaching would prohibit their employment.

DEVELOPMENT OF RESEARCH PERSONNEL

Vocational education, a traditional advocate of intensive planning and organized instruction, should make new applications of its principles to the development of an adequate and effective research corps. We need research based on the assumptions and techniques of education, sociology, economics, and psychology and in the various subject-matter areas, such as mathematics and science. In addition to an effective recruitment service, the following (and many other) development activities may be productive:

1. Early identification and stimulation of research interest and potential of professional personnel at all levels.
2. Deliberate, planned instruction in research in the professional preparatory and in-service programs of teacher and supervisor education.
3. Generous, research-encouraging provisions and standards in administrative regulations to make research-personnel-in-training eligible for employment in a multitude of research-personnel categories.
4. Provision of many formal and informal research activities to foster research interest, experience, and competency development.
5. Delineation of research-personnel classifications as aides, assistants, interns, technicians, and the like, and education and utilization of persons with research potential in appropriate classifications.
6. Recognition of and granting credit for research experience not limited to that acquired in the field of education.
7. The stimulation of interest, participation, and development of competency through grants, loans, scholarships, and fellowships specifically for research that may or may not have direct application.
8. Concentrated attention to broadened *research activity* (as differentiated from *teaching* and *supervisory* activity) in programs of college Seniors and graduate students.
9. Pre- and in-service program development of interdisciplinary research activities including research design, methodology, and experimentation employed in the major disciplines and professions.
10. Planned interdisciplinary seminars of varying degrees of sophistication and research understanding.
11. Realistic allocation of the work loads of supervisory and teacher-education personnel to permit developmental research activities and programs to be planned and carried forward.
12. Employment of interdisciplinary research talent and leadership to develop research and research personnel.

The foregoing activities should also be conceived as means of influencing the recruitment, enrichment, and development of research administrators, supporting personnel, reporters, writers, and other needed personnel. In short, if we are serious about the task of research, we must construct a research hierarchy parallel to the one we have maintained to develop teaching and administrative personnel. To do less will be to unduly restrict teacher and supervisory development. To do more will give greatly needed insight into and direction to the shaping of our vocational effort and the changes which must take place.

Organizational Structure and Financial Support of Research

IMPORTANCE OF ADEQUATE FINANCING AND REALISTIC ORGANIZATION

The fact that public vocational education has placed all its eggs in the basket of *program operation* has been made clear in a previous section of this chapter. Documentation of this weakness (and strong criticism from the popular press and the profession) has been presented in such publications as the John Dale Russell Report and the report of the President's Panel of Consultants on Vocational Education.[6] The latter group notes again the dearth of vocational-education research as it was indicated in a position paper of the Research Committee of the American Vocational Association:

> The Research Committee is not optimistic for the future of vocational education if research needs and implications continue to be ignored and by-passed because of supreme concerns for program operation and lack of vision for the magnitude of responsibility for future programming. It is still further concerned lest research become primarily a crash concern at times of national stress in tangential aspects of the overall occupational education program. Almost half a century of vocational education as we have come to know it in our time verifies the need for research activity in all parts and levels of the total occupational education program. If occupational education has come of age, research must permeate all aspects of its planning, operation, organization, administration, and evaluation. Lacking the contribution of meaningful research, occupational education will play, at best, an impotent, hit-and-miss function in the lives and welfare of few citizens.[7]

This is not to say that there has been no worthwhile research by colleges, universities, state and local systems, the United States Office of Education, and organizations within agriculture, distribution, home economics, and industry. But, too often, the relatively meager research of the past has been descriptive, normative, and superficial, emanating chiefly from the individual efforts of graduate students.

6. (a) John Dale Russell and Associates, *Vocational Education*. Prepared for the Advisory Committee on Education, Staff Study No. 8. Washington: Government Printing Office, 1938.

(b) *Education for a Changing World of Work*. Report of the Panel of Consultants on Vocational Education. United States Department of Health, Education, and Welfare, Office of Education, OE-80021. Washington: Government Printing Office, 1963.

7. Quoted in *Education for a Changing World of Work, op. cit.*, p. 199.

Generally, a passive administrative attitude which exemplified little faith in research has prevailed. The extent to which this attitude can be overcome and the speed with which a bold research effort can be initiated on problems of high priority are matters of opinion.

At this time in our history there is neither definition of our overall research problem nor assessment of our research resources. We do know that the complexity of expanding vocational education in these critical times has been compounded by the gross and overpowering dimensions of our social, economical, and technological problems. Our resources to support and disseminate research have not been identified, much less inventoried. Despite positive evidence that new and promising research activities are taking place, that new interests are being created, and that researchers are acquiring increasing competence and sophistication in performing and administering research, we are flying blindly without either flight plan or instruments to keep us on course. This confused condition is dismaying to vocational educators.

Obviously, we must look at our *research problem* in aggregate and at our *total capability* to overcome it. This challenge, in itself, presents an interesting and major research problem. Assuming that our *research problem* can be approached on the basis of Rupert Evans' supply-demand theory or alternatively on a quantitative-qualitative basis, it is essential that we know our research problems and their order of priority. Our total *research capacity*, which likewise must be determined, must be brought to bear on our research priorities. It should not be an insurmountable task to assess our research capability if we realistically examine research interests, facilities, personnel, relationships, and resources represented in departments of the federal government, the states, the local schools, and colleges and universities. Essentially, our inventory of research potential should list for examination the unique and specialized interest and the type of research effort which each potential contributor wishes to make and can realistically perform. Ultimately, all our planning and assessment must produce a model or system of feasibility which will concentrate action on research priorities and simultaneously stimulate and strengthen each aspect of our research capability.

Now that authorizations of the Vocational Education Act of 1963 are supported by realistic appropriations, the outlook for research is bright. Barring serious breaches in federal and state research administration, important new steps toward realization of our research purpose may be implemented. The new steps should be regarded as "first steps," take-offs, and *minimums*. We should fully realize that the new legislative minimums for research and program development are *minimums* indeed. Additional ways and means to promote and sustain research at an effective level must be discovered through administration of other provisions of the new law, to add to the research formally designated in the Act.

Legislation will continue to demand adequate *evaluation* and *accountability*, both of which are highly related to research but neither of which is the exclusive responsibility of it. It will be tragic to our development if responsibility for appraisal becomes the deserted foundling on the research doorstep. Balance and accommodation should characterize the research function, and so should the realization that research can and should discover new knowledge and methods of appraisal; evaluation, however, should neither be its sole function nor accountability its exclusive obligation.

The concern for vocational education and for provisions to sustain it adequately goes beyond that represented in educational legislation. Mounting needs in the field of labor, particularly those related to unemployment, manpower development, training, and retraining, strongly indicate the importance of some relationships which are not new. The total federal, state, and local legislative provision must be geared for an across-the-board effort to meet vocational-education demands. At every level of program development, operation, and evaluation (together with the accompanying research activity), our new role as professionals requires a large measure of co-operation. Multibureau investments and efforts to overcome vocational problems will move the vocational program to its proper place in the total educational endeavor.

Despite the relatedness of vocational education to the farm, shop, store, office, and home, and their contributions to our nation's development, it is ironic that our research effort has been diametrical in production and resources. As vocational educators we have failed to make clear to our institutional affiliates that education and educational research are inseparable. Faced as we are with staggering research needs, it should be obvious that legislative provisions can never financially provide for complete research fulfilment. In addition to research support from legislative provisions, there is critical need to investigate and enlist the interest and financial assistance of research foundations, private agencies, philanthropic groups, and those from the broad fields of agriculture, business, and industry at the local, state, national, and international level. Accompanying investigation should also be made of numerous co-operative plans of funding research which may be peculiar to certain types of educational and occupational projects.

Research support should also be realistically conceived to include a wider realm of human and physical resources than funding per se. We should become much more knowledgeable of the total occupational- and personnel-research complex within the broad fields of government, industry, agriculture, business, and education. Undoubtedly we shall find data, methods, and experimental evidence relevant to our problems. We may also discover research personnel having diversified interests and special competencies. The assistance of and exchange of ideas with such personnel is needed.

The enlistment and utilization of various resources to support the research and development effort should be regarded as functions of research administration. A clear-cut distinction should be made between researcher and research administrator. With the increased complexity of the vocational-education program and the scope and nature of needed research, there will be little progress if vocational administrators (*a*) attempt themselves, without delegation, to administer both the vocational program and the research program, (*b*) throttle researchers by assigning to them the total responsibility for research administration, (*c*) weaken research activity by combining it with other functions, such as leadership development, evaluation, curriculum development, and demonstration activities, and (*d*) make judgments, without competent research opinion, which affect the research program.

RESEARCH ADVISORY COMMITTEES

Over the years we have developed many techniques and principles of great value relating to organization, operation, and evaluation of advisory groups in vocational education. Research advisory groups, their membership, and their consultative functions should observe appropriate principles of operation. First, the *presence* of the advisory committee does not relieve the administrator of bearing the ultimate responsibility for decisions which affect research; it would follow, then, that research advisory groups should be made up of competent researchers with experience, preparation, and ability to determine the soundness of research design, to closely estimate the cost of research, to pass on possible alternatives, to inventory and recommend the use of specialized research personnel and resources, and to weigh the values of short- and long-range plans for over-all research programs. Administrators will need the specialized wisdom and advice of these groups as well as of their own research staffs. Advisory groups can also be of invaluable aid in assisting individual researchers and staffs of research programs and projects, in evaluating and disseminating the results of research, and by serving (for the administrator) on executive research committees in whose delicate operation the fine lines of research and administration should be carefully delineated.

There is a delicate balance somewhere between allowing the researcher to study exactly what he pleases and allowing administrators to command the services of researchers. Neither extreme is practical, but each group resists surrendering too much authority to the other. One of the best ways of achieving a balance is for the researchers to prepare proposals which are evaluated by research advisory committees and approved by administrators, while at the same time administrators suggest ideas for studies which they will support if researchers will prepare adequate proposals for such studies.

Dissemination and Acceptance of Research

Extensive research activity carried on outside the realm of needs and reality will not provide the evidence for making desirable changes which should take place in vocational education now and in the future. It is also quite likely that new research knowledge if not communicated, disseminated, and applied will not have the needed impact upon change and readjustment. Obviously, the dissemination and application of research must go hand in glove with research activity itself to such an extent that one without the other is inconceivable. Vocational education, with its great strength in its traditional categories, is particularly vulnerable to the violation of this principle as seen in the chain of research-reporting-dissemination-application. The creation of separate research centers for each of the vocational services would make us even more vulnerable. More important than adding "leadership development" to the list of purposes of the individual research centers is the clarification of the simple objective of discovering, reporting, and applying new knowledge relating to vocational-education problems.

Despite the strength of organization of the vocational categories over the last half-century, the organization and operation of a separate research center for each category violate the principle of *similarity* of teaching and learning in vocational education and the spirit of current legislation which supports it. Vocational-research centers should be established at strategic locations in the states, and their programs should be co-ordinated with a national plan to avoid duplication of activity and effort. This objective would not have been realized if a separate center had been established for each vocational category or service. It is much more realistic to organize centers with specific, designated research functions in curriculum development, student selection and follow-up, evaluation, education of professional vocational personnel, programed-learning media, and in other problems areas which are common to all vocational categories. Each center should assume that the accompanying obligations of reporting, disseminating, and implementation are mandatory.

Most researchers complain that operating personnel do not understand research results or the problems of the researcher. Research results are usually greeted either with, "Why, I knew that all the time. You certainly didn't need a research study to learn that fact," or "That result is impossible. There must be a flaw in your study." Unfortunately, communication between researchers who are working in different fields is of much the same order.

One of the most serious difficulties at the moment is that, for example, agricultural-education researchers talk only to each other and know little or nothing of the work done in home-economics education. We have at present no researchers concerned with the whole of vocational education. Certainly persons studying skill development in trade and industrial education, agricultural education, or business education have more in common than they have with persons within their own area of occupations who are studying attitude development.

If an effective research-abstracting service in our field can be developed, or if computer-based information retrieval achieves full development, and if we are able to establish vocational education (rather than occupational areas) as our research field, many of the problems of communication between researchers will be minimized.

DEMONSTRATION PROGRAMS

When results from experimental or pilot programs indicate the desirability of a change in operating practices, states or regions should establish demonstration programs incorporating the desired changes. These demonstration programs should be established in reasonably typical local or area schools. There is considerable evidence to indicate that publications and conferences do not accomplish change, but that change can be accomplished if administrators can visit and study demonstration programs which are actually operating.[8]

Research on Research

The earliest attempts to increase the quantity and improve the quality of research in our field consisted of conferences which produced long lists of "needed research." While these meetings probably served a cathartic purpose for the participants, they produced little or no other results. More recent attempts to find a solution for this problem through seminars for training researchers have not been evaluated.

Comparisons of the effectiveness of various research techniques in other educational fields indicate that matched-group studies, single-variable studies, and pretest, post-test, and control-group studies are largely invalid. They indicate further that the Hawthorne effect is

8. H. Brickell, "Organizing New York State for Educational Change," in *Dissemination and Implementation*, chap. iv. Bloomington, Indiana: Phi Delta Kappa, 1962.

rarely controlled, that statistical techniques are frequently misused, and that randomness is usually not achieved.

Effectiveness of much of the research in education is difficult to measure. Curriculum research which results in new course content and methods would appear to be easy to evaluate, but efforts to do so have been disappointing. Studies aimed at predicting student success in vocational education, on the other hand, have been relatively profitable, as is shown by the studies of Margaret Crawford at the Los Angeles Trade-Technical College.

Researchers and administrators of research must take the initiative in evaluating the progress of their research. It is too easy to ride the present vogue for research of any and every type and to forget that every vogue ends as quickly and surely as it begins. Only solid logical and empirical testing will improve research to the point that it can stand on its own merits.

CHAPTER XIII

A Platform for Vocational Education in the Future

MELVIN L. BARLOW

Introduction

The common conception of vocational education has changed over the years. Once regarded as "those knacks in education," as an early writer described the program, it is now perceived as an integral, essential part of education. But attitudes toward work have changed much more slowly: We still find people who measure a man by the kind of work he does rather than by the quality of performance, whatever his work may be.

Vocational education has been reaching toward its destiny continuously since the inception of the movement near the turn of the century. The struggle has not been easy, and vocational education has been called upon time and again to justify its existence in the imperative educational experiences of society.

Vocational education has always had a strong social bearing. Vocational education is concerned with people: people who are going to become members of the labor force; people who are members of the labor force; in fact, most of the people who produce the goods and services required by our society.

Vocational education, the thing itself, has changed much during the first half-century of its existence. Rigidity of operation yielded slowly but certainly until vocational education abandoned its early sheltered existence, to become in practice what it was intended to be in theory. More and more of the disciplines have contributed to the evolution of vocational education, and more and more of the citizens at large have given advice concerning its direction. Emphasis has shifted from the strong back to the alert mind.

Society requires most of its members to do something concrete, actual, finite, real. Some of the vocations in society have protected themselves from the interloper, the misfit, and the unprepared by establishing laws, regulations, and certificates of competency. In the same sense that a person must possess more than a bottle of iodine in order to practice medicine, a person must have more than a hammer to practice carpentry. Standards are moving upward, and people are as likely to require competence in their plumber as in their dentist. Most occupations are setting higher requirements for those who desire to enter.

All occupations must be developed upon a basis of general educational achievement, which includes a wide variety of school experiences. We expect the historian and the baker to contribute as effective citizens. Their occupations are different and equally honorable, but their fundamental obligations as citizens are the same.

Elements of the Platform

CULTURAL ELEMENTS

Social and economic mores.—Vocational education was born of social and economic needs. Its purposes are now and must continue to be close-linked to the needs and behaviors of the total population and to its economic well-being. Planning for vocational education must be conducted by persons well informed about key trends in population growth and in general social development. The coming of age of minority groups with their strivings for recognition cannot go unnoticed in the future of vocational education. Urbanization provides a new challenge to vocational education. The general mobility of the population must change the narrow "community" concept of occupation into concepts having relevance for a much larger geographical area. Women in the labor force, the scope of their employment, and their entrance into new occupational fields are among the most important items to be considered in the future. Vocational-education programs must be closely related to the established patterns of employment of women and the changes in these patterns. Composition of the population—the 18-year-old bulge of the present—and the vocational requirements of various segments of population are giving rise to new plans and programs for meeting these requirements.

Improving the ability of the individual to produce and to compete effectively is directly related to the improvement of the national economy. Demands for highly trained workers and the general tendency to reject poorly or untrained workers are problems that point to the tasks of vocational education. The shortened work week and rural depopulation are other factors in the economic background of our culture and, in turn, have implications for vocational competency to be provided through schools, colleges, adult education, and apprenticeship.

Current trends and problems related to social and economic needs vividly imply that community co-ordination and general co-operation of all concerned are necessary in order that the functions related to the needs may be carried out.

Centrality of technology.—Our newly developing technology has reached deeply into American life and has become thoroughly entrenched as a dominant influence. Whether it becomes a disease or a boon (current odds seem to favor boon), it unquestionably has many implications for vocational education. The vital organ of technology is the computer, whose extraordinary achievements have brought reality to theory. Technology working under the direction of man, the master, has produced an "explosion of knowledge." Information-retrieval systems shorten to seconds the time required to reproduce knowledge, thus giving man seven-league boots, king size.

Vocational education has included in its theory and practice such self-adjusting characteristics that occupational change is reflected in the program of vocational education. Representative advisory committees, instructors, supervisors, and administrators who are in tune with occupational requirements and change have aided in this continuous appraisal of vocational instruction. However, in the midst of rapidly changing technology, one problem with two parts must be solved more effectively than it has in the past. The problem is the need for statistical information related to vocational programs, on the one hand, and labor requirements, on the other.

The platform for the future recognizes the centrality of technology and the imperative need for statistical information about many facets of the technology. The Division of Vocational and Technical Education of the United States Office of Education will supply increasing amounts of statistical data about vocational-education programs. The Bureau of Labor Statistics of the United States Department of Labor will supply reliable occupational information. The advisory committee to the United States Commissioner of Education (and the advisory councils) will provide policy and procedures for effective use of this information. Such information will strengthen one plank in the platform of the future: vocational education closely related to the labor market.

Conceptual understanding of vocational education in the educative process.—Vocational education is an accomplished fact in the common school, but not in all schools. Only about two million students a year have an opportunity to take advantage of the vocational offerings. A variety of claims is being made upon the instructional time of the common school. Division of opinion among educators arises from a number of conflicting points of view. Necessity for general courses, strong emphasis upon so-called disciplinary requirements, growth of post-high-school institutions, and a long historical background which has tended to be largely antivocational are some of the forces which slow the development of vocational education in the common school. Opposed to these forces are the increasing demands for job competency of high-school graduates, a high degree of success among existing vocational programs in the common school, and the rising national interest in vocational education. These conflicting forces are exceedingly complex, and the educator is, therefore, presented with puzzling and uncertain choices.

The platform for the future of vocational education in the common school cannot disregard any choices which appear to enhance the future employability of students. The problem cannot be solved by strengthening a dichotomy of antivocational and pro-vocational forces. The problem, simply stated, is to have your cake and eat it too. Balance of contemporary opinion among vocational educators tends to place value upon extensive vocational-education programs in the setting of the comprehensive common school. A strong possibility exists that for many students the vocational-education program can make the academic program important and valuable. A student in vocational printing soon learns the value of English, a student in vocational electronics is faced immediately with the necessity for skill in mathematics and science; such motivation can possibly overcome previous mediocrity of performance in English, mathematics, and science. Although this has not been tested by conclusive research, there is just enough evidence available to suggest that vocational education may have a strong supportive role in relation to disciplinary values.

The common school in transition is faced with the cold hard reality of three facts: (*a*) some students do not stay in school through high-school graduation, (*b*) more than half of those who are graduated attempt to enter the labor force, and (*c*) a large percentage of those who continue their education has occupational goals that can be satisfied in one or two years of additional study. It is apparent immediately that vocational education is concerned with most of the students in the common school. A platform for vocational education for the future in the common school will include an equitable resolution of the complex problems involved, to the end that students may enter occupational life thoroughly prepared from the standpoint of vocational skills and from the standpoint of the common learnings required for vocational competence.

Reality of the actual program in the secondary schools.—Chapter v of this yearbook presents a brief overview of the vocational-education program in the secondary schools. In addition to factual statements about the program, it presents a rationale and, in light of this rationale, discusses trends, emerging points of view, areas of emphasis, and numerous relevant problems. It is important to describe the existing program not only to inform the reader of the contemporary nature of vocational education but also to provide a point of departure for the building of a platform for the future.

The contemporary program has been valuable in satisfying individual needs and in meeting national goals. Present development, however, is far from satisfactory in terms of anticipated future requirements. The platform for the future will probably include many elements that cannot be identified at this time. However, the following items will likely be included in it.

1) Segregation of vocational programs by occupational categories will tend to disappear under the general emphasis of *vocational preparation*. This trend will be more noticeable from an organization and administration point of view, in that no occupational area, as previously, will be outside artificially established occupational boundaries.

(The exception is that occupational preparation requiring a baccalaureate or higher degree as a part of the initial preparation will not
be included.) Under these conditions it is relatively unimportant
whether a program is administered by one department or another.

2) Flexibility in organizing vocational-education programs will
develop in an entirely new perspective. If an opportunity to provide
occupational instruction exists, and if a job market is available for
qualified persons, the school simply provides the instruction. The
key point here is that vocational-education needs are to be served on
a broad basis. Obviously, national and state policy will exist relative to
the use of federal and state vocational-education funds. Such policy,
however, will likely represent a consensus drawn from experience
about standards and quality control. Flexibility cannot be carried to
the extreme of complete casualness.

3) Local supervision of vocational programs by qualified persons
who are specialists in the field of supervision and who are competent
in the area of *vocational education* will be the rule where quality
programs are developed. Vocational programs cannot operate successfully without adequate supervision.

4) Interdepartmental co-operation in secondary schools in relation
to the vocational-education program is imperative. This program
belongs to the school—not to one department in a school, sealed off
from the total school operation and environment. Obviously, the vocational program will have its own administration for day-to-day
operation of the program, but standards of performance of students
in areas such as mathematics, physics, art, English, and the like, must
continue to be the concern of these departments.

5) Community involvement in advisory committees and in many
other ways is necessary in the future program. National, state, and
local labor-force needs must be reflected in the "going" vocational-
education program of the school. Representatives of specific occupational groups—labor, employees, and employers—can and should provide advisory services.

Emphasis upon vocational goals.—One problem which has not been
adequately solved in public education is guidance toward a vocation.
It is strange that this has been the case, when almost 100 per cent of
the students will be involved in the matter of vocational choice. This

failure in public education cannot be placed entirely on the doorstep of the public school because it is obvious that the parent and the community have not placed sufficient emphasis on this problem.

However, the problem has not been ignored universally. There are many schools that do have excellent programs of vocational guidance, and the results are most satisfying. Other schools make a start in the right direction, but somehow attention to vocational choice gets lost in the process. What is needed in the platform of the future is a total dedication by public education to its responsibility for the child's vocational orientation. This responsibility must be shared by the parent and the community. This is not an impossible task when one considers the excellent progress made in counseling and guidance in general. We already know a great deal about children and youth, and we must use this information to take the important step toward preparing them for a vocation.

Preparing for a vocation is becoming exceedingly complicated by the fact that our occupational structure cannot guarantee stability of an occupation. The job may not exist by the time the student is ready for it, and he may be confronted by job opportunities which were unknown when he began his vocational preparation. The "broad field" approach has merit, but the present state of development of the idea is somewhat intangible and seemingly related to vocation only by chance. The attitude of "keep him in school as long as you can" or "send him on to college" may increase the student's chances of employment, but, since employment takes up such a large part of a person's life, it seems unreasonable that so much should depend upon "chance."

It is of utmost importance that the platform for vocational education in the future should include an all-out development of vocational guidance.

Extensive development in post-high-school institutions.—For more than a decade vocational education has found fertile ground for growth and development in institutions beyond the high school. Such development is consistent with labor-force requirements of more education and of preference for maturity in job applicants. The labor market and the productive capacity of the nation are such that delayed entrance upon an occupation caused by continued schooling is not a handicap to national economic stability.

In the platform of the future, development of post-high-school institutions with an emphasis upon vocational education will be encouraged. The success of some states with their area schools and junior colleges has encouraged other states to plan similar educational institutions. The post-high-school institution is ideal for the student who continues in school immediately after completing high school, and it is similarly ideal for the employed worker who wishes to continue his education. Evening or extended-day programs provide opportunities to retrain unemployed workers and to provide a variety of related educational services which improve the productive capacity of individuals.

One could say that the future of vocational education belongs to the post-high-school institution, provided of course that the inference is not made that this point of view suggests a lack of enthusiasm for high-school programs. As long as students tend to drop out of high school and as long as half of the high-school graduates go to work immediately, there will continue to be intensive interest in and concern about vocational education at the high-school level. But that the trend in vocational education is toward more extensive development in post-high-school institutions there can be no doubt.

ENABLING ELEMENTS

Federal encouragement and review.—Federal participation in vocational education has been justified on the basis that the vocational preparation of the American labor force is a national problem. Financial aid since 1917 has made it possible for each of the states to develop vocational-education programs. Federal encouragement and program review have provided in each of the states a plan prepared by the state to signify its intentions in relation to the vocational-education acts for state-wide development of vocational education. National conferences and the work of professional associations have strengthened all aspects of the vocational-education program. Rededication of the federal government to the purposes of vocational education was manifest in the Vocational Education Act of 1963. Federal legislation and policies have had a significant impact upon the development of vocational education.

Vocational educators in their platform for the future accept fully the necessity of continued federal financial support and consultative services. The Division of Vocational and Technical Education of the United States Office of Education must be expanded in terms of personnel and professional services in order that the states may have available continued competent professional resources. The success of vocational education in the future will depend to a large extent upon the quantity and quality of assistance from the federal government.

Adequate state and local policy.—An essential item in the platform for the future of vocational education is the updating of state and local policies in regard to vocational education. Such policy must be prepared with due regard for policies developed in response to the Vocational Education Act of 1963. National policy will be developed from the Act and will unquestionably reflect to a large extent the points of view of the Panel of Consultants on Vocational Education. Such policy will be limiting upon the states only to the extent of requiring the states to plan appropriately for the expansion of offerings in the various states; the Act of 1963 prohibits federal control.

The key point in regard to state and local policy is that "there is much more danger of undue and unwise state control over vocational education than there is of federal dictation." Such policies should be carefully reviewed and reconstituted to maximize the opportunity for local schools to develop completely adequate programs of vocational education.

An effective administrative structure.—The administrative structure of vocational education appears to be sound, but its actual effectiveness depends upon the persons who hold administrative, supervisory, and co-ordination responsibilities in the state and local programs.

The platform of the future demands that those who have any degree of administrative influence on the vocational-education program strengthen their skills and deepen their understanding of vocational education. National and state conferences will provide much of the opportunity for professional growth of the contemporary administrative group. Review of the administrative role and evaluation of administrative plans and procedures are high-priority items in the platform of the future.

Expansion of the vocational-education program will provide many new administrative positions. Vocational-education's platform for the future must make adequate provision for leadership development in order to provide the new competencies required for future administration of vocational education.

Interests "outside" public education.—Business, industry, the military services, and the private schools make extensive contributions toward building and maintaining a high level of vocational competence in our technological society. The role of vocational education in business, industry, and the military services is directed primarily toward vocational competence related to the interests of the agency or institution involved. Some of the programs are broad and extensive and are capable of providing high-quality training.

Despite extensive developments "outside" public education, such programs do not provide vocational education for all persons who need to update and upgrade their skills or who require retraining for a new occupation. However, within the future development of vocational education in public institutions must be found a more extensive pattern of co-operative relationships with the "outside" agencies. It is obvious that vocational education directed toward "families" or "clusters" of occupations must be based upon information provided by industry and business. Closer working relationships between schools and other agencies will provide new understanding of the human factors involved in educating persons for work in a changing technological society. The familiar advisory committee, long a characteristic of good vocational-education programs, must have an even higher priority in the future.

Critical analysis.—The future of vocational education belongs to research. Vocational education has been research-starved for such a long period of time that data necessary for evaluative review are meager. New responsibilities of vocational education, youth with special needs, and leadership development, for example, will require extensive experimental study. In addition, a number of dimensions must be identified and subjected to a sufficient degree of analysis so that adequate comparative data may be obtained about vocational education on a nation-wide basis.

The Age of Vocational Education

The purpose and function of vocational education in the contemporary program of public education have been clarified considerably since World War II. During this period, evidence has accumulated which shows the growing dependence of the American economy upon the vocational competence of the masses of the people.

Change in vocational education has not been so much in its content and direction as in its relationships to other cultural forces. Concurrent demands upon every segment of American life have brought into the open new relationships of these segments to our national well-being. Our average general educational achievement has risen rapidly to a point between eleven and twelve years of schooling. Productive capacity has improved and increased to almost unbelievable heights. The recent achievements of "inventing invention" speeds up the rate at which technology creates new designs for living. Scientific progress has outdistanced social progress. We are confronted with "time on our hands," but for what purpose? Leisure? Advanced preparation for keeping up with our jobs? Both? Neither?

Education has budged very little under the impact of the new dimensions for living. We hold school five days a week, six hours a day, for about 60 per cent of each year. We have crammed many things into the curriculum, let the subject-matter areas fight with each other for a claim to space, and have insisted upon holding to some arbitrary number of years, or semesters, of study of a subject rather than finding out what competencies are to be achieved. There are relatively few preferred pathways through the subject-matter maze, and most of the students have been forced into one pattern because we have said that only this one has the greatest ultimate value. We believe in tempting students to *think*, but it only counts when they *think* about a few special elements of our total culture.

It used to be possible to enrol the school failure—the one weeded out of the preferred pathway—in the vocational program on the pretext that if he couldn't work with his mind then obviously he could work with his hands. This was sugar-coated by talking about students with many intelligences—mechanical, clerical, social, abstract, and others—but we didn't really carry the rationale into practice. Then technology played a dirty trick. Occupational tables were upset. In order to succeed in an occupation, the worker had to be able to work with his hands and his mind. The other occupations—those in which he only worked with his hands—ceased to exist. So the students who couldn't read, write, and calculate were returned to their classes with the demand: "Teach them to read, write, and calculate; otherwise we can't teach them to work!"

During its infancy, vocational education was placed in a strong crib, and a hands-off policy prevailed. In its age of maturity, social and technological forces have removed the formerly strong barriers and have made the vocational preparation of the youth of America a responsibility of all subject-matter areas in the school. "It has taken the American people a long time to see the need for vocational education," wrote Joseph S. Taylor in 1914. Fifty years later he might have written, "The American people have at last learned to place value upon vocational education."

Index

INFORMATION CONCERNING THE NATIONAL SOCIETY FOR THE STUDY OF EDUCATION

1. PURPOSE. The purpose of the National Society is to promote the investigation and discussion of educational questions. To this end it holds an annual meeting and publishes a series of yearbooks.

2. ELIGIBILITY TO MEMBERSHIP. Any person who is interested in receiving its publications may become a member by sending to the Secretary-Treasurer information concerning name, title, and address, and a check for $8.00 (see Item 5), except that graduate students, on the recommendation of a faculty member, may become members by paying $6.00 for the first year of their membership. Dues for all subsequent years are the same as for other members (see Item 4).

Membership is not transferable; it is limited to individuals, and may not be held by libraries, schools, or other institutions, either directly or indirectly.

3. PERIOD OF MEMBERSHIP. Applicants for membership may not date their entrance back of the current calendar year, and all memberships terminate automatically on December 31, unless the dues for the ensuing year are paid as indicated in Item 6.

4. DUTIES AND PRIVILEGES OF MEMBERS. Members pay dues of $7.00 annually, receive a cloth-bound copy of each publication, are entitled to vote, to participate in discussion, and (under certain conditions) to hold office. The names of members are printed in the yearbooks.

Persons who are sixty years of age or above may become life members on payment of fee based on average life-expectancy of their age group. For information, apply to Secretary-Treasurer.

5. ENTRANCE FEE. New members are required the first year to pay, in addition to the dues, an entrance fee of one dollar.

6. PAYMENT OF DUES. Statements of dues are rendered in October for the following calendar year. Any member so notified whose dues remain unpaid on January 1, thereby loses his membership and can be reinstated only by paying a reinstatement fee of fifty cents.

School warrants and vouchers from institutions must be accompanied by definite information concerning the name and address of the person for whom membership fee is being paid. Statements of dues are rendered on our own form only. The Secretary's office cannot undertake to fill out special invoice forms of any sort or to affix notary's affidavit to statements or receipts.

Cancelled checks serve as receipts. Members desiring an additional receipt must enclose a stamped and addressed envelope therefor.

7. DISTRIBUTION OF YEARBOOKS TO MEMBERS. The yearbooks, ready prior to each February meeting, will be mailed from the office of the distributors, only to members whose dues for that year have been paid. Members who desire yearbooks prior to the current year must purchase them directly from the distributors (see Item 8).

8. COMMERCIAL SALES. The distribution of all yearbooks prior to the current year, and also of those of the current year not regularly mailed to members in exchange for their dues, is in the hands of the distributor, not of the Secretary. For such commercial sales, communicate directly with the University of Chicago Press, Chicago 37, Illinois, which will gladly send a price list covering all the publications of this Society. This list is also printed in the yearbook.

9. YEARBOOKS. The yearbooks are issued about one month before the February meeting. They comprise from 600 to 800 pages annually. Unusual effort has been made to make them, on the one hand, of immediate practical value, and, on the other hand, representative of sound scholarship and scientific investigation.

10. MEETINGS. The annual meeting, at which the yearbooks are discussed, is held in February at the same time and place as the meeting of the American Association of School Administrators.

Applications for membership will be handled promptly at any time on receipt of name and address, together with check for $8.00 (or $7.50 for reinstatement). Applications entitle the new members to the yearbook slated for discussion during the calendar year the application is made.

5835 Kimbark Ave.   HERMAN G. RICHEY, *Secretary-Treasurer*
Chicago 37, Illinois

PUBLICATIONS OF THE NATIONAL SOCIETY FOR THE STUDY OF EDUCATION

NOTICE: Many of the early yearbooks of this series are now out of print. In the following list, those titles to which an asterisk is prefixed are not available for purchase.

POSTPAID
PRICE

Distributed by

THE UNIVERSITY OF CHICAGO PRESS, CHICAGO 37, ILLINOIS
1965